ROAD RAGE

AND
AGGRESSIVE
DRIVING

**Steering Clear
of Highway Warfare**

D1258299

DR. LEON JAMES
& DR. DIANE NAHL

(PB) **Prometheus Books**

59 John Glenn Drive
Amherst, New York 14228-2197

Published 2000 by Prometheus Books

Inquiries should be addressed to
Prometheus Books
59 John Glenn Drive
Amherst, New York 14228–2197
VOICE: 716–691–0133, ext. 207
FAX: 716–564–2711
WWW.PROMETHEUSBOOKS.COM

04 03 02 01 00   5 4 3 2 1

Library of Congress Cataloging-in-Publication Data

James, Leon, Dr.
    Road rage and aggressive driving : steering clear of highway warfare / Leon James and Diane Nahl.
        p. cm.
    Includes bibliographical references and index.
    ISBN 1–57392–846–1 (pbk. : alk. paper)
    1. Road rage. 2. Automobile drivers—Psychology. 3. Automobile driving—Safety measures. 4. Aggressiveness. I. Nahl, Diane. II. Title.

TL152.35 .J35 2000
629.28'3'019—dc21   00–040662
                                                                              CIP

Printed in the United States of America on acid-free paper

In memory of

Dixie Camilla Coke Nahl
(1898–1993)

who inspired us to begin this work and watches over us.

CONTENTS

ROAD RAGE AND AGGRESSIVE DRIVING

PART TWO: DRIVING PSYCHOLOGY

5. Emotional Intelligence for Drivers   111

6. Three-Step Driver Self-Improvement Program   133

7. Children and Road Rage   151

ROAD RAGE AND AGGRESSIVE DRIVING

Contents

ACKNOWLEDGMENTS

Diane's grandmother, Dixie Camilla Coke Nahl, who drove throughout the twentieth century with several aggressive drivers, was the first one to openly complain about Leon's aggressive driving, and was instrumental in helping us conceive the idea for this book. She would have loved to see it in the bookstores. Thanks goes to our parents, brothers, sisters, nieces, nephews, and friends who shared their aggressive driving experiences and provided enthusiastic and unflagging support for the book.

Our children, Joy and Rex, deserve special thanks for their support of this project, and we ask their forgiveness for the suffering we caused them because of our aggressive driving and road rage. They helped us to see that we were passing on dangerous habits to them, making us realize that we needed to change for their sakes. One of them has overcome the aggressive driving habit that we helped to instill, and we hope the other will follow, for the sake of their children.

Our deepest appreciation goes to our gem of an agent, Roger Jellinek, who gave moral support throughout the process. He was the first to acknowledge that the book was viable. His vision steered the book toward road rage, and his expertise guided us from proposal to contract. Roger astonished us with his generous editorial wisdom that significantly improved the book.

Special thanks wholeheartedly goes to Ellen Chapman, who made our job easier and reminded us along the way that people need this book. As a professional librarian and indexer, Ellen is an information filter extraordinaire. When we mentioned we were working on this project she instantly wanted to read the first version and she kept us continuously up to date as the topic evolved over three years in the news media. Ellen also created the index with her astute sense of topic structure that makes it easy to find information in the text.

We wish to thank the people across the country and the world who emailed Dr. Driving to express their views, to seek advice, and to share their often harrowing experiences. We are thankful that they are safe and hope that from this moment on they will drive with Aloha.

PREFACE

Grandmother: Leon is not a good driver!
Diane: Yes he is . . . what do you mean?
Grandmother: He scares me when he flies around the corners so fast. I have to brace myself to keep from falling.
Diane: Oh, really? I didn't realize that. Maybe you should sit in front.
Grandmother: It wouldn't make a difference because he just drives too fast and it knocks me around. I don't like it. It's undignified.

DIANE'S STORY

Over the years I couldn't tell Leon that his driving scared me because whenever I tried he became irritable or angry. So when I told Leon what my eighty-five-year-old grandmother had said, he scoffed at her "backseat driving." His position: He is the Driver, the Driver is in charge—and passengers should only be cooperative and grateful. Passengers have nothing to say about the driving, for that is the Driver's domain. "Backseat driving" is simply not allowed under any circumstance.

Grandma's need to feel safe and comfortable was perfectly normal and reasonable, especially since she had arthritis pain. Yet as far as Leon was concerned she was simply a backseat driver, so her complaints could be dismissed. I was confronted with the harshness of this reality when Leon refused to slow down around turns even after he knew she wanted him to. It became a power struggle between them. At each turn, as she lost her balance and tried to right herself, she would gasp dramatically and grab the seat back for support. After each trip, she complained about his driving to me because she was afraid to confront him. Then I would repeat it to him, provoking his anger or skepticism.

It was hard for me to accept that my nice-guy husband apparently didn't care about Grandma's feelings—or about mine. She and Leon were good friends otherwise, so I couldn't understand why this usually sweet man would permit himself to dismiss our feelings when he got behind the wheel. When I tried to get him to talk about his driving, he simply refused and put on a bad mood to keep me away from the topic.

This was a taboo subject with him for several years, until Grandma finally broke through. One day she got up her nerve and shyly said directly to him, "You drive too fast, and when you go around corners you knock me over. I have to hold on for dear life and I don't like it. That's not how it's supposed to be." Miraculously, Leon responded with friendship and vowed to change his ways, and with concerted effort over time, he did. Grandma was quite satisfied, especially because she could claim all the credit for inspiring Leon to reform his driving behavior. And I'm happier now that I feel free to talk to Leon about the things that scare me in traffic without getting into trouble. Leon himself became happier when he discovered how rewarding it is to include the passengers' feelings as part of the driver's domain.

LEON'S STORY

The idea of "driving psychology" was born in my mind when I began to realize how difficult and painful it was for me to accommodate my driving style to the needs of Diane's grandmother. But I didn't like it—I resented her dictating to me how I should drive. It seemed ridiculous for anyone to drive so slowly and to have to worry about passengers when turning corners. Couldn't she just hold on to the door handle like everyone else? I thought she was just being demanding, and she got away with it because I didn't feel like arguing with her every Sunday.

Diane had suffered my aggressive driving in silence for ten years. Once in a while she tried to express her anxiety, but I shot her down instantly with my unfriendly reactions—denying it happened, questioning her right to tell me what to do behind the wheel, arguing against the obvious, being sarcastic, frowning, raising my voice, threatening, ridiculing, denigrating, ignoring, fuming, and giving her the silent treatment. I often watched her silent tears in her seat, knowing she was depressed and hopeless, feeling abandoned. At first, my heart hardened and I became distant, remote, and cold. Sometimes I kept silent for the entire trip to punish her for being so unreasonable as to remind me that I should courtesy wave to drivers who let me into their lane. I would fume to myself.

> Big deal. So I didn't wave to the other driver. It's up to me whether I want to wave or not. I don't feel like it. It makes me feel stupid, on stage or something. I don't even know the jerk who let me in. Besides, he's not even looking at me. What's this to her? Why does she have to care? She shouldn't keep reminding me. She should just take it, ignore it, and shut up about it.

Once in a while I would make a feeble effort to patch things up to get her off my back.

Leon: OK, I'm sorry I made you cry. I'll watch it next time. All right, honey?

Diane: That's what you said last time this happened . . . yesterday.

Leon: Oh, yeah. Well, I still think it's better to drive in the left lane. In the middle lane you have cars on both sides. You're totally locked in. There's danger on both sides. But in the left lane you have the wall on one side and you only have cars on your right.

Diane: I'm talking about how I feel riding in the fast lane, and the fact that you're acting like you don't care. You make me cry every time I bring up something that scares me.

But when her grandmother complained about me, Diane found a new freedom to speak against my "driving personality." I became aware of all sorts of conflicting feelings when her grandmother rode with us. We decided it was time to investigate this problem as social scientists. Our systematic efforts to understand and respect her grandmother's needs led us to create the new field of driving psychology.

This book brings together resources and discussion on road rage and aggressive driving from research studies, news media, government agencies, law enforcement, and citizen groups. A variety of Web-based resources are listed in the end-of-chapter notes. For easy, one-click access to these resources, visit DrDriving's site for the book at www.DrDriving.org.

THE CONFLICT
MENTALITY

PART 1

ROAD RAGE: REAL OR MEDIA HYPE?

In 1996 the American media began to write stories about violent highway incidents using warlike language that highlights a spirit of battle on the roads:

> It's high noon on the country's streets and highways. This is road recklessness, auto anarchy, an epidemic of wanton carmanship.[1]

> Armed with everything from firearms to Perrier bottles to pepper spray and eggs . . . America's drivers are taking frustrations out on each other in startling numbers.[2]

Stories listed in Yahoo! in 1999:[3]

- A driver intentionally rammed his vehicle into a car with three kids and their parents in it, after the children gave him an "obscene finger gesture."

ROAD RAGE AND AGGRESSIVE DRIVING

- A man was stabbed repeatedly by another motorist when a traffic disagreement escalated from obscene gestures to violence.
- A motorist spit on the driver of a bus after he was cut off, then as the bus driver got out, the enraged motorist severely beat the bus driver.
- A forty-nine-year-old father of five was shot to death by another motorist, who has been charged with capital homicide.
- A woman got a fifteen-year sentence for gunning the engine and hitting another woman in a fender-bender dispute.
- A man was shot at after he had honked at another car who passed him.
- A delivery van collided with a pickup truck, breaking a side mirror. An argument ensued and the van driver punched the other driver, who then pulled out a handgun and shot the van driver in the chest.
- A seventeen-year-old boy was tailgating a motorist. They both pulled over, a dispute ensued, and the boy was shot.
- An elderly driver, peeved that another driver honked at him, hurled his prescription bottle at the honker, then smashed the man's knees with his car when he got out.
- A bicyclist, enraged after being knocked off his bike by a car, pulled out a handgun and shot the driver to death.

The expression "road rage" was introduced into the public vocabulary by the popular media. Though there has been no agreed-upon definition, people use the phrase to refer to an extreme state of anger that often precipitates aggressive behavior, sometimes restricted to words and gestures, sometimes as assault and battery. A variety of factors have been named to account for the increase in aggressiveness between drivers, such as traffic congestion, feeling endangered, being insulted, frustration, time pressure, fatigue, competitiveness, and lapses in attention.

A much quoted article in the August 1998 issue of the *Atlantic* questions the existence of road rage, claiming that it's "merely media mayhem."

> Like any other fabricated epidemic, the more you tell people it's there, the more they see it. Tailgating used to be called tailgating. Now it's road rage. The *New York Daily News* assures us that using a car phone is road rage. Saying "Hi, honey, I love you; be home soon." is now no different than bowling over bicyclists with your Buick. . . . The term, and the alleged epidemic, were quickly popularized by lobbying groups, politicians, opportunistic therapists, even the U.S. Department of Transportation.[4]

The writer, Michael Fumento, isn't impressed by "research evidence," such as the AAA Foundation for Traffic Safety's 1997 studies that reported 218 police records of deaths following disputes between drivers between 1990 and 1996. During the same period, Fumento points out, 290,000 Americans died from vehicular accidents, but this large number, he feels, is not due to road rage.

> America's roads become safer by the year. . . . At first, "road rage" meant one driver acting against another. But by last year it had come to include a Washington, D.C., bicyclist who shot the driver of a car who ran into him, and a Scottish couple who threatened a driver with a knife after his BMW ran over their dog.[5]

In theory, it's possible to restrict "road rage" to felonious or criminal acts of violence by one driver against another. Even if people could agree on that usage, there's a similar problem with the term "aggressive driving" referring to reckless behavior, such as running red lights or giving someone a "brake job," as well as to speeding, tailgating, and lane hopping. To many, these maneuvers are merely a preferred style of driving that is assertive and competitive, not aggressive or hostile. However, word usage can almost never be legislated according to ideological preference, and society has been using "road rage" and "aggressive driving" to designate many forms of both hostile and illegal driving.

Beginning in the late 1980s, talk about road rage and aggressive driving increased tremendously, while the number of deaths due to crashes gradually decreased from around fifty thousand deaths per year in the 1950s and 1960s to about forty thousand deaths per year in the 1980s and 1990s. This healthy change reflects improvements in safety and design introduced since 1970, including mandated seat belts, air bags, better brake systems, upper tail lights, and crash-absorbing devices. In addition, seat belt and child seat restraint legislation, improved highway engineering, and the expansion of limited-access divided highways contribute to better driving safety.

Cars are safer, roads are safer, medical emergency operations are faster and better, saving more lives. Still, the annual death toll remains at a plateau around forty thousand per year, while the yearly toll in crash injuries has reached six million per year. The combined cost to society is a whopping $250 billion per year, not counting human suffering. Human error figures prominently in these statistics. We can say that this horrendous situation is due to road rage, aggressive driving, incompetent driving, impaired driving, risk taking, or frustration in congested traffic. Does the phrase really make a difference? Aggressive drivers have always been responsible for traffic problems. In the nineteenth century, some English authorities attempted to reduce the "furious driving" of horse-drawn vehicles with drunk drivers on their way home from bars. Gilbert and Sullivan's play *Mr. Jericho*, first performed at the Savoy Theatre in London in 1893, contained this reference to a problem everyone recognized:

Horace. There would be no more exhilarating rides for you to Marshall and Snellgrove's, with your Horace at the ribbons.

Michael. These are vain regrets, my boy. Remember that your 'bus is totally disabled, and that the last post tonight will probably bring you a dismissal from the Company's service for furious driving.

Horace. True, father.[6]

The phrase "furious driving" is still in use in England, for instance in the Dangerous Driving Road Traffic Act of 1988 in which these illegal driver behaviors are listed:[7]

- Competitive driving, racing, showing off
- Excessive speed
- Prolonged, persistent, deliberate bad driving
- Wanton and furious driving
- Driving with disregard for road safety taking account of road, weather, and traffic conditions
- Deliberate acts of selfishness, impatience, or aggressiveness, causing inconvenience

In another 1999 story widely reported in the press, a thirty-nine-year-old New York prosecutor faced murder charges for allegedly running down a roller skater, then driving a half mile with the body on the hood of his car.[8] He then allegedly stopped his car, stole a parked car and drove a short distance before he was stopped by police.

In Philadelphia, the city of brotherly love, a *Daily News* staff writer warned the world in 1997:

Welcome to the mean streets of Philadelphia, where speeding, lane-changing, tailgating, white-knuckled drivers are Hell on Wheels. To those who survived the Independence Day weekend of driving madness, congratulations. But watch out when you drive today, tomorrow and the next day: Hell on Wheels is a daily, unrelenting phenomenon.[9]

On the average, more than one person per hour is injured in auto accidents in Philadelphia. Acts of aggression have replaced carelessness as the main source of the danger: running stop lights (the number one traffic problem in Philadelphia and many other cities), tailgating or following too closely, improper turning or lane changes, and failure to yield.

Aggressive drivers kill two to four times more people than drunk drivers. The aggressive driver typically denies that these accident-causing behaviors are aggressive. Yet it's clear that motorists who put others in danger by the way they choose to drive are indeed aggressive, hostile, dangerous, and selfish because they attempt to impose their will on others who are considered to be "in the way." They feel justified in dominating others, and that's what makes it aggressive driving.

Formal attention to aggressive driving as a widespread problem began to heat up in the late 1990's. As recently as 1997 one major city had not yet awakened to it:

> As the *Daily News* documented in February, traffic-law enforcement nationwide—but especially in Philadelphia—has disintegrated into irrelevance. City police, for example, write about one-quarter of the red-light tickets that they did 20 years ago. "Right now, drivers know there's little chance of being caught. . . . The cat's out of the bag. Drivers realize they can run red light after red light and never get a ticket. It promotes unsafe behavior." Seen from that perspective, lax enforcement is part of a social phenomenon that Sen. Patrick Moynihan has described as "defining deviancy downward." "It's a question of what will we tolerate?" AAA President Faul said. "In Harrisburg, for example, yield means stop. But if you see one person running a light, you'll try it, too. Soon, the whole city is doing it. It's kind of a culture of driving." A review of city accident records suggest Philadelphia's driving culture is pure hell. Injuries from accidents caused by aggressive driving have climbed in each year since 1991.[10]

Our driving psychology approach to the problem received early national attention through an Associated Press news service release in 1996:

> Nasty driving attitudes have become a subject of scholarly study since University of Hawaii psychology professor Leon James began researching the minds of drivers. James' study turned up that "drivers are stressed out, threaten each other, are in a bad mood, terrorize their passengers, and often fantasize violent acts against each other." He says this shows there is a strong need for driving psychology which can reverse this trend and alter our driving style.[11]

A WORLDWIDE PHENOMENON

The forecast for a natural decline in aggressive driving is not positive and evidence of the problem continues to surface around the globe. Official recognition of the new travel danger is increasing, illustrated by this warning on a government Consular Information Web page:

ROAD RAGE AND AGGRESSIVE DRIVING

As the number of cars in Slovenia continues to rise, roads are becoming more heavily congested during the weekends on major routes and during rush hour. Parking is difficult.... Travelers should be alert to aggressive drivers both in cities and on highways. Many of the serious accidents in Slovenia occur as a result of high speed driving.[12]

A Philippine resident wrote to us in July 1999:

You hardly hear complaints here about road rage because we got so used to it that it seems normal. Things like swearing, tailgating, reckless driving, and cutting off. Yesterday, a man was sentenced to death for killing a pregnant woman due to a dispute about a parking space. People feel helpless about road rage since there is not much we can do. ... I refuse to drive here due to the stress I observe on the road. I cannot handle it. In order to control the traffic, our government has implemented the "odd-even" scheme for driving on alternate days. One of my aunts who now lives in Pennsylvania visited us two years ago and she was so affected by the traffic situation that I saw her praying the rosary while we were in the car. That's how bad it is here.

Research at the University of Southampton in New Zealand, supported by the Automobile Association and the AA Driver Education Foundation, released the results of their study on the aggressive driving behavior of 526 motorists.[13] Their findings give us pause. Almost two in three (64 percent) said they think that overall, the behavior of motorists has changed for the worse in recent years. When asked what types of aggressive driving behavior they had experienced in the last twelve months, 62 percent named aggressive tailgating, 59 percent had lights flashed at them in annoyance, 48 percent received rude gestures, and 21 percent had been deliberately obstructed or prevented from maneuvering.

In all categories, men reported receiving nearly 10 percent more highway abuse than women, and were 12 percent more likely to experience an aggressive incident. When asked about their own aggressive behavior, 45 percent admitted to flashing lights when annoyed and 22 percent made rude gestures, but only 6 percent admitted to aggressive tailgating and only 5 percent said they had deliberately obstructed another vehicle. More of the younger drivers under thirty-five admitted to aggressive behavior (76 percent) than drivers over fifty-four (34 percent).

Several Associated Press and Reuters reports in 1998 and 1999, posted on CNN's Web site, document aggressive driving problems in a variety of countries:[14]

CALGARY (Reuters)—December 8, 1998. The spirit of the Wild West is very much alive on the streets of the Canadian city of Calgary, where motorists are more prone to road rage than those in the country's biggest cities, according to a survey released Tuesday. Calgarians, known for their cowboy heritage, are more likely to mete out vigilante justice by punching out fellow drivers, cutting off other cars, yelling and making obscene gestures than are motorists in Toronto and Montreal, according to the study by an insurance company.

Meanwhile, 43 percent of the Calgarians said they had been victims of aggression when behind the wheel, compared with 30 percent of the Torontonians and 28 percent of the Montrealers. The survey cited several examples of road rage, ranging from the tame—muttering to one's self when irritated by a fellow motorist—to the more extreme—dangerously close tailgating and physical violence.

ATHENS, Greece (AP)—December 13, 1998. Even motorists accustomed to Athens' epic traffic problems are showing signs of frustration at the staggering tie-ups during the traditional pre-holiday wave of protests. Choking traffic in Athens is not difficult. It is now home to more than 4 million of Greece's population of 10.2 million. In Salonica, after a local soccer team was punished for crowd violence, furious soccer supporters staged a giant demonstration in the city center, and briefly blocked the highway to Athens.

BANGKOK, Thailand (AP)—December 24, 1998. With a burst of road rage in which he allegedly almost killed a policeman, a freshman member of Parliament has emerged as the latest symbol of what many regard as the Thai elite's contempt for the law. Now, all of Thailand is waiting to see what price he will pay—if any.

An eyewitness description of New Delhi road users:

When traveling in India a few years ago, I was blown away by the sort of highway travel that I experienced there. While traveling by bus on the highway from Dehra Dun to New Delhi, I quickly noticed that buses, trucks, bicycles, and all sorts of other vehicles were barreling down a narrow piece of pavement in both directions. When the bus I was on wanted to pass another, or if a truck approached from the other direction, the driver would honk the horn like hell until, miraculously to me, a path cleared for the bus to pass.

While this driving technique—the constant blasting of horns—was obnoxious and terrifying to me, it was acceptable and standard behavior in that country, or at least on that expanse of highway. In fact, most trucks had signs—decoratively painted on the tailgates—stating, "Horn Please," which I took to mean something like, "Honk with impunity to let me know you're behind me."[15]

There is no doubt that road rage and aggressive driving are worldwide phenomena, rooted in cultural ideology.

ROAD RAGE AND AGGRESSIVE DRIVING

FACING THE CULTURE OF DISRESPECT

Media reports and driver opinion surveys illustrate the need to place aggressive driving within a cultural context to answer the question: Why is this happening and why is it on the rise? At the 1996 National Women's Political Caucus, Sharon Rodine discussed the need for greater "civility in society." She noted that culture influences the level of intolerance and violence by promoting and supporting the acceptance of aggressive behavior. It's essential, she said, to differentiate between "stupid acts" and "stupid people" by looking beyond facile polarization and stereotypes. And the president warned us about the decline of sportsmanship, where "winning ugly" has become the popular model and unrepentant bullies deliberately contribute to an atmosphere of unsportsmanlike behavior with profanity, kicking trash cans, insulting referees, making ugly shows of defiance, participating in field brawls, and denigrating fans in media interviews. One of the most commercially successful events on TV is wrestling, where enthusiastic crowds, including children, applaud the simulated violence, insults, and enraged acts of wrestlers.

A culture of rage also prevails in the driving arena. Everyone knows about it, and everybody talks about it. It's estimated that there are billions of road rage exchanges annually among the 177 million U.S. drivers, not including the twelve hundred road rage assault-and-battery incidents reported each year by police. But the vast majority of the billions of road rage exchanges, each lasting mere seconds or minutes, don't end up with shootings and battering. Nevertheless, it's appropriate to designate these hostile mini-exchanges as instances of road rage because each involves the two symptoms that define road rage: (a) the feeling of rage accompanied by mental violence, and (b) the desire to punish and retaliate.

Few of us can claim to be free of hostile encounters when we drive. Mostly, the little incidents are easy to ignore. We get used to them and consider them normal. But we run a risk each time because it's not possible to predict which little incident will turn violent. The cumulative effect of our daily encounters with pervasive hostility toughens our hide, and promotes a culture of mutual disrespect on highways.

Deborah Tannen examines the dynamics of the culture of disrespect in everyday life.[16] Tannen's analysis of the problem of contentiousness in society is applicable to driving. The adversarial attitude common in driving is similar to disputes and disagreements in the workplace, in the family, and in personal relationships. Aggressiveness among motorists adds a dysfunctional element to driving as a social institution or activity. Some drivers go overboard in applying the defensive driving principle, emphasizing suspiciousness and a readiness to criticize or expect the worst of others.

Tannen's view of how social disputes are sequenced and practiced in daily life leads to an obvious recommendation: Society must find constructive ways to resolve disputes and differences. One of the prominent characteristics of "the argument culture" is the use of war metaphors. On the highway front it's common to hurl expletives: stupid fool, road warrior, Sunday driver, Mad Max, maniac, slimeball, airhead, and worse. When a driver enters our lane immediately ahead of us in order to get to an off ramp, we have a choice of labels for this action. We can call the action "cutting me off" or "entering my lane." Often the latter is more accurate, but we prefer the former. Why? The argument culture inspires a knee-jerk defensive response that makes opposition the norm. According to Tannen:

> Everywhere we turn, there is evidence that, in public discourse, we prize contentiousness and aggression more than cooperation and conciliation. Headlines blare about the Star Wars, the Mommy Wars, the Baby Wars, the Mammography Wars; everything is posed in terms of battles and duels, winners and losers, conflicts and disputes.[17]

This generation will be characterized as the "Age of Rage," typified in popular book titles and headlines that herald, and accurately reflect, society's deep involvement in the rage experience:

- *The Culture of Rage*
- *The Culture of Criticism*
- *The Culture of Violence*
- *The Culture of Disrespect*
- *The Culture of Aggression*
- *The Culture of Cynicism*
- *The Culture of Fear*
- *The Argument Culture*

Deborah Tannen writes that young men drive more aggressively because in driving they express a "ritual opposition in their struggles for status." Drivers have become specialized in a mental driving economy that keeps track of how many times their "face" (or ego) has been ritually "injured" (or disrespected) by an exchange with another driver. In this status-seeking mentality, the actions of other drivers take on dramatic and symbolic meanings that either insult us ("Who does he think he is?") or make us feel superior ("Gotcha!"). But in a diverse and congested highway community, the sense of entitlement to drive the way we want engenders unfair and unrealistic expectations of other drivers. Since the roads are also shared by inexperienced, unfamiliar, impaired, and unsure drivers, it's unreasonable and unrealistic to demand that all drivers engage in one style or level of driving. This despotic orientation leads to a deprecating attitude about the intelligence, motives, the capacity of others, and a self-righteousness that permits us to become anonymous vigilantes. Since this harsh approach to driver relations is a culturally transmitted norm, we all practice it to some extent, under circumstances that vary with individual background and personality. But we pay a price in terms of diminished quality of life because disrespect increases risk, danger, stress, defensiveness, and dehumanization.

Ned Megargee's research in criminal psychology resulted in a classification system for prison inmates based on studies of aggressive and violent behavior.[18] His research determined that violent behavior is the outcome of a number of factors converging to produce the aggressive response. The source of all aggressive behavior lies in an individual's motivational structure, or "the sum of the forces that drive an individual to commit a violent act." Human motives that often accompany aggression include greed, jealousy, hate, anger, revenge, need for status, need for acceptance, lust for control, lust for excitement, and thrill seeking. The presence of any of these motives leads an individual to build up a repertoire of aggressive and violent behaviors, performed repeatedly under favorable conditions when inhibitions are weakened.

The more violent behaviors are reinforced or rewarded through success and avoidance of punishment, the stronger the "habit strength" of the behavior and the more frequently it occurs. That's why the best predictor of future violence is past violent behavior.

> Megargee wholeheartedly agrees that how children are raised—the values they're exposed to by parents, peer groups or the media—can have an incalculable effect on their inhibitions against criminal behavior and violence. The "family values" crowd has it right when they argue that such things as a cohesive neighborhood, an intact family and religious instruction can contribute enormously to a child's sense of propriety. "Chances are, if the environment you grow up in disapproves of violence, you're going to disapprove of it as an adult. If your neighborhood approves of violence, that's the attitude you tend to take with you as you grow up. There's little debate about that."[19]

Though Megargee doesn't discuss aggressive driving and road rage, it's clear that his research and theory apply. Think of millions of parents driving aggressively in the presence of millions of children, all future drivers.

> But even adults with strong senses of right and wrong can suffer lapses of moral inhibitions several ways. One of the most effective means is by seeing others commit crimes with impunity. By seeing repeated exam-

ples of criminals going unpunished, with miscreants benefiting from their misdeeds, individuals of even the stoutest moral character are likely to experience an erosion of their inhibitions over time.[20]

Few of us are ready to accept the idea that our daily aggressive driving behaviors fall in the "criminal" category making us "miscreants," yet aggressive driving is a criminal misdemeanor and felony in several states, and does go "unpunished" in most cases, contributing to erosion of inhibitions over time. Megargee warns, "it's a lot easier to lose your inhibitions than it is to foster them."[21] The hostility experienced daily on streets creates a subculture of aggressiveness that couples disrespect with lowered inhibitions, adding up to oppositional driving styles.

Daily, millions of motorists have to manage hundreds of social exchanges with strangers such as when to brake, when to speed up, when to yield. Most driver interactions are minor, lasting only a second or two, yet their spirit of execution has a cumulative impact on our moods, feelings, and thoughts, sometimes lasting for hours through the day. Some drivers report that after driving to work, their mood negatively affects their productivity and exchanges with coworkers:

> When I'm in a bad mood and I have to sit in bumper-to-bumper traffic, I'm not a very friendly person. I usually get very aggressive and angry at anyone and everyone for everything. For instance, the person could have the blinker on and assume that I'm letting them in, so the car merges into my lane and because I'm in a bad mood, I'll say something derogatory even though the person waves to thank me. When I'm in this kind of mood, it's really difficult for me to lessen the negative.

Negative thoughts behind the wheel act like mental pollutants, decreasing the enjoyment of driving and increasing its noxious by-products—stress, higher blood pressure, frustration, pessimism, and less effective mental productivity that influences health, workplace, and family life. For millions, driving has become an emotional irritant that daily contaminates their mood. According to research in the United States and Sweden, the longer the commute, the higher the blood pressure, and commuters facing congested drives have a greater incidence of absenteeism. Men and women of all ages, ethnic, and income groups experience frustration on crowded freeways and at red lights. While this is an understandable reaction to congestion, few realize that frustration in traffic is a learned habit, and therefore it can be unlearned.

Learned negativity is characteristic of this generation's driving norms. For years we imbibe our parents' attitudes as we ride with them. Watching drivers behaving badly on TV, enjoying it and getting away without consequences, further reinforces the norm of aggressiveness. When teenagers obtain that coveted driver's license and claim their independence, the negativity they've imbibed in childhood takes over and fortifies the culture of disrespect. And we are passing it on to the next generation—unless we decide to do something about it. Social methods have been used to counteract the stressful effects of negative thoughts. For example, commuters who switch to ride sharing arrangements show a significant reduction in blood pressure within a few days. Carpoolers, both drivers and passengers, are less bothered by congestion, possibly because socializing shifts their focus away from what other drivers are doing or not doing. This book presents self-change methods that substitute habitual negativity with learned optimism and a positive outlook behind the wheel.

THE EXPANDING AGE OF RAGE

There are indications that the culture of disrespect is opening new venues for expressing anger. As usual, media mavens have a finger on new cultural developments and the word is out: Rage is spreading! Many headlines proclaim:

- Parking lot rage
- Sidewalk rage
- Surf rage
- Air rage
- Neighbor rage
- Shopping mall rage
- Workplace rage
- Cafeteria rage
- Customer rage
- Keyboard rage
- Desk rage

Surf rage? There is "Surf Rage Shock in Laid-Back West Coast of the United States," according to *World News Online*:

> The normally relaxed beaches of southern California are becoming a hazardous place, following a series of "surf rage" attacks. Undercover police officers clad only in swimming trunks and wrap-around sunglasses are watching the waves on beaches where the problem of violence is so severe that some surfers have been admitted to hospital. Several surfers face charges of using their boards as deadly weapons by launching them at interlopers.

There are now about 1.5 million surfers in America, competing for waves on a relatively small number of beaches in Hawaii, Florida and California. A surf-rage offender is as likely to be a lawyer as a thug. Surf etiquette requires that those nearest to a breaking wave should be allowed to ride it first, but the ocean is now often so crowded that protocol fails.

Lawmakers are considering adding surf rage to a list of federal hate crimes that includes attacks on racial and religious minorities and homosexuals.

The worst assaults involve the boards themselves, deliberately aimed at unsuspecting swimmers. Once the ultimate symbol of a carefree and peaceful way of life, the Open Waves Act would reclassify many models of surf board as deadly weapons.[22]

While Britons and Aussies report on Californian surf rage, a Hawaii newspaper headlines "Surf Rage Sweeping British Beaches":

Violence is erupting on British beaches as angry surfers fight to ride the best waves. Fists have been flying and tempers have been flayed. Newquay in Cornwall, the Mecca of British surfing, has witnessed the worst outbreaks. An estimated 250,000 people a year in Britain now try their hand at surfing.[23]

Did someone say "desk rage"?

Just when you were finally getting a handle on your road rage problem, along comes a new anger epidemic to ruffle your feathers—desk rage. A new British study shows that mounting workplace pressure is leading to an increasing incidence of squabbles and outright slugfests between colleagues who are stressed out.

A survey of more than 600 workers in England revealed that . . . 28 percent had suffered a bout of desk rage that led to a "stand-up row" with a colleague. . . . According to one estimate, job stress costs U.S. industry $300 billion annually due to absenteeism, diminished productivity, employee turnover and medical, legal and insurance fees. Stress is linked to a long and varied list of ailments including cardiovascular disease, cancer, cirrhosis, gastrointestinal foul-ups, emotional disorders, herpes, arthritis and the common cold.[24]

Richard Denenberg, codirector of Workplace Solutions, a Red Hook, New York–based consortium of conflict and crisis management professionals, reports that European officials refer to the malady as "mobbing" and in the U.S. it's known as "workplace bullying."[25] The Campaign Against Workplace Bullying (CAWB) calls it an epidemic.[26]

A recent New Yorker cartoon captioned "Sidewalk Rage" pictures a spacious sidewalk divided by double lines into four lanes, each marked with a sign: Speed Walkers (far-left lane), Walkers Who Veer, Walkers Who Reverse Direction, and Walkers Who Inexplicably Stop (far-right lane). This unfortunate episode reveals the ugly reality of sidewalk rage:

> It seems road rage doesn't end at the curb. World champion cyclist Larry Zimich became the victim of sidewalk rage Tuesday afternoon on the Lions Gate Bridge. On Wednesday, the 32-year-old North Vancouver rider woke up at St. Paul's Hospital in Vancouver. "Right now I can't even get up," said Zimich, who's suffering from broken bones in his shoulder and a displaced hip after a roadside confrontation with bridge workers.

One of the pedestrians on the bridge yelled an obscenity about cyclists and is reported to have "raised his elbow and clipped Zimich with it as Zimich rode slowly by," causing the cyclist to fall over.

> "I ended up on the bridge deck and in the middle of the lane," said the 156-pound rider. "I heard something crack. Then I heard the screeching of the cars. I look up and there's this guy's bumper right above me. He just managed to stop in time. The poor guy thought he had hit me. He was just shaking.[27]

These worrisome news items illustrate the severity of the expanding rage problem.

> *Car show rage:* At the New York International Auto Show, two men are rushed to hospital after a knife fight at the BMW display. Witnesses say the altercation began when a man stepped in front of another who was trying to photograph a white convertible.

> *Express lane rage:* A Milwaukee grocery shopper follows a woman to the parking lot and cuts off part of her nose because the woman went through the express checkout with more than ten items. The man, forty-one, is charged with second-degree reckless endangerment.

Rage problems vary, but violence remains the typical response.

> *Parking lot rage:* In Ottawa, CFRA open-line host Lowell Green tells listeners he is fed up with picketing Corel Center cleaners delaying his entry into the arena's parking areas. He adds, "The next time it happens, I'm going to run over them." However, Mr. Green later said his comments were "just satire."[28]

> *Parking rage:* On April 2, 1998, a Cal State student almost died over a parking space. The suspect, whose name is being withheld, became involved in a verbal argument with another student, who was driving a

Porsche, after parking his GMC truck. The driver of the Porsche then stabbed the GMC owner in the torso four times as he walked away.[29]

A new permissiveness frees more people to become openly enraged in a wide variety of public places, sometimes in jest—but sometimes not.

THE ANGER CHOICE

According to Deborah Tannen, anger is the main method people use to negotiate dominance levels in power games.[30] Carol Tavris describes Darwin's theory of human aggression as a biologically programmed response no different from the rage reflex of animals when they are attacked or threatened.[31] Tavris thinks this model is too simplistic for humans, since threat does not always elicit anger and anger does not always elicit aggression. Humans have mediating processes such as judgment and choice that interrupt automatic connections. In this view, expressing anger is not a triggered response but a learned habit. The habit specifies when anger can be expressed as aggressiveness, and when it must be inhibited or hidden. Thus, anger is a habit that can be modified to restore human choice in provocative situations.

Even if it feels as though anger is automatically aroused, it does not automatically lead to aggressiveness. The connection between anger and aggressiveness is mediated by norms and principles, by what a person feels is or is not allowed. If a philosophy or value system permits the expression of aggressive behavior, a person might act out when angry under certain conditions. The aggressiveness in road rage is a behavioral strategy used to enforce domination of a stranger—someone who is seen as deserving punishment for having inconvenienced us, or for having placed us in danger out of stupidity, incompetence, or a lack of consideration or caring.

Daniel Goleman writes that anger "is energizing, even exhilarating."[32] Venting rage behind the wheel feels like a catharsis—"Isn't it better for me than holding it in?" Does this justify hostility or uncivility? While long-held popular belief says that venting anger is healthy, recent medical research concludes that venting instead increases stress and depresses immune system functioning.[33] The new message is this: anger kills.[34] However, our culture has inherited the ill effects of the "venting is good" model. Goleman points to the "seductive, persuasive power" of anger, of the illusion that it is uncontrollable, triggered automatically; that we're not really responsible when it just comes out.[35] But actually, the "triggering" stimulus is merely the sudden realization of physical endangerment. Someone cuts us off and we hit the brakes. As the foot moves, the brain reacts simultaneously and prepares for the worst. For a **35** few moments we experience overwhelming physical sensations. This is the moment of choice.

It is a free choice and its outcome depends on the symbolic value we attach to the event. If we attach the event to our self-esteem, we may go down the road of rage, feeling insulted, wronged, disrespected, demeaned, and thwarted from our legitimate goal. The emotional brain takes over and leads us to emotionally challenged behavior like retaliating. But there is another choice that is equally available to us in that emotional moment. If we realize that the driver's prime directive is to stay in control of the vehicle and of the situation, we can see that we give up control by responding in kind. We don't know what the other driver might do next, but we have the freedom to transform the symbolic value of the "triggering" event, to inhibit the impulse to kill. Following the prime directive gives us the opportunity to remain cool-headed and to respond from the new, cortical brain: "Hey, be my guest," or "Let it go, it's not worth it," or "Maybe the guy has an emergency or something," or "That could be my grandmother." The essence of emotional intelligence for drivers is consciously transforming the critical reaction to something less painful. That's a big victory!

GEORGE WASHINGTON'S RULES OF CIVILITY

Reporter Michelle Malkin, in an article on road rage, reminds us of George Washington's Rules of Civility as the cement that binds a nation together. Malkin believes that following these rules can cure road rage and aggressive driving:

> The problem isn't absence of self-esteem—but an utter lack of self-restraint. Two-and-a-half centuries ago, our Founding Father, George Washington, subscribed to a more cost-effective and time-tested program for reining in one's inner dragons. He carried a hand-copied list of self-improvement rules, originally set out by 16th-century Jesuit priests, wherever he went—from Valley Forge to Yorktown and throughout his presidency. The original manuscript is kept at the Library of Congress.
>
> Like many modern road-ragers, Washington was a hothead who faced mounting stress at work and at home. As Brookhiser notes, "Washington had a lot to be angry about over the course of his career: untrained soldiers, incompetent officers, difficult allies, quarrelsome associates (including Thomas Jefferson)—to say nothing of his own mistakes from losing battles to misjudging people. . . . But if he had gone into uncontrollable rages at every disappointment or disaster, he would have ruined his health, besides ruining his effectiveness as a leader." Rather than let it all hang out, Washington tempered his temper by adhering to some basic rules of civil life.[36]

This is the simplest and nicest solution available, more effective than law enforcement surveillance: Civility, a true American virtue! For instance, Washington's Rule 1, translated for the traffic world: "Every action done to another driver ought to be done with some sign of respect." This alone could solve the epidemic of the century and stop it from reproducing itself in the next. Washington's Rule 22 had a moral implication for character development: "Shew not yourself glad at the misfortune of another though he were your enemy." This is the basis of supportive driving, a driving orientation that emphasizes compassion, tolerance, and wisdom. Further advice from our founding father for aggressive drivers, as recast by Malkin:

- Don't show any sign of anger in your interactions with other motorists, but show instead signs of "sweetness and mildness" (Rule 45).
- Don't use insulting language against another driver or pedestrian, neither curse nor revile your passengers (Rule 49).
- Labor to keep alive in your breast that little spark of celestial fire called your driving conscience (Rule 110).

Malkin also refers to our approach:

Naturally, a new breed of experts in "traffic psychology" has arisen to provide a cure. They converged upon Congress last week peddling 3-step, 5-step, and 10-step programs to "acquire inner power at the wheel" and "engineer your own driving personality make-over." These gridlock gurus warned the House Transportation Committee that the world's car-bound population is facing a mental health crisis.

Most rage-related incidents, the experts explain, arise from trivial causes over parking spaces, obscene gestures, tailgating and turn signals. Thus the need, says renowned traffic psychologist Leon James (aka "Dr. Driving") at the University of Hawaii . . . to "slay your driving dragon" and "acquire personal self-management techniques as a driver."[37]

Malkin concludes her report with this reminder: "For motorists who aspire to something higher than boorishness, the 'Rules of Civility' serve as clear and fundamental rules of the road. . . . Simple good manners, Washington taught, are the first step to greatness—and they may even save lives." And that's precisely what it takes to remain a polite and civilized driver in all circumstances. We can no longer afford to treat road rage like Goofy did half a century ago:

There is a 1950s cartoon about it. Kindly "Mr. Walker" (played by Goofy) turns into the ill-mannered, and aggressive "Mr. Wheeler" when he drives his car. Maybe Disney should be credited as the discoverer of Road Rage, and Goofy can be the poster child.

DEVELOPING EMOTIONAL LITERACY

We pay a high price for being emotionally challenged. Depression and social conflict are the twin scourges affecting the individual and society. Depression is a symptom of our hurt self-esteem, and social conflict is a symptom of the prejudice and lack of education that tear a community apart. Emotional literacy can be taught in courses or self-taught. The three-step program for lifelong driver self-improvement (see chapter 9) teaches drivers to become aware of and to monitor the sequence of their emotions and thoughts behind the wheel. The purpose of monitoring thoughts while driving is to acquire systematic information about oneself. Our research shows that we typically hold exaggerated beliefs about ourselves as drivers, and this creates conflict when someone complains about it: "No way—I'm an excellent driver!"

Without emotional literacy a person can neither recognize aggressiveness nor feel personal responsibility for the mayhem. The injury we cause others is threefold: Injury to their cars and bodies; injury to their mental state and happiness; and injury to the nation by contributing to social conflict and disunity. The shift from "aggressive driver" to "supportive driver" comes only through developing a consciously benevolent feeling, supporting community values over individualistic desires. The benefits of greater emotional self-awareness are impressive for the individual and for society. Caging rage is a civilized necessity. This book details the breakdown of the highway community with the passing of civility and the institutionalized tolerance of highway aggression and automotive vigilantism (see chapters 3 and 4). To reverse the accelerating trend of highway violence and hostile attitudes, we need to restore the forces of cohesion that bind us together as civil drivers. According to some current theories of human evolution, our original ancestors shared positive qualities such as community and belongingness that were unifying forces in culture. Over the course of time new qualities emerged that gave us more power over the environment, such as creating technology and social organization. These later traits tended to suppress the earlier and milder traits of social cohesiveness and equality.[38] Fortunately, we are still capable of drawing on these community-building forces.

Highway and car design must integrate and incorporate positive paradigms of cooperation and caring to counteract the current trend of competition and hostility. The social organization of traffic can be achieved through methods of sociality and mutuality, not individuality, competition, and defensiveness. The shift from adversarialism to mutuality marks the coming of age of driving society. All nations go through the first phase of evolution in driving governed by the old emotional brain. But even if aggressive driving is a natural phase in driving evolution, society cannot survive if antisocial driving continues unchecked. As an external management system, law enforcement is incapable of exerting an inner influence on the social conscience.[39] It is the task of safety experts and driver education specialists to build viable training programs that give drivers the inner power tools needed to develop compassion on the roads. Chapter 9 outlines a proposal for an inexpensive and effective delivery mechanism for a new paradigm to achieve lifelong driver self-improvement training.

PROTECTING YOURSELF FROM AGGRESSIVE DRIVERS

Typical advice from a traffic safety organization:

- Do not make obscene gestures.
- Use your horn sparingly.
- Don't block the passing lane.
- Don't switch lanes without signaling.
- Avoid blocking the right-hand turn lane.
- Do not tailgate.
- If you travel slowly, pull over and allow traffic to pass.
- Avoid unnecessary use of high-beam headlights.
- Don't let the car phone distract you.
- Don't stop in the road to talk with a pedestrian or other driver.
- Don't inflict loud music on neighboring cars.
- Assume other drivers' mistakes are not personal.
- Be polite and courteous, even if the other driver isn't.
- Avoid all conflict if possible. If another driver challenges you, take a deep breath and get out of the way.
- Reduce your stress: Allow plenty of time for the trip; listen to soothing music.[40]

It's one thing to be able to recite good advice and quite another to follow it. Knowing or memorizing the list is only the first step in the change process; this book describes the tools needed to turn these ideals into reality. The driver's prime directive is to stay in control of the vehicle and of the situation, and aggressive driving violates this principle because it contributes to more crashes between cars and duels between drivers.

ROAD RAGE AND AGGRESSIVE DRIVING

CHECKLIST: YOUR ROAD RAGE TENDENCY

For each statement, circle "Yes" if it applies to you reasonably well, or "No" if it doesn't.

1. I swear a lot more in traffic than I do elsewhere.
   Yes   No

2. I normally have critical thoughts about other drivers.
   Yes   No

3. When a driver in a parking lot tries to steal the space I've been waiting for, I get furious.
   Yes   No

4. I fantasize about doing violence to other drivers (e.g., using guns or blowing them up or sweeping them aside)—but it's just fantasy.
   Yes   No

5. When drivers do something really "stupid" that endangers me or my car, I get furious, even aggressive.
   Yes   No

6. It's good to get your anger out because we all have aggressive feelings inside that naturally come out under stressful situations.
   Yes   No

7. When I'm very upset about something, it's a relief to step on the gas to give my feelings an outlet.
   Yes   No

8. I feel that it's important to force certain drivers to behave appropriately on the highway.
   Yes   No

9. Pedestrians shouldn't have the right to walk slowly in crosswalks when cars are waiting.
   Yes   No

10. Pushy drivers really annoy me so I bad-mouth them to feel better.
    Yes   No

11. I tailgate when someone drives too slow for conditions or in the passing lane.
    Yes   No

12. I try to get to my destination in the shortest time possible, or else it doesn't feel right.
    Yes   No

13. If I stopped driving aggressively, others would take advantage of my passivity.
    Yes   No

14. I feel unpleasant emotions when someone beats me to the light or when someone gets through and I'm stuck on red.
    Yes   No

15. I feel energized by the sense of power and competition I experience while driving aggressively.
    Yes   No

16. I hate speed bumps and speed limits that are set too low.
    Yes   No

17. Once in a while I get so frustrated in traffic that I begin to drive somewhat recklessly.
    Yes   No

18. I hate large trucks and I refuse to drive differently around them.
    Yes   No

19. Sometimes I feel that I'm holding up traffic so I start driving faster than feels comfortable.
    Yes   No

20. I would feel embarrassed to "get stuck" behind a large vehicle on a steep road.
    Yes   No

Scoring your answers: Give yourself 1 road rage point for every "Yes" answer. How many do you have?

Interpreting your score: Scores range from 0 to 20. Few drivers score 0 because road rage emotions are habitual and cultural. We all have some tendency toward it. The higher the score, the more likely it is that you will become involved in road rage trouble. Typical scores range from 5 to 20, with an average of 12.

If your score is less than 5, you're not an aggressive driver and your road rage tendency is manageable. **Scores between 5 and 10** indicate that you have moderate road rage habits. **If your score is greater than 10,** your road rage tendency is out of control, enough to compromise your ability to remain calm and fair in certain routine but challenging driving situations.

By examining the pattern of your answers, you can gain valuable insight about your current level of emotional intelligence as a driver (see chapter 5). Many drivers are able to reduce their score to under 5 after conscious practice with the techniques described in this book. This checklist helps you assess four critical elements that create habitual road rage:

ROAD RAGE AND AGGRESSIVE DRIVING

- your anger theory (questions 1 to 7)
- your driving philosophy (questions 8 to 11)
- your habit of compulsive rushing or feeling competitive (questions 12 to 17)
- your oversensitivity to social pressure by motorists (18 to 20)

A word of caution is in order. You cannot fully trust the reliability of the answers, especially when your score is low, because it only represents your opinion of your driving. You may have an excellent opinion of yourself as a driver, but it may not be objective or accurate. Our research shows that when 10 is perfect, most people choose 8, 9, or 10 when asked to rate their skill as a driver. Clearly, if most drivers were close to perfect, there wouldn't be six million collisions and billions of hostile incidents each year. The following chapters describe various convenient methods you can use to make objective observations about yourself as driver. Accuracy in self-assessment is essential for identifying and modifying unsafe components in your driving habits. We recommend that you fill out all the checklists and do all the exercises because they supply the knowledge needed to practice a lifelong driver self-improvement program (see chapter 9).

CHECKLIST: WINNING AND LOSING IN THE DRIVING GAME

The culture of disrespect on highways is a worldwide phenomenon that is part of car society. A negative car culture has created a competitive mental driving economy for keeping track of what happens to us on the roads. People often have personal contests with themselves, counting the seconds, minutes, or landmarks that pass before they must apply their brakes. Never having to stop is a sign of skill, power, and victory. The inherited culture of disrespect subconsciously embroils us in a gaming method of accounting that elevates or lowers our self-esteem, determined by the actions of others. Even for the smallest events we keep track of supposed insults or when someone's action forces us to do something. You gain or lose points in the daily driving game by counting:

1. ____ How many cars you passed
2. ____ How many cars passed you
3. ____ How well you managed by choosing the fastest lane
4. ____ How many times you had to brake
5. ____ How many lights you made without having to stop

6. ____ How many times you were the leader of the pack
7. ____ How fast you made it somewhere
8. ____ Whether someone was pushy toward you
9. ____ How often you got away with speeding over a stretch of road
10. ____ How many cars cut into your lane, forcing you to brake
11. ____ How many times you felt insulted, wondering whether you're a wimp if you don't retaliate
12. ____ How many cars you were able to keep out of your lane by closing the gap
13. ____ How many cars you passed in a long line before cutting in
14. ____ How many minutes you were able to shave off the trip
15. ____ How many times you were thwarted from doing something
16. ____ Others: _____

INSTRUCTIONS: Which do you typically give yourself points or credit for when driving? Which ones make you lose points? Add others that are not on this list. Review the list immediately before your next drive. Make a mental note each time you become aware of giving or taking away driving points. Build greater awareness by repeating this exercise on several trips. Keep a driving diary or log, or think out loud into a voice-activated tape recorder.

This mental driving economy maintains an aggressive culture on highways and streets. As soon as the gunnysack of minus points is full on any particular trip, the passion of self-righteousness swells in the chest and we feel justified in letting it fly, exploding in rage and disapproval, with condemnation and violent thoughts. A spirit of territorial competition governs this mental gaming economy. Society needs to see the driving game as a harmful cultural practice that requires a psychosocial solution. Driving psychology provides the tools needed to curb aggression in driving. In the following chapters we discuss the self-instructional methods needed to reclaim our freedom from the current emotional terrorism that highway culture has unthinkingly created.

NOTES

1. Andrew Ferguson, "Road Rage: Aggressive Driving Is America's Car Sickness Du Jour," *Time*, January 12, 1998 [online], www.time.com/time/magazine/1998/dom/980112/society.road_rage_.html [May 19,2000].

2. Paula Story, "Americans Often Take Out Their Frustration behind the Wheel," *Centre Daily Times*, July 2, 1997.

3. Yahoo! [online], headlines.yahoo.com/Full_Coverage/US/Road-Rage [June 3, 1999].

ROAD RAGE AND AGGRESSIVE DRIVING

4. Michael Fumento, "Road Rage vs. Reality," *Atlantic Monthly*, August 1998 [online] www. fumento.com/atlantic.html [May 19, 2000].

5. Ibid.

6. "An Operetta in One Act, Words by Harry Greenbank, Music by Ernest Ford," Gilbert and Sullivan Archive [online], diamond.idbsu.edu/gas/companions/jericho/jericho06d.html [May 19, 2000].

7. British Home Office, "Dangerous Driving Road Traffic Act of 1988" [online], www.homeoffice.gov.uk/cdact/finalann.htm [May 19, 2000].

8. "N.Y. Prosecutor Faces Murder Charge," AP Online, June 30, 1999 [online], www.ap.org [May 19, 2000].

9. Don Russell, "Driving Ourselves into Early Graves: Angry Motorists Kill More Than Drunks Do," Philadelphia Online [online], www. philly.com/packages/hellonwheels/hell07.asp [May 19, 2000].

10. Ibid.

11. Associated Press Honolulu [online], www.honoluluadvertiser.com [October 14, 1996].

12. Slovenia Consular Information Sheet [online], travel.state.gov/slovenia.html [May 19, 2000].

13. "Road Rage," AA Driver Education Program New Zealand [online], www.aadef.co.nz/roadrage.html [May 19, 2000].

14. CNN.com World News Asia-Pacific [online], cnn.com/WORLD/asiapcf/9812/23/PM-Thialand-LawlessLawma.ap/index.html [December 23, 1998].

15. Personal anecdotes quoted throughout this chapter were sent to us by e-mail correspondents.

16. Deborah Tannen, *The Argument Culture: Moving from Debate to Dialogue* (New York: Random House, 1998).

17. Deborah Tannen, "For Argument's Sake: Why Do We Feel Compelled to Fight About Everything?" *Washington Post*, March 15, 1998 [online], www.georgetown.edu/tannen/argsake.htm [May 19, 2000].

18. Frank Stephenson, "The Algebra of Aggression," *Research in Review*, spring 1996 [online], www.research.fsu.edu/ResearchR/spring96/features/algebra.html [May 19, 2000].

19. Ibid.

20. Ibid.

21. Ibid.

22. James Langton, "Surf Rage Shock in Laid-Back West Coast," *Sydney Morning Herald*, March 2, 1999 [online], 203..26.177.61/news/9903/02/world/world14.html [May 19, 2000].

23. Denis Campbell, "Surf Rage Sweeping British Beaches," *Honolulu Star-Bulletin*, July 28, 1999, p. A15; Tim Ryan, "Surfing Solitaire," *Honolulu Star-Bulletin*, February 16, 1999, p. D6.

24. Jon Bowen, "Fisticuffs in the Cube: Stressed-Out Office Workers Are Succumbing to 'Desk Rage,'" Salon.com Health & Body [online], www.salon.com/health/log/1999/09/07/rage/index.html [May 19, 2000].

25. Richard Denenberg and Mark Braverman, *The Violence-Prone Workplace:*

A New Approach to Dealing with Hostile, Threatening and Uncivil Behavior (Ithaca, N.Y.: Cornell University Press, 1999).

26. Campaign Against Workplace Bullying (CAWB) [online], www.bully-busters.org/home/bullybust.html [May 19, 2000].

27. Ian Noble, "Nightmarish Encounter Recounted: Cyclist Bumped from Bike on Bridge," *Northshore News*, October 20, 1997 [online], www.usnews.com/issue/w102097/10179701.html [May 19,2000].

28. Phillip's Volkswagen News [online], www.ingear.net/users/Phillip/vwnews/98-12-01.html [December 12, 1998].

29. Nick Brennan, "Parking Rage Leads to Stabbing at CSUDH," *Daily Titan Interactive* [online], dailytitan.fullerton.edu/issues/spring_98/dti_04_15/news/parkingrage.html [May 19, 2000].

30. Tannen, *Argument Culture*, chap. 1

31. Carol Tavris, *Anger: The Misunderstood Emotion* (New York: Simon and Schuster, 1982), p. 36.

32. Daniel Goleman, *Emotional Intelligence* (New York: Bantam Books, 1995), p. 59.

33. Paul Pearsall, *The Pleasure Prescription: To Love, to Work, to Play–Life in the Balance* (Alameda, Calif.: Hunter House Publishers, 1996).

34. Redford Williams and Virginia Williams, *Anger Kills* (New York: Harper Perennial, 1993).

35. Goleman, *Emotional Intelligence*, p. 59.

36. Michelle Malkin, "A Founding Father's Rules Might Cure Raging Drivers," *Seattle Times*, July 22, 1997 [online], www.seattletimes.com/extra/browse/html97/altmalk_072297.html [May 19, 2000]. These quotations are used with permission from Ms. Malkin.

37. Ibid.

38. James A. Vela-McConnell, *Who Is My Neighbor: Social Affinity in a Modern World* (Albany: State University of New York Press, 1999).

39. Jay Earley, *Transforming Human Culture* (Albany: State University of New York Press, 1999).

40. "Road Rage," NETS Network of Employers for Traffic Safety [online], www.trafficsafety.org/library/roadrage/protect.cfm [May 19, 2000]. A collection of thousands of tips culled from the Web may be found on our Web site at www.aloha.net/~dyc/tips.html.

AGGRESSIVE DRIVING AND MENTAL HEALTH

DENIAL AND THE SEMANTICS OF AGGRESSIVE DRIVING

In April 1998, the U.S. Department of Transportation's National Highway Traffic Safety Administration (NHTSA) released its Capital Beltway Update study of sixty-four miles of roadway surrounding Washington, D.C.,[1] a unique longitudinal study of aggressive driving patterns. The first study was done in 1994 and was repeated in 1995 and 1997. A team of experts, led by officials from Maryland and Virginia, was formed to address aggressive driving issues on this urban interstate highway. The drivers who participated represented three groupings of Beltway drivers: normal drivers, aggressive drivers, and commercial drivers. The aggressive drivers were recruited among motorists who met the general qualifications and who scored high on eight screening questions designed to measure anger, impatience, competitiveness, and vindictiveness of the driver in frequently encountered driving situations.

Aggressive Driving and Mental Health

Results from the focus group discussions confirmed that the aggressive group was more likely to engage in risky driving practices:

Focus group participants listed and ranked perceived causes of Beltway crashes. There were some remarkable differences between the 1994 and 1997 groups. Unsafe driving behaviors were among the most important factors in both years, but the 1997 participants ranked them among their top three causes twice as often as the 1994 participants. Excessive speed, aggressive driving, inattention, unsafe lane changing, and tailgating were most frequently designated major crash causes in the 1997 focus groups. Aggressive driving was the number one concern among the "general" motorist groups. It was mentioned as one of the three most serious crash causes by 53 percent of the participants. This compares with only 2 percent among the 1994 participants. Interestingly, the aggressive driver groups were less concerned about aggressive driving, since only 15 percent of them mentioned aggressive driving as one of the major crash causes.[2]

In a key early finding about the psychology of aggressive driving, three out of four participants reported feeling competitive with other drivers on a constant basis:

Drivers in the aggressive group also said they more frequently got angry when cut off, had passengers tell them to calm down, blocked other cars trying to pass, and blocked cars trying to change lanes. One woman called driving on the Beltway "a competitive sport." Aggressive drivers spoke differently from the general drivers. Both groups blame much of the unsafe driving on the Beltway on the "other driver." General groups expressed dismay at specific unsafe driving maneuvers that make them nervous on the Beltway—the drivers who speed, change lanes frequently, cut them off, and force their way ahead. Aggressive drivers, on the other hand, blame those who are going too slow in the passing lane, cars at the speed limit who "force" them to change lanes and weave in and out of traffic. As one young woman phrased it, "Get out of my way, please."[3]

Aggressive drivers typically blame other drivers for their conduct. They are vehement about left lane etiquette. One young man said, "If I'm going 80 MPH in the fast lane and someone comes up behind me, I should move out of his way." Aggressive drivers want minimum speed limits, not maximum. They express annoyance at other drivers who hinder their progress. At the same time, when these drivers feel provoked, which is often, they go out of their way to block another car trying to pass or cut in front of them. With respect to speeding, most of the drivers, aggressive and nonaggressive, acknowledged driving fifteen miles per hour above posted limits, and consider this to be safe.

ROAD RAGE AND AGGRESSIVE DRIVING

Remarkably, most forms of driving considered aggressive by law enforcement are not considered aggressive by the majority. This disparity in legal versus popular meanings excites the conflict between what is allowable and appropriate. Table 2.1 illustrates the results of a 1999 survey comparing attitudes of Los Angeles drivers with those across the nation, showing that there are large variations in what people consider aggressive driving.[4]

Table 2.1
Common Driving Behaviors and the Percentage of Drivers
Who Do Not Consider Them Aggressive

Behaviors	United States	Los Angeles
Making obscene gestures	14	30
Passing on the shoulder	17	38
Failing to yield to merging traffic	17	42
Pulling into a parking space and making others wait for you	20	33
Flashing high beams at other drivers	32	40
Waiting until the last minute to merge (not waiting in line)	40	54
Speeding up to a yellow light	42	50
Changing lanes without signaling	42	47
Blocking the left (passing) lane	45	53
Honking the horn	45	53
Going at least 10 MPH over the speed limit	53	54
Driving too slowly (at least 10 MPH below the speed limit)	74	66
Tailgating	12	36

These percentage distributions may vary in different geographic locations or specific highway segments, but whatever these specific variations may be, each location is marked by a combination of several forms of aggressive behavior that constitute the norms of aggressiveness typical in that location.

DRIVERS BEHAVING BADLY ON TV

A crucial question many have asked in the past decade is, why has road rage exploded in the 1990s? Traffic congestion has existed since the 1950s and has worsened since the 1970s. The root of road rage is a "culture tantrum," because the way we express anger and when we do it is culturally condoned or sanctioned. What has happened to promote this cultural norm of highway hostility? Psychiatrist John Larson attributes this new attitude to "the Road Warrior type movies of the 1980s" and today's television that teaches impressionable individuals that "vigilante behavior, even that which harms others, is virtuous, associated with heroic figures, and easy to do."[5] This reveals that the readiness to use violence is a cultural habit.

One of our students' favorite research activities is watching popular television programs and taking notes on scenes that portray drivers behaving badly:[6]

July 17, 1997, 6:17 P.M.: *The Simpsons* (adult cartoon series)
First incident: The three kids were watching TV, the cat was trying to kill the mouse and as the cat was running from the house, the cat runs onto the road and gets run over by a speeding truck. The Simpson kids watching the show are laughing very hard at this scene.
Second incident: Homer Simpson is late for work again and speeds into a public parking stall, almost hitting a pedestrian. Homer doesn't slow down, he just chases the pedestrian until the person moves out of the way. Homer yelled at the pedestrian for being in the way.

October 3, 1997, 6:42 P.M.: *Clueless* (movie for teenagers)
In this scene we see three of the main characters, Cher, Dion and Dion's boyfriend, traveling down a city street. Somehow, Dion manages to take the on ramp to an L.A. freeway. Screaming ensues, and mass chaos becomes the new theme of the scene. Trucks are honking, old ladies are passing by in other cars and giving the finger. Dion panics and with luck manages to make it to an off ramp.

October 5, 1997, 10:45 P.M.: "I'd Rather Ride Around" (music video)
Singer Reba McEntire and her boyfriend are getting ready for her cousin's wedding. Reba is supposed to be the bridesmaid. Together, they get carried away and end up driving around in a convertible on the beach. "Let go of the wheel" is sung as the driver takes his hands off and raises them up high. The driver throws his head back in laughter taking his eyes away from the road. The lyrics are brought to life by the actions of the actors in the video. The realism factor is high because many young people tend to joke and play behind the wheel.

In the 1970s a national debate raged on the issue of whether television violence encourages violence in homes and on streets. Some argued that it's just entertainment and everyone knows the difference between fantasy and reality. But by the 1980s the weight of research had persuaded society as a whole to accept the opposite view. Studies showed children playing more roughly after watching aggressive behaviors portrayed by a bully. Children imitated the aggressive behavior they observed in other children. It has been shown that continuous exposure to shocking and cruel behavior reduces sensitivity to it, so that school bullies deny that what they do "really" hurts. While there is no scientific research that proves that television's frequent portrayal of drivers behaving badly promotes aggressive driving, the conclusion is not unreasonable given the findings on the connection between television and violence.

PLAYERS BEHAVING BADLY
WITH ROAD RAGE VIDEO GAMES

In July 1999 GT Interactive Software shipped one million units of the PlayStation® game console version of Driver in the U.K., where it rose to the top of the charts. U.S. retail outlets reported sellouts within five minutes. The manufacturer's description of the highly realistic interactive software is noteworthy for its explicit appeal to a driver's baser instincts:

> Driver delivers the clutch-your-seats, adrenaline-charged action of a heart-stopping, Hollywood-style car chase, propelling players along a high-speed, all-out thrill ride through the wild streets of four major U.S. cities. . . . Extensive pre-production filming of each city [New York, Los Angeles, San Francisco, and Miami] brings home an unprecedented level of realism to the interactive arena, where players can clearly pick out such notable landmarks as the Empire State Building, Golden Gate Bridge and South Beach. In addition, each city has working traffic lights, wandering pedestrians who manage to get in the way, moving traffic and vigilant cops on patrol, making getaways more challenging and dynamic, immersing the player into a world that lives life on the edge.[7]

Computer games and simulations are becoming more graphic and intense in nature. The most popular games are those with the most blood and carnage. The gaming genre is evolving to reflect the interests of the most involved customers, older young-adult males 18–25 years old, the age group with the highest number of traffic fatalities. The Entertainment Software Rating Board (ESRB) alerts parents of gaming content by placing ratings on software packaging, but few believe this keeps violent games out of the hands of impressionable teenagers. In the 1990s, several games came out using road rage scenarios to entertain. These aren't typical racing games where players get points for driving skillfully and avoiding crashes. The road rage games are based on how badly players behave as aggressive and killer drivers. The object of some games is to crash into as many people or animals as possible.

For example, Carmageddon offers a triple combination of road rage, racing, and a demolition derby. In this highly intense game—which features races with names like "Maim Street" and "Coastal Carnage"—running down pedestrians and performing high-risk moves with a car earns players points and extra play time, enhanced with messages like "Splatter Bonus," and players are rewarded for smashing pedestrians and killing them in every way possible. One of our student reviewers commented on this game:

> Pretty intense. When I played this game for the first time, I immediately thought, "This game is definitely NOT for children!" Even I, a video game junkie, had to widen my eyes at the violence depicted in this game. But even so, I thought this was one of the most fun games to play. I mean, I'm not the only one who thinks this way.

The media reinforce the game's success:

> Carmageddon is the most impressive racing game around, and the most original game I've played for ages. . . . [I]f anyone is thinking of getting this but is weak of stomach, try starting the game by typing 'carma-German' which will let you play the non-bloody German version of the game. A stonker of a game![8]

After the demo was released in March 1998, pressure was brought on the manufacturer to provide less gory alternate versions. For instance, in the U.K. version, a scene showing "the old woman crossing the street and the weird guy in the trench coat was replaced by zombie-looking characters, with green instead of red blood." Mike Johnson, a spokesperson for the Automobile Association (AA), was unhappy with the potential negative impact of the game: "Despite the changes to the game, we still don't think it's an appropriate message to be sending out."[9]

Roadkill is a driving game that could be downloaded free from the Web in its beta stage. Its introduction on the Web site says, "The road is your hunting ground, a car is your weapon, the mission, to turn as many animals as you can into Roadkill." After trying it, one college student wrote:

> Everything about this game was pathetic. The graphics were horrible, sound effects were horrible, gameplay was horrible, blah. Everything was horrible! You are put in this awful-looking vehicle, and you drive along this road, killing old ladies and animals walking across the street.

In Interstate '76, another game that can be downloaded from the Web, the object is to destroy other cars and their drivers using a choice of available weapons: light firearms heavy artillery rockets, cannons, grenade launchers, and flamethrowers. To get points, players run people off the road or shoot them down with weapons.

ROAD RAGE AND AGGRESSIVE DRIVING

A distributor of these road rage games asked us to endorse its product as a safe method for harmlessly expressing natural road rage. We declined because we disagree with the notion that expressing rage in a game reduces rage in reality. In fact, the opposite is the case: Practicing acts of murder and torture, especially with graphic multimedia effects, can weaken inherent inhibitions against performing acts of violence. These inhibitions depend on developing a social conscience. Repeatedly practicing games that allow antisocial violence can interfere with the ability to empathize with others in distress. Thankfully, awareness of the problem is growing. For example, a Detroit shopping mall video arcade used by children prohibits games that simulate violence and death, stressing instead nonviolent games, driving simulations, and kiddy rides.[10]

WHY DRIVING AROUSES ANGER

Driving in traffic routinely involves events and incidents. Events are normal sequential maneuvers such as stopping for lights, changing lanes, or braking. Incidents are frequent but abnormal events. Some of these are dangerous and frightening, such as near-misses or violent exchanges, while others are merely annoying or depressing, such as being insulted by a driver or forgetting to make a turn. Driving events and incidents are sources of psychological forces capable of producing powerful feelings and irrational thought sequences. Driving is a dramatic activity performed by millions on a daily basis. The drama stems from high risk, interactivity, and unpredictability. Predictability creates safety, security, and escape from disaster. Unpredictability creates danger, stress, and crashes.

For many, driving is linked to a value of freedom of locomotion. On one hand, we can get into our cars and drive where we please, the very symbol of freedom and independence. But on the other hand, we encounter restrictions and constrictions—regulations, congestion, and the unexpected actions of other motorists that prevent us from driving as we wish. The following list identifies fifteen conflicting aspects of driving that act as stressors. The list represents emotional challenges that are common occasions for expressing hostility and aggressiveness on highways and streets:

1. *Immobility*: Most of the body remains still and passive during driving, unlike walking, where the entire body exerts effort and remains continuously active. Tension tends to build up when the body is physically constricted.
2. *Restriction*: Motor vehicles are restricted to narrow bands of

highway and street lanes. In congested traffic, progress will inevitably be continually blocked by numerous other cars. Being prevented from going forward when you expect to arouses frustration, and along with it anxiety and an intense desire to escape the restriction. This anxiety prompts drivers to perform risky or aggressive maneuvers to get away or get ahead.

3. *Regulation*: Driving is a highly regulated activity. Government agencies and law enforcement officers tell drivers how fast and where they may drive, but cars and trucks have powerful engines capable of going much faster than is allowed. Drivers are punished for violating regulations. This regulation, though lawful and obviously necessary, feels like an imposition and arouses a rebellious streak in many, which then prompts them to disregard whatever regulations seem to be wrong or inconvenient.

4. *Lack of personal control*: Traffic follows the objective laws that govern flow patterns, like those we see in rivers, pipes, blood vessels, and streaming molecules. In congested traffic the flow depends on the available spaces between the cars. When one car slows down, hundreds of other cars behind run out of space and drivers must tap their brakes to slow down, or stop altogether. No matter how we drive, it is impossible to beat these traffic waves, whose cause may start miles away. This lack of personal control over traffic events is frustrating and often leads to venting anger on whoever is around—usually another driver or a passenger.

5. *Being put in danger*: Drivers love their cars and car repairs are expensive. Even a scratch is aggravating because it reduces the car's value. Congested traffic filled with impatient and aggressive drivers can create hair-raising close calls and hostile incidents, sometimes within a few minutes of each other. This results in physiological stress, along with many negative emotions—fear, resentment, rage, a sense of helplessness, and a depressed mood.

6. *Territoriality*: The car is symbolically associated with individual freedom and self-esteem, promoting an attitude of defensiveness and territoriality. Our car is our castle and the space around the car is our territory. When other drivers invade our space and threaten our castle, we often respond with hostility, even with warlike postures and aggressive reactions to routine incidents. We often perceive such incidents as skirmishes and battles. For many motorists, driving has become a dreaded emotional roller coaster.

7. *Diversity*: There are currently 177 million licensed drivers in the United States and they represent a breadth of experience, knowledge, ability, style, and purposes for being on the road. These social

differences reduce predictability because drivers with different skills and purposes don't behave according to the expected norms. Motorists' confidence is shaken by unexpected events, and driving becomes more complex and more emotionally challenging.

8. *Multitasking*: The increase in dashboard complexity and other in-car activities like talking on the phone or checking e-mail challenge our ability to remain alert and focused behind the wheel. Moreover, we become more irritated at others—and they at us—when our attention as drivers is perceived to be lacking due to multitasking behind the wheel.

9. *Denial*: Typically, most driving is automatic, using unconscious habits learned and compiled over years. Drivers tend to exaggerate their own excellence, overlooking their many mistakes. When passengers complain or when other drivers are threatened by these errors, there is a strong tendency for the individual to deny such mistakes and to see complaints as exaggerated, hostile, or unwarranted. This denial causes us to feel indignant and self-righteous enough to wish to punish and retaliate.

10. *Negativity*: When learning to drive, we don't just learn to manipulate the vehicle; we also acquire an overly critical attitude toward other drivers. As children we're exposed to the judgmental behavior of our parents and other adults as they drive us around. It's also reinforced in movies portraying drivers behaving badly. This culture of mutual hostility among motorists promotes an active and negative emotional life behind the wheel.

11. *Self-serving bias*: Driving incidents are not neutral; someone is always considered to be at fault. The tendency to attribute fault to others is natural, but it influences our memory of what happened, and we easily lose objectivity and judgment in a dispute.

12. *Venting*: Our culture permits and even encourages venting anger. It's supposed to be healthy to "let it out" instead of keep it inside. But venting has its own logic, and vented anger tends to expand until it breaks out into overt hostility. Venting is felt as an energizing "rush." This seductive feeling is short-lived, and is accompanied by a stream of anger-inspiring thoughts that impair judgment and tempt us into rash and dangerous actions. Habitual venting can have serious physical consequences by weakening the immune system. But motivation and self-training can help drivers learn not to explode.

13. *Unpredictability*: Streets and highways create an environment of drama, danger, and uncertainty. Competition, hostility, and stress further intensify negative emotions. Even noise and smells aggravate feelings of frustration and resentment. The driving environ-

ment requires constant emotional adjustment to unexpected, tedious, brutish, and dangerous occurrences.

14. *Isolation*: Motorists cannot communicate. There is no easy way of saying, "Oops, I'm sorry!" as we can in a bank line. This leads to ambiguity and misunderstanding: "Did he just flip me off or was that an apology?" It would be helpful if vehicles were equipped with an electronic display allowing drivers to flash appropriate prerecorded messages that facilitate coordination and positive interaction in driving.

15. *Emotional challenges*: Traditionally, driver education teaches students some general principles of safety, with a few hours of supervised hands-on experience behind the wheel or on a driving simulator. Developing awareness of common and problematic driving behaviors and the application of sound judgment and emotional self-control have not been part of the training. Most nonprofessional drivers today are insufficiently trained in cognitive and affective skills. Cognitive skills are good habits of thinking and judgment in challenging situations. Affective skills are good habits of attitude and motivation in challenging situations. Drivers often lack the emotional intelligence coping skills essential for driving on today's roads, including how to:
    - cool off when angered or frustrated;
    - retain focus when multitasking;
    - cooperate with the traffic flow and not hinder it;
    - allocate sufficient time for the trip;
    - feel responsible for obeying traffic regulations; and
    - be a supportive, noncompetitive, compassionate driver.

The common element in all fifteen driving stressors is anger, possibly the most frequent of human emotions. Anger has always been closely linked to aggressive behavior. It is common to relate aggressiveness to social and environmental factors, in addition to individual personality factors. For instance, under certain critical conditions, congestion on highways and anonymity in cars interact with faulty attitudes and inadequate coping skills to produce aggressive traffic behavior. These apparent triggering conditions are unpredictable and hold symbolic meaning to the interactants, who may report having felt insulted or threatened.

Sigmund Freud held a Darwinian theory of human aggression, still popular today, that views anger as a biological instinct. Aggression and violence are ultimately forces of self-destructiveness in the innate struggle between life and death.[11] Aggressiveness and assertiveness are clearly different in intention, but sometimes they are difficult to distinguish behaviorally. In our society, competition and disagreement are often used as mechanisms for establishing identity, as in athletics and the marketplace. Biological theories of aggressiveness have also been used to rationalize aggressive driving. According to a U.K. study, an increase in road rage incidents occurred throughout the various layers of society: young and old, men and women, the public and law enforcement alike.[12] Furthermore, road rage behavior could not be predicted on the basis of personality or reputation, so that those committing violent roadway behavior do so uncharacteristically.

Roland Maiuro, M.D., director of an anger management program at the University of Washington School of Medicine, summarizes three sets of factors that influence aggressive driving:

> *Socioenvironmental factors:* population growth and traffic congestion, faulty highway engineering that impedes traffic flow, inadequate regulation of aggressive driving habits, and the anonymity and sense of power many drivers feel sitting behind the smoked glass and bullet-shaped armor of the car itself
>
> *Mental illness factors:* anger disorders that can be triggered by the pressures of driving
>
> *Cultural habit factors:* faulty attitudes, inadequate driving skills, need for education relevant to our challenging and stressful world; symptomatic of society's growing loss of community, a decay of moral values, and, essentially, a mobile form of rudeness and aggression[13]

The anger management program at the University of Washington looks at high-risk populations, safe and unsafe behavioral practices, and strategies for personal and public intervention. An attempt to profile the typical high-risk driver who engages in road rage suggests these recurring characteristics: males under twenty-six years of age, the Type A personality, persons with displaced anger or projected rage, the passive-aggressive "Jekyll and Hyde," and the "polite" rule enforcer. According to Dr. Maiuro:

> The Type A profile includes a broader age range, but also predominantly male, who may be well established and successful as business people and professionals in the community. Previously described as "coronary prone" in behavioral medicine research, the Type A individual has a cluster of attitudes and a pattern of reactivity that appear to interact with the stresses of driving. The cluster includes time urgency, competitiveness, and hostility toward anyone perceived as delaying or blocking their progress.
>
> Such was the case with Mr. A, a thirty-four-year-old computer technologies executive from an affluent Seattle suburb who rammed his

Mercedes-Benz into the rear bumper of a driver of a BMW when the latter failed to yield to Mr. A's tailgating and horn honking as he drove to an important meeting with a client. Although he had no previous criminal record, Mr. A got so caught up in the heat of the moment that he followed the BMW driver home, drove up on his lawn, and physically assaulted him. Mr. A was arrested and never made the appointment with his client.[14]

The anger we feel behind the wheel may have either (or both) of two sources: another driver's behavior or some earlier event unrelated to driving. *Displaced anger* is a common defense mechanism used in many situations. On the road, displaced anger seems to be triggered by a driving incident, and the other driver becomes the enemy target. Some drivers seek medical help after a scary driving incident, even when not obviously injured. These symptoms of post-traumatic stress disorder can last for months, even years, according to Dr. Arnold Nerenberg, a noted road rage psychotherapist.[15] There are few self-referrals at the Harborview Anger Management clinic, according to Dr. Maiuro:

> People exhibiting road rage often do not seek help because of their limited self-awareness and a tendency to see the "other guy" (perceived as provocative and deserving of retaliation) as the problem. Consequently, self-referral to programs such as ours is rare, and an afflicted driver usually arrives for help at the request of a traffic court judge, lawyer, or family member concerned about the person's own safety and the risk to others.[16]

Our research in Hawaii shows that aggressive drivers resist change primarily because they deny that they have a driving problem. Our three-step program for recovery from aggressive driving begins with the most difficult step, "I acknowledge that I need to retrain myself as a driver" (see chapter 6). The hallmark of today's driving culture is denying aggressiveness or calling it assertive, efficient, or progressive instead.

THE GENDER EFFECT

The cultural component of aggressive driving also shows when comparing men and women drivers. One of the items in our Web-based Road Rage Survey asked the two thousand respondents how often they experience certain emotions behind the wheel, on a scale of 1 (never) to 10 (quite regularly).[17] In the results for men and women we found differences in certain behaviors and similarities in others. The response confirms that when it comes to feeling negative emotions behind the wheel— **57**

ROAD RAGE AND AGGRESSIVE DRIVING

rage, impatience, danger, violence, and competition—men experience them more frequently than women. It's the opposite when it comes to feeling compassion for other drivers: Women report positive emotions while driving more often than men do. These emotional differences between men and women carry over to specific aggressive driving behaviors.[17]

Table 2.2
Percentage of Men and Women Self-Reporting Aggressive Driving Behaviors

Aggressive driving behavior	Men	Women
Making illegal turns	18	12
Not signaling lane changes	26	20
Following very closely	15	13
Going through red lights	9	7
Swearing, name calling	59	57
Speeding (15–25 MPH above the speed limit)	46	32
Yelling at other drivers	34	31
Honking to protest	39	36
Revving engine in retaliation	12	8
Making insulting gestures	28	20
Tailgating dangerously	14	9
Shining high beams in retaliation	25	13
Braking suddenly in retaliation	35	29
Deliberately cutting off other drivers	19	10
Using car to block other drivers	21	13
Using car as a weapon to attack	4	1
Chasing other cars in hot pursuit	15	4
Getting into physical fights	4	1

For each aggressive driving behavior, more men report doing it than women. The differences in percentage points are statistically significant for all of these items. Though percentages look close, this means that in any sample more men than women will report aggressive behavior. These results confirm what earlier surveys have found: Men drive more aggressively than women and manifest road rage symptoms more routinely. However, a growing number of women engage in each aggressive driving behavior:

Over the last twenty years, the number of fatal traffic accidents involving women drivers is up 18 percent, and women are involved in a higher rate of non-fatal accidents than men. Though men are still more likely to be involved in aggressive driving accidents than women, the number of women involved in these incidents is on the rise.[18]

The greater aggressiveness of men and the increasing aggressiveness of women drivers are cultural trends reflecting a rise in permissiveness toward expressing anger. Some of the increase in women's aggressive driving is attributed to the growth in the number of women in the workplace. The proportion of women in the driving population rose from 43 percent in 1963 to 50 percent in 1999, amounting to 88 million licensed women drivers in the United States. More women are stuck in congested traffic, experiencing the same stress and frustration as men. Additionally, women often have more stops to make, carting children to school, sports, and lessons as well as driving to work, running errands, shopping, and banking. A 1998 Johns Hopkins University study surveyed a group of female telecommunications workers and found that the majority confessed to driving aggressively at times during their commute (56 percent), yelling or gesturing at other drivers (41 percent), and taking their frustrations out behind the wheel (25 percent).[19] The most important factor linked to road rage in this group of women was a high level of home responsibility coupled with a low level of emotional support for their hard work. Women are often forced to drive on congested roads under time pressure. As a result, auto insurance rates for young women are now close to those for inexperienced young men, who are still being charged 18 percent above the base rate.

DRIVING IMPAIRED

Impaired driving results from both physical and emotional factors that interact and can contribute to driving aggressively or driving in rage. Driving under the influence of fatigue, a chemical substance, or strong emotion is a form of aggression because the impaired driver chooses to operate his vehicle in that condition. Whenever we decide to risk the lives of others, that decision is inherently antisocial. The most common physical impairment factors include:

- Alcohol
- Illegal drugs
- Over-the-counter drugs
- Prescription medication
- Extreme fatigue or sleep deprivation (driving while drowsy)
- Incapacity due to disability, pain, aging, or illness

ROAD RAGE AND AGGRESSIVE DRIVING

Most of the thirty-five million people who use legal and illegal drugs every day drive at some point. People read the warnings against operating heavy equipment on their prescription bottles, but they drive anyway. Perhaps they think they can handle it, perhaps they don't even think about it, or perhaps they feel they have no choice. Still, it is estimated that fifteen thousand people die every year in crashes caused by drug-impaired driving. Drug-impaired driving aggravates and contributes to other driving problems such as road rage, aggressive driving, driving while drowsy, inattention, lack of emotional self-control, and excessive risk taking, often contributing to the road rage of others.

Driving requires interaction between the body and mental processes of judgment. People routinely drive in mental states that distort body reactions and thinking processes. This lowered ability to manipulate a moving vehicle is impaired driving. Alcohol in the blood slows motor movements and distorts visual perception, and alcohol in the brain disrupts normal thinking. Warning signs are ignored and erroneous conclusions are drawn, often leading to catastrophe. Mental impairment leads to unpredictable behavior and the impaired driver becomes a menace to all. Driver fatigue leading to drowsiness is a form of mental and physical impairment. During a state of sleep deprivation, the biochemical composition of the blood and brain fluids create an overwhelming desire to close the eyes and fall asleep, but also increases irritability and risk-taking behavior. Driver fatigue leads to impaired driving as dangerous as that caused by alcohol or road rage.

The emotional impairment factors are just as treacherous, but are more difficult to manage because they often arise suddenly, without warning—for example, an unexpected feeling of anger after missing a light, followed by gunning the engine and racing ahead when it turns green again. The most common emotional impairment factors include:

- Anger or rage
- Anxiety, fear, or panic (irrational thought sequence)
- Depression or suicidal tendency
- Speed addiction ("It's worth getting a ticket for," or "I can outrun the cops.")
- Risk addiction ("It's no fun driving normally.")
- Habitual self-appointed vigilante or road warrior ("Can't let them get away with that.")
- Habitual rushing mania or feeling panic or claustrophobic when blocked
- Emotionally challenged behind the wheel (biased assumptions, wrong conclusions)
- Habitual disrespect for the law

- Habitual negativity that condones the expression of hostility on highways
- Habitual and automatic denial of own driving mistakes

These factors are characterized by an unwillingness to exercise emotional self-control because of fear, fun, vengeance, prejudice, or disrespect.

Health professionals generally attribute some of the increase in driving pugnacity to stressful social factors such as increasing road congestion, urbanization, dual-income families, workplace downsizing that increases crowding, family discord, job dissatisfaction, and physical illness. The connection between stress and illness was established in medicine with Hans Selye's pioneering work fifty years ago.[20] New research shows that driving-related stress is no different from other life stress in the way it affects our health. Stress, then, is a form of potential impairment that mixes physical with emotional factors. Raymond Novaco, a psychologist at the University of California Transportation Center, found that people with longer commutes report more overall stress. And studies indicate that traffic jams and other driving stressors can affect mood, health, work attendance, job stability and life satisfaction:

> People who have long commutes to work, for example, are found to have higher blood pressure than those who commute shorter distances. And people who have more roads to travel to get to their jobs call in sick more frequently than those who drive on fewer roads, Novaco added. The frustration and stress resulting from traffic conditions don't automatically generate aggressive actions, but they do increase the risk for such behavior, researchers say. Some believe traffic-induced aggression stems in part from territorial defensiveness. They describe the car as an extension of personal space. People become contentious when someone encroaches upon that private territory, such as bumping their car from behind.[21]

Experts at the American Heart Association have linked chronic activation of the fight-or-flight response to damage to the heart and coronary arteries, due to the receptors of stress hormones in the heart. If a driver sits fuming in traffic thinking "I'm going to explode," it may be literally true! Anger management workshops in the workplace are becoming commonplace and they tend to deliver the same message: You can choose to vent your anger and stress out, or you can learn to cope with the provocations in an emotionally intelligent way, by modifying your reactions rather than fruitlessly trying to control the objectionable behavior of others.

It is well known that anonymity weakens inhibitions against expressing anger. Crowds of normal individuals can become ugly and uncivilized under the cloak of anonymity. Individuals who are nice and polite in a bank line sometimes feel free to be uncouth and nasty inside their moving castles that allow them to "curse and run." We support law enforcement efforts to restrict tinting because impenetrable windows add to a driver's false sense of isolation and increases the sense of anonymity. Researchers at Maryland's Towson State University measured people's use of car horns in an attempt to find out if anonymity increased hostility. In the study,

> a confederate driver looked for convertibles or jeeps approaching a stoplight, and pulled in front of them before they reached the signal. When the light turned green, the confederate driver remained idle and recorded the subject's reaction, particularly their use of the car horn. Subjects driving their vehicles with the tops up began honking their horns sooner, and kept at it longer, than those with their tops down. "It appears that an enclosed automobile may provide the occupant with a sense of anonymity which, in turn, serves to facilitate aggressive behavior."[22]

EMOTIONAL SELF-CONTROL BEHIND THE WHEEL

Research on how people manage to control their feelings shows that the ability to regulate our emotions is a learned skill with two main components. The first is accurate *self-appraisal*. This skill depends on how carefully we monitor our emotions and how we express them, verbally or by silence, gesture, and tone. The second is effective *self-regulation*. This skill depends on acquiring methods to self-regulate the intensity and expression of our emotions. Self-appraisal and self-regulation are skills that can be learned by anyone who is dedicated to practice. Exercising discretion and control over our emotional lives is a necessary coping skill that determines success and health. Some are able to learn these skills on their own, through experiences, but many others do not, and need to be given self-training techniques for accurate self-appraisal and effective self-regulation. Motorists are constantly exposed to risky situations that generate intense emotional involvement. The driver's prime directive is to maintain control of the vehicle and the situation, so it's smart to train yourself to exert self-control over the emotions behind the wheel because emotions impact the situation.

To develop emotional competence as a driver you need a basic understanding of mental control. When sitting behind the wheel and exerting control over your vehicle, what is happening in the brain and mind to carry out the driving task? Many know that the neocortex has two subparts, the left brain and the right brain. Our emotional life correlates with the action of the right brain, while the left brain correlates with our intellectual life. Everyone can become aware of their thoughts through systematic self-observation. If you are serving as a juror or testifying as a witness, you are expected to report what you saw, what you said, what you decided, what you concluded, what you thought, or why you did something. We are expected to be able to account for our inner life when it impinges on others. In conversations we're expected to remember what we said and what the other person said. If someone asks, "What are you thinking about?" we can often describe the topic and sometimes even the words that occurred in the mind. But if someone asks, "What are you feeling?" many times we show little capacity for accurately describing our ongoing feelings. We can't always put feelings into words. We can easily become aware of the left brain activity correlated to thinking or cognitive processes, but only with difficulty and practice can we become aware of the right brain activity correlated to emotions, feelings, moods, or what's called "affective behavior."

Most people aren't able to accurately gauge their mood, and lack of emotional awareness is a primary problem for motorists because negative emotions encourage and even invite negative, judgmental, and self-serving thoughts. We're aware of the negative thoughts, but not the emotions and mood that helped those thoughts grow. Pretty soon we're preoccupied with distressing ruminations: "Why is everybody against me?" or "Who does he think he is?" or "How can he do this to me?" As long as we remain unaware of our mood and emotions, the thoughts will take a negative turn, becoming biased, inaccurate, inflexible, and inappropriate. These negative emotions work behind the scenes to encourage and invite negative thoughts. These negative thoughts and the hostile verbal expressions that go with them are easily observed because they're out in the open. The intense negative emotions impel us to make incorrect judgments that lead to regrettable acts and to fabricate neat justifications for these acts. Negative emotions also act to keep more rational alternatives out of awareness, leading us down the path of impulsive, inappropriate, and often dangerous or injurious behavior. This is emotional driving.

Some individuals are able to progress on their own beyond emotional driving. They raise their level of emotional intelligence as drivers by improving emotional awareness behind the wheel. They learn to recognize the rage rush and how to manage when it is present. But many, even experts in human services, believe that emotions just happen to people or that it's a permanent personality trait. Others find out that they can influence their emotions by "not going there." There are three mental control techniques to suppress distressing ruminations behind the wheel, and avert blind negative emotions that can lead to catastrophe:

1. Postponing the immediate satisfaction you intensely desire
2. Avoiding savoring the victory and the pleasurable anticipation of punishing and taking revenge

3. Redirecting negative scenarios of justifications that give you permission to engage in hostile acts

In the heat of emotional arousal, the overwhelming sensation is of being carried away, of loss of control. At that moment we sit on the cusp of a free choice: to go along and be carried away—which seems deliciously seductive—or to refuse to be carried away and choosing a more benevolent course of action. The altruistic choice seems unattractive and difficult to achieve, but society holds us responsible for going one way or the other because this is a free choice. If you're motivated toward self-regulation for the sake of positive social values, you will be able to resist the downhill slide into angry aggression. You learn how to redirect thoughts by postponing or giving up the impulse to express negative emotions.

After deciding to postpone gratification, it becomes easier to take the second step, to avoid fantasies of retaliation and the associated enjoyments of vengeance. Before the first step, it is not possible to quit savoring the victory when anticipating all that you plan to do to make sure that the "offender" understands your disapproal and to ensure that the offender won't think of trying to get away with such behavior again. But as soon as you make the decision to postpone satisfaction, you also gain control over the retaliation fantasy. Then you can take the third step.

Redirecting mental focus requires consciously rejecting the justifications that your mind fabricates, no matter how familiar and "right" they sound. Your thinking responds to the negative emotion and produces justifications that validate it at a fast and furious pace, while the emotional arousal level climbs. If you avoid savoring thoughts of vengeance, you free your mind to switch to more adaptive scenarios of what's going on and what to do about it. In this way, you're able to short-circuit the buildup of rage. It's emotional judo.

It's hard to believe that ordinary, good folk are capable of murderous feelings, and yet that's a common occurrence behind the wheel. Motorists who would never assault anyone overtly do so mentally and privately. Some drivers do this only with a vague global feeling as they grit their teeth and shake their heads, muttering words of deprecation; others do it in graphic detail. The intensity of the sense of endangerment can be turned up by savoring revenge fantasies, or it can be turned down by redirecting focus and reappraising the situation. Our research shows that drivers cannot spontaneously redirect their attention to positive scenarios, but that it is possible if they learn to handle confrontations. Motorists who are successful in overcoming their bad moods and negative emotions in traffic rely on positive distractors. Whether it's the radio, CD, books on tape, voice e-mail, or self-regulatory sentences, these motorists have learned to occupy themselves with positive thoughts.

Actions we take now determine in part how we feel later. Knowing this, we can exert control over our feelings behind the wheel.

CHECKLIST: AGGRESSIVE THOUGHTS AND FEELINGS

This checklist helps to identify aggressive feelings and thoughts that are part of a road rage habit. The items are based on self-witnessing tapes of drivers in traffic and cover three common areas:

- Fantasies of retaliation and revenge
- High-pressure driving and competition
- Impulsiveness and reckless driving

Since these are actual statements made by drivers, the style may not suit you perfectly but you may recognize the feeling or sentiment. Check each that applies to you.

Driving Area 1: Fantasies of Retaliation and Revenge

1. ___ When others cut in front of me so that I have to brake, I feel like crashing into them to teach them a lesson.
2. ___ When I encounter road-hugging pedestrians, I feel like pushing them out of my way.
3. ___ When drivers become aggressive by tailgating me, I enjoy slowing down to pay them back.
4. ___ When I'm under stress due to work, I get very edgy and take it out on other drivers.
5. ___ I don't think passengers should tell me how to drive and I let them know if they try.
6. ___ If motorists around me act cocky and drive recklessly, I get into a rebellious mood.
7. ___ I passionately hate drivers who think that they are the only ones on the road and act carelessly.
8. ___ When a driver cuts me off and then slows down, I feel like ramming that car.
9. ___ I get nasty thoughts about drivers who force their way into my lane, especially without signaling.
10. ___ I feel like ramming them to smarten them up about doing dangerous things (eating, putting on makeup, reading, talking on the phone, etc.) while they should be paying attention to the road.

11. ___ When people run or walk on the shoulder of the highway I feel like swerving toward them to scare them off the road for good.

12. ___ When slow cyclists take up a whole lane so I can't pass and refuse to move when I honk, I feel like whipping by so close they lose their balance and fall.

Driving Area 2: High-Pressure Driving and Competition

13. ___ When a car gets in my way I don't like it and I try to get around it even if it means taking some risks.

14. ___ In heavy traffic I feel a constant desire to weave across lanes, trying to get ahead.

15. ___ I'm a "gap closer" and I make sure no one enters my lane in front of me.

16. ___ When I'm late, I have no patience and tailgate slower motorists in my way.

17. ___ If it was up to me, I'd have everybody else get off the road until I pass—like the president.

18. ___ I like the idea of saluting careless drivers "with respect" (flipping them off with my hand safely out of view under the dashboard).

19. ___ I don't have respect for drivers who forget to turn their blinkers on or off.

Driving Area 3: Impulsive and Reckless Driving

20. ___ Showing off for friends is something I do because I'm expected to take risks and not act like a coward.

21. ___ I enjoy loud, fast music while I drive—lets me feel free!

22. ___ When I drive late at night and the road is clear, I like to go fast no matter what the signs say.

23. ___ When I'm in a rush and upset I cut in front of cars and rush through yellow lights.

24. ___ If I had a few drinks but feel all right, I take a chance and drive home anyway.

25. ___ When I'm tired I become less alert, but I still need to drive. I have no choice.

26. ___ Going through red lights should only be done when you're absolutely sure there are no cars that can show up in your way.

27. ___ I love to hear the tires screech when I take turns fast. It's a nice sound. Makes me feel alive.

NOTES

1. U.S. Department of Transportation National Highway Safety Administration (NHTSA), "Capital Beltway Update: Beltway User Focus Groups," April 1998 [online], www.nhtsa.dot.gov/people/injury/research/aggressive/final. rpt.html [May 20, 2000].

2. Ibid.

3. Ibid.

4. Kenny Morse, *Mr. Traffic Newsletter*, October 1999 [online], mrtraffic.com [May 20, 2000].

5. John Larson, *Steering Clear of Highway Madness: A Driver's Guide to Curbing Stress and Strain* (Wilsonville, Ore.: BookPartners, 1996); John Larson with Carol Rodriguez, *Road Rage to Road-Wise* (New York: Tom Doherty Associates, 1999).

6. Leon James and Diane Nahl, "Drivers Behaving Badly—DBB Ratings," DrDriving.org [online], www.aloha.net/~dyc/dbb.html [May 20, 2000].

7. "Driver" [online], driver.gtgames.com [May 20, 2000].

8. "Carmageddon," CitySearch Chicago [online], chicago.sidewalk.com [March 7, 1999].

9. Ibid.

10. Hawke Fracassa, "Arcade will Pull Plug on Violent Games," *Detroit News*, October 16, 1995 [online], www.detnews.com/menu/stories/20296.htm [May 20, 2000].

11. Sigmund Freud, "Instincts and Their Vicissitudes," in *The Collected Papers* (New York: Collier, 1915).

12. "Transport Research Library (TRL)," *Police Review* 105, no. 5417 (1997): 20.

13. Roland Maiuro, "Rage on the Road," *Recovery* 9, no. 2 (summer 1998) [online], www.icbc.com/oldrecover/Volume9/Number2/RageOnTheRoad [May 20, 2000]. Other theories promote the notion of social or emotional contagion, or the idea that people are infected by others' behavior and moods. See Elaine Hatfield, John T. Cacioppo, and Richard L. Rapson, *Emotional Contagion* (Cambridge: Cambridge University Press, 1994).

14. Ibid.

15. Arnold Nerenberg, Ph.D., personal correspondence with the authors, 1998.

16. Maiuro, "Rage on the Road," www.ibc.com/oldrecover/Volume9/Number2/RageOnTheRoad.

17. Leon James and Diane Nahl, "Aggressiveness in Relation to Age, Gender, and Type of Car," DrDriving.org [online], www.aloha.net/~dyc/surveys/survey2/interpretations.html [May 20, 2000].

18. Karyn Sultan, "Women's Role in Road Rage Up, Statistics Show," WomanMotorist [online], www.womanmotorist.com/sfty/female-roadrage.shtml [May 20, 2000].

19. Dan Vergano, "Tough Workplace, Homelife Can Create Road Rage," *Medical Tribune* News Service, March 30, 1999 [online], 199.97.97.16/

contWriter/yhddepression/1999/03/31/medic/0983-0364-pat_nytimes.html [May 20, 2000].

20. Hans Selye, *The Stress of Life* (New York: McGraw Hill, 1956).

21. Scott Sleek, "Car Wars: Taming Drivers' Aggression," *APA Monitor*, September 1996 [online], www.apa.org/monitor/sep96/drivinga.html [May 20, 2000].

22. Ibid.

CAUSES OF HIGHWAY HOSTILITY

3

DEFENSIVE DRIVING

In 1996, drivers in the United States caused five million accidents, forty thousand deaths, and $150 billion in health and related costs. To reduce these losses, safety officials and the insurance industry have recommended defensive driving practices and more vigorous law enforcement for offenders. Despite these efforts, aggressive driving worldwide continues to increase in frequency and seriousness. Clearly, new approaches are needed. How do we prepare millions of drivers for the emotional challenges of congested driving? Neither conventional driver education nor defensive driving courses include training for emotional intelligence on the road. According to a resource curriculum on defensive driving, it is better to assume the worst from other drivers, and not have it happen, than to ignore the worst and have it occur. This defensive orientation is logical and saves drivers from some collisions, but it has unintended consequences that can increase rather than decrease risk in driving. What

69

happens when things are competitive and motorists adopt the view that the best defense is a good offense? One correspondent, a defensive driving instructor who has logged millions of miles, wrote:

> Only by expecting other drivers to do it wrong can you be prepared to cope safely and smoothly with their actions. If they do surprise you, it's for the good and no allowances are necessary on your part and you have lost nothing.[1]

But the defensive orientation can become a problem when people abuse it. Defensiveness can create suspicion and encourage the tendency to see other drivers as the enemy. A defensive attitude doesn't explicitly encourage mutual support and compassion. We propose "supportive driving" as the new model, because it encourages anticipating what others might do, accepting errors as normal, and trying to provide for errors by making room or by yielding (see chapter 8).

Sliding into an offensive driving style is inevitable because fear and anger disorganize rational responses and distort judgment. Clearly, drivers need training in emotional control in traffic so that they can better manage routine experiences such as panic, fear, stress, provocation, anger, competition, and impatience. Professionals generally concede that the majority of accidents are caused by "driver factors" such as inattention, risk taking, and conflict between highway users. The American Driver and Traffic Safety Education Association handbook includes a section on interacting with other highway users in various situations:

> Competent drivers make well-timed and accurate turning movements and maintain safe braking distances. When you encounter a compulsive gap-filler, drop back and re-open a space for your own protection. Avoid tailgaters by accelerating, decelerating, or moving into a slower lane. Finally, operators who can control themselves in an emergency are the people who would be more apt to control their vehicles.[2]

This is good advice, but we need to learn how to accomplish these things. The handbook has learning modules with exercises for each item except for the last: "operators who can control themselves in an emergency." It gives good advice on what to do with tailgaters (accelerate-decelerate; get out of their way) and gap fillers (let them in and stay behind). But what about bad moods, frustration and anger, fear from near misses, impatience, desire to retaliate and teach a lesson, peer pressure, competitiveness, lack of respect for regulations—how are you to handle these feelings and attitudes that affect the quality of driving? This is why drivers need training in emotional intelligence. This is an inner training, dealing with our habits of thinking and ranking the importance of things. Our driving emotions have become ingrained habits, no longer questioned or even admitted, but the same social principles that taught to us to be aggressive drivers in this generation can be used to teach us to become supportive drivers in the next.

The traditional paradigm in driver education and safety teaches defensive driving that promotes an orientation to be permanently on guard against the mistakes of unpredictable drivers. Defensive driving has for decades been promoted as the key to survival on the road. It's a pragmatic philosophy that has undoubtedly prevented an untold number of collisions and saved thousands of lives. Unfortunately, defensive driving is an inadequate solution to the escalating problem of aggressive driving. Our research on the thoughts and feelings of drivers indicates that defensive driving itself can become a form of offensive driving when it promotes mutual suspicion. An unpredictable mistake by one driver is easily taken as an insult by another. An insulted driver is more likely to respond with hostility, and the vicious cycle of aggressiveness escalates. A defensive driving strategy may encourage a competitive driving philosophy that can make it harder for motorists to back out of their negative emotional involvement. The new paradigm in driver education and safety focuses on preparedness and alertness within a context of tolerance (see chapter 9).

STRESSFUL CONGESTION

Traffic congestion has become a universal problem plaguing many parts of the world, both rural and urban, because there are never enough miles of road for the number of vehicles in use. The annual costs associated with traffic congestion in the United States are astronomical—and rising.[3]

- One-hundred-billion-dollar loss in productivity
- Two billion hours spent in traffic
- Six billion gallons of extra gasoline
- Two billion incidents of aggressive driving
- Increase in air pollution
- Increase in number of collisions, injuries, and fatalities
- Discourages tourism and diminishes quality of life

Because it inconveniences, delays, and frustrates drivers, congestion increases the number of crashes due to aggressive driving. People experience time pressure when they can't predict travel time accurately; they feel caged or trapped with no way out, and some become incensed and drive on the shoulder to pass unwitting motorists waiting it out. The **71** emotional dynamics of congestion are mostly private—until someone takes chances and tries to make a break for it, accelerates too fast to avoid collision at a merge point, or tries to get the advantage by cutting in line. Whether or not a crash occurs, congestion is a major source of frustration and anger that simmers daily in the minds and bodies of motorists, increasing their stress. Researchers at the University of California, Irvine, found that drivers who face frustrating commutes have more job frustration and illness than drivers whose commutes aren't as congested.[4]

Frustration and stress will increase once drivers discover that congestion can cost individuals up to twelve hundred dollars each year in extra gasoline burned while sitting in traffic. A 1998 study found that the amount of time commuters spend stalled in traffic in small and medium-sized cities has more than quadrupled since 1982, growing at a much faster rate than it has in larger cities. To quantify density of congestion, researchers used a roadway congestion index that considers traffic volume (demand) and the number of freeway and major street lanes (supply) in an area. An index value of greater than 1.0 indicates problematic congestion. The top five congested cities:

1. Los Angeles (1.57)
2. Washington, D.C. (1.43)
3. Miami-Hialeah (1.34)
4. Chicago (1.34)
5. San Francisco-Oakland (1.33)

The least congested cities:

1. Bakersfield, Calif. (0.68)
2. Laredo, Tex. (0.73)
3. Colorado Springs, Col. (0.74)
4. Beaumont, Tex. (0.76)
5. Corpus Christi, Tex. (0.78)[5]

Surprisingly, the difference between rush-hour and non-rush-hour travel times was only 50 percent in heavily congested cities and less than 10 percent in the less congested areas. Since the average commute is around thirty minutes, even a 50 percent increase in time travel is only a few minutes, so not much time is saved by rushing and lane hopping.

Researchers also calculated the amount of fuel wasted as a result of congestion, noting that drivers stuck in traffic wasted more than six billion gallons of fuel in 1996—enough to fill 670,000 gasoline tank trucks or 134 supertankers. In the nation's most congested cities, the waste amounts to more than 100 gallons per eligible driver per year. Drivers in the least congested cities waste about 20 gallons per year. The total cost of traffic congestion in the cities studied amounts to almost $74 billion. Delay costs account for 88 percent of that total, with the remainder due to wasted fuel. The annual congestion cost per eligible driver ranged from $1,290 in Washington, D.C., to $125 in Boulder, CO.[6]

The study concludes that solving the urban congestion problem requires a variety of engineering approaches, including building more road space; slowing the growth of vehicle volume on the road with bus and carpool lanes and transit service; staggering the times that vehicles use the road with flex time and telecommuting techniques; more efficient traffic management with coordinated signals and incident management; and more land-use alternatives that might reduce the need for vehicle travel. But since some congestion is inevitable, commuters still need better methods for coping with its ill effects.

INEVITABLE UNPREDICTABILITY

Driving is a truly remarkable achievement: tons of steel and glass hurtling along narrow lanes, avoiding disastrous collisions most of the time. Who controls this potentially lethal activity? We, the individual drivers, do. Our thoughts and feelings, values and decisions determine management of this risk. Millions spend hours every day interacting with others behind the wheel. In a few minutes you have hundreds of exchanges in which you and others make critical split-second decisions. Avoiding collisions requires complex and coordinated responses, and each driver counts on the others to be rational and predictable.

But uncertainty is a factor in all human endeavors, including driving. Every driver at some time acts unpredictably. This becomes more significant as the number of cars increases and people drive more miles. The farther you travel or the more congested the traffic, the more interactions you're bound to have and the more frequently you'll be confronted with incidents where someone behaves unpredictably. Some events are minor and can be compensated for by slowing down, tapping the brakes, or swerving. The more serious events result in threat, injury, or death.

PEER PRESSURE

Driving is a social activity that requires constant and instantaneous cooperation between strangers, and this requires that we be sensitive to one another in order to anticipate what other drivers are likely to do. Some people feel excessive pressure to do things they don't want to do, like going faster than it's safe because of fear of disapproval. A number of drivers report feeling embarrassed making a full stop at a stop sign when there are no cars in sight. One older female driver shared her fears about not wanting to lose face, to be "the one who's stuck back there" at the intersection:

> I should go, I should go. Will I run the light? I should go. They expect me to go. If I don't go they'll think I'm a wimp. I hate that. I have to go, oh wow, I'm going.

She sees making a mistake or "missing" a light as an opportunity to berate herself and feel ashamed, increasing her stress.

Drivers, both young and old, need to be equipped with the inner tools to resist perceived peer pressure that increases risk and stress.

> I read that young drivers are less likely than older drivers to wear their safety belts. I can truly relate to this so-called trend. As a teenager, you are so worried about fitting in and looking good. You want to do what others are doing. I recall the whole idea of wearing a safety belt as being "so lame." I couldn't imagine cruising around Vance Point with my seat belt on . . . "What a geek!" That would be unheard of, and what would people think of me? I think for many of us we knew the importance of safety belts, but because it wasn't "cool," we didn't use them. The norm in the eyes of my teenaged friends is not to use safety belts, so I, as well as others, conformed to this expectation. Conformity in this situation is the same as peer pressure.

In the absence of emotional intelligence training or a naturally positive driving philosophy, drivers can believe that they have a right to respect or disrespect both people and laws, to justify hostile feelings and give themselves permission for violent retaliation, giving in to the rationale that since some people drive crazy, we all must.

> It's ridiculous. I have finally reached the point where I have had to pull totally off the highway, onto the shoulder, to let some speeder pass (at 70 to 80 MPH) who absolutely refused to pass on any of the other three lanes to our left. I find that these days there are so many people out of control on the highways that a person who tries to drive at the speed limit and within the law actually becomes a traffic hazard to the speeders. It becomes safer to drive just as crazy and fit in with the crowd.

Going with the flow of traffic is widely considered the safest course of action, but bowing to peer pressure can result in citations and fines, even loss of license. The safety conflict over obeying traffic laws and keeping up with traffic is played out millions of times daily.

> Wow, it just happened to me. My first ticket, and I guess the officer was having a bad day. At least he didn't just take my license on the spot. I have to go to court, pay court and lawyer costs, and then have this wonderful state take it away. The dilemma is obvious: Go the speed limit and have people tailgate you or explain in the courtroom why 79/55 [79 MPH in a 55 MPH zone] is an OK speed. "Your honor, I was only going with the flow." "Guilty." *Bang*. (Yes, 55 MPH is the speed limit on the Beltway.)

AUTOMOTIVE VIGILANTISM

One of the more revealing results in our Web-based 1998 Road Rage Survey is that there are, broadly speaking, two types of drivers in the United States and Canada: those who drive "tough-minded" vehicles like sport-utility vehicles (SUVs), sports cars, and light trucks versus motorists who drive "soft" vehicles like family and economy cars and minivans. There is a substantial and significant difference between these two groups in driving style and attitude, and always in the same direction. In our survey, people driving tough-minded cars confessed to more frequent and more severe aggressive driving behaviors, and this difference was even more pronounced with young people, both men and women. Equally revealing was the finding that those who remember their parents being aggressive drivers were themselves more aggressive than average.[7]

John Larson, director of the Institute for Stress Medicine in Norwalk, Connecticut, has been working with problem drivers since 1963. He identified three types of highway incidents that have made media headlines:

- A driver harms or kills another driver whose driving behavior has provoked him.
- Two drivers, aggressively racing each other, lose control of their vehicles and collide with other cars, injuring or killing themselves or others.
- A driver impulsively takes risks, for example, passing in a no passing zone, going through a red light, or crashing into a vehicle that has the right-of-way.[8]

ROAD RAGE AND AGGRESSIVE DRIVING

In our survey, we explored three levels of intensity in aggressive driving: impatience, hostility, and violence. At the start of a road rage duel, there may be nothing more than a grimace, gesture, or curse, but the crucial part to understand is its main symbolic function. It is usually the desire to punish the other driver that motivates the first step toward road rage. The desire to punish or retaliate divides those at risk for road rage from those who are not. One of our correspondents called it "automotive vigilantism." These results for three items on our Web-based driver personality test illustrate the prevalence of the mindset that's responsible for automotive vigilantism.

Given the statement "You must retaliate against aggressive drivers in order to maintain law and order on highways," 25 percent agreed; for the statement "It's justified to resist bad drivers by scaring them a little so they don't think others are unaware or powerless," 32 percent agreed; and for the statement "It's important to prevent aggressive drivers from pushing you and other drivers around by blocking their way or giving them a scare," 28 percent agreed.[9] In any group of five drivers, one or two of them will have the mindset that legitimizes automotive vigilantism. The root of this attitude is the erroneous belief that aggressive driving can be prevented by aggression against aggressive drivers. Millions of drivers are caught in this delusional logic. As one convicted road rager claimed brazenly, "I am as much a victim as the person who got killed." A correspondent suggested we adopt his logic on automotive vigilantism:

> So, then, maybe aggression could be a positive concept when the aggression is lawful. But then again, aggressively driving down a sidewalk to avoid robbery is not lawful yet positive aggression. So positive aggression would be to act in a manner such that the end result makes things better and negative aggression would be one that makes a circumstance worse. Don't you agree?

We don't agree. Aggression is neither lawful nor effective. With drivers, aggressive behaviors stem from cultural and psychological roots, including the way we view and explain anger and rage.

TRIGGER THEORY OF ROAD RAGE

Even the best and most experienced drivers have problems managing negative emotions. Many drivers believe that expressing anger is a basic right; pop psychology has promoted it as healthier than holding it in and retaliation is accepted as a punitive method for keeping control on the highway. But playing war games undermines self-control, and many drivers are incapable of holding back outbursts of rage once they make the critical choice to go along with their wild emotions. People justify aggression by fabricating an illogical sequence: "They provoked me. I can't help it. They deserve it." There's a feeling of being "right" in the show of aggression: "They're breaking a basic rule and they shouldn't. Therefore, I can't let them get away with it by doing nothing." This serves as the excuse for instant retribution and dangerous, risky behavior. But is this logical, effective, or fair?

There is no direct connection between "They provoked me" and "They deserve punishment," but people make an indirect connection when they describe the situation this way: "They broke an important rule, which makes me feel bad. Therefore I want to punish them, which will make me feel better. Besides, it's dangerous to let them get away with it. So I must help society and myself by teaching them a lesson they won't forget." It's tempting to use driving incidents as an opportunity to take charge and play the disciplinarian for the public good. Raging aggressively is a way of striving for control, attempting to coerce, imposing our will on others. Habitual aggressive driving is a strategy for gaining supremacy over others. Suddenly, we see an opportunity to become a member of a highway posse, out to enforce vigilante law and order. It feels good to take control as the keeper of the rules of the road. Much of the time everyone gets away unscathed, so there appear to be no serious consequences to our unrestrained acts. But don't count on it.

One sure sign of a high road rage tendency is the strong desire to let the other person know how you feel. Everyone can list driving pet peeves on the road, the things other drivers do that get us going or push our hot buttons, and *seem* to act like triggers. But actually, we give ourselves permission to rage because someone has "broken an important rule." A young woman describes how she got upset when a motorist failed to courtesy wave after her kindness to him:

> Just before the on-ramp entrance I let one of the cars go in front of me. I thought I had saved this person a great deal of trouble and that he would be thankful that I let him go ahead of me. But instead of getting the wave, I got nothing. I didn't even see a quick gesture of thanks. Immediately, I became infuriated.

Physiologically, anger is a momentary flare-up that quickly dies down. At this point she's angry, but not quite angry enough to create a road rage incident. However, she fans the flames of righteous indignation, escalating her anger and turning it into wrath:

> I don't understand why some people are so rude. I feel like tailgating this person to let him know how I feel. What would society be like if

everyone were like this rude person? Maybe I should've just made him wait his turn. How hard is it to wave anyway? Any civilized person would do it. But this person is hardly civilized. I didn't have to do this person a favor, and I felt as if that rebuff ruined my whole day. I felt hurt and insulted as well as angry. All I could think about was revenge.

I wanted to teach that person a lesson. I wanted that person to crash, to run out of gas, or get pulled over by the police. I wanted that person to feel like I did—angry. I knew the chances were pretty small that he would be plagued by any of my curses. So I decided not to leave it to other forces to teach him a lesson. I had to be the punisher. By this time we were both on the freeway. I tailgated him in the fast lane going 60 MPH. I must have been no more than a few feet away from his car. I was aware how dangerous it was in the stop-and-go traffic of rush hour. Then as I passed him, I revved my V-8 engine and gave him the meanest glare I could muster.

She accuses the "uncivilized" driver of rebuffing her and ruining her day. Because she feels she was hurt by him, she wants to retaliate to avenge the injury. She feels helplessly driven by her angry emotions, which she attributes to the man's act of neglect. She doesn't see that this cause-effect assumption is a self-fulfilling prophecy. In reality she is her own trigger and emotional amplifier. The other driver's behavior appears to be the trigger or cause of her anger, but this is an illusion.

Some people get incensed at drivers who don't get going right away when the light turns green. When another driver disregards this "rule" they automatically become offended, thinking, "He's not paying attention. But he should." The implication is, "Drivers who don't follow this (my) rule need to be taught a lesson by me." This may seem extreme, but in fact many of us behave this way in numerous situations. Mental inflexibility is a characteristic of lower emotional intelligence that is activated by assuming the worst of others. We have a clear choice of whether to go along with self-righteous indignation or not. Choosing to go along with indignation churns up the anger with justifications and venting.

The fuel that drives aggressiveness on the road is the false assumption that the action of another driver makes us hostile because it triggers our aggressive response. But the offending act doesn't automatically trigger the aggressive response, it merely creates an opportunity to deliver a hostile act in order to express intense righteous indignation. We have the power to turn down the opportunity to retaliate. If other drivers were the actual trigger for our rage we'd have no choice but to get furious every time something goes wrong. Yet this isn't what happens. Most angry motorists retaliate some of the time, but not every time. This proves that there is no automatic trigger mechanism between an insult or provocation and an angry retaliation.

Despite claims to the contrary, drivers don't have any real power to suppress or change the bad behaviors of other drivers, but they do have the power to be obnoxious and create hazardous conditions. There's a certain feeling of satisfaction in being rude to drivers who behave unreasonably, and we might enjoy the idea of paying them back, correcting them, or making them feel bad. We may even take pleasure in calling them fools, bozos, and slugs. Shaken by the fear of impending disaster, we try to make ourselves feel better by condemning those who offend us, and standing up for ourselves in the face of uncalled for provocation. Our mental and verbal aggressiveness seems to us to be warranted and just. But this is only an appearance, an illusion.

Even if we never intend to become physically violent, we don't hesitate to engage in lesser forms of aggression. We may speed up to a car or pedestrian, though we wouldn't actually bump them. We may honk, gesture provocatively, or yell and move on down the road. Or we may disguise feelings of aggression with muttering, gestures hidden below the dashboard, and private fantasies of torture and beatings.

> The driver in front of me was holding up traffic and could have easily caused an accident. I honked for him to go and he very rudely showed me his middle finger and sped away, glaring through his rearview mirror. My first reaction was to tailgate him and ask him if he would (just as rudely) like to show that finger to one of my three grown sons or maybe my husband? Just about any one of them could show him just where he could appropriately place it. (Yes, I can be very aggressive also.)

Habitual road rage is one way to retaliate against drivers who behave badly. Whatever the form of aggression, either visible or hidden, its purpose is to make us feel better about ourselves, to gain relief from fear and frustration or to feel superior to another. For example, suppose someone who's been following too close passes on the left then comes back into your lane and slows down, forcing you to brake or pass. It's natural to feel annoyed. But there is a critical choice: to heat up the intensity of your annoyance or to cool it down, to vent or to backpedal.

Habitual road rage is a mental state of learned aggressiveness justified by feeling contempt for other drivers, or the compulsion to rage about road events and participants. When do people give themselves permission to act aggressively? We don't try to take control in every situation, only in certain ones where we might have an advantage. For instance, you see a car with its turn signal still on after the driver switched lanes. You watch the signal light blink on and off for a long time, wondering when the numbskull is going to turn it off. Finally, you can't stand it and mentally bad mouth the driver. It may not show but inside your mind is filled with contempt, ridicule, denigration, and name calling.

ROAD RAGE AND AGGRESSIVE DRIVING

Some people draw the line at going public with their rage because they don't think it's appropriate to show it. They hide their gestures out of view or cuss under their breath with a neutral face. Others feel that it's all right to express aggression—"to let it out"—but that it's not right to do anything physically injurious like ramming or beating. Then there are those who condone acts of violence as long as they were provoked by stupid, inconsiderate, or irresponsible behavior. But wherever one personally draws the line of hostility, there's a common feeling that the other driver is guilty. We feel justified in responding when that line is crossed. Some have it to a slight degree while others have it continuously while behind the wheel.

CAUTION—VENTING IS HARMFUL TO YOUR HEALTH

Giving in to anger is harmful in many ways. Scientists have discovered that routine anger makes people sick by weakening the cardiovascular and immune systems.[10] Each anger episode sets up a fight-or-flight survival response that makes the heart beat faster and the blood thicken. Each episode is cumulative, and if you have dozens of angry or hostile reactions on one trip, the effect on the coronary system can be damaging enough to shorten life.

An experiment at Mount Zion Medical Center in San Francisco showed that patients' heart palpitations were reduced 60 percent when they received counseling to reduce hostility and time urgency.[11] It's been shown that "Type A" behaviors can be modified through special practice, reducing by half the recurrence of heart attacks. For heart attack victims, a single angry episode doubles the risk of another attack for two hours. A study at the Harvard School of Public Health showed that men who score high on an "angry response scale" were three times as likely to develop heart disease over a seven-year period.[12]

Contrary to popular belief, expressing or venting anger is literally bad for your health and well-being. Writer and psychoneuroimmunologist Paul Pearsall gives the "pleasure prescription" for hostility: "Don't express it, don't suppress it, confess it."[13] Suppressing and expressing anger have similar negative effects because letting it burn in your mind while trying to hide it takes tremendous energy, and neither resolves the corrosive negative attitude that is the source of stress. A healthy approach to take when anger strikes your heart is to transform it by confessing to yourself that you've lost your cool, and now you'd rather be free of that sort of compulsive reaction. This admission prepares your mind to be less susceptible to giving in to anger by venting and getting worked up. It helps to think of anger as an inner tyrant that we don't want to let out of the cage. When provoked, we are at risk of letting the fiend out, so we need to prepare better responses.

Reacting with anger affects health because physiology is driven by how we mentally construct and interpret reality. Getting angry is actually a weakening response that makes you ineffective because you're handing over power to an opponent—the power to injure your health through venting and dangerous retaliation. Anger is self-punishing and self-defeating. In an experiment at Iowa State University, people who were given a way to vent their anger showed more aggressiveness afterward than people who were encouraged not to vent.[14] Contrary to popular opinion, the punching-bag theory is wrong. It's less frustrating when you don't vent.

CHECKLIST: YOUR RANGE OF HOSTILITY

The following twenty steps are arranged along a continuum of escalating degrees of hostility, beginning with relatively milder forms of aggressiveness (step 1) and going all the way to extreme violence (step 20). How far down the uncivilized path do you allow yourself to go? The majority of drivers we tested go as far as step 13.

(1) Mentally condemning another driver
(2) Verbally denigrating another driver to passengers in your vehicle
(3) Closing ranks to deny someone entry into your lane because you're frustrated or upset
(4) Giving another driver the "stink eye" to show your disapproval
(5) Speeding past another car or revving the engine as a sign of protest
(6) Preventing another driver from passing because you're mad
(7) Tailgating to pressure a driver to go faster or get out of the way
(8) Fantasizing physical violence against another driver
(9) Honking or yelling at someone through the window to indicate displeasure
(10) Making a visible obscene gesture at another driver
(11) Using your car to retaliate by making sudden, threatening maneuvers
(12) Pursuing another car because of a provocation or insult
(13) Getting out of the car and engaging in a verbal dispute on a street or parking lot
(14) Carrying a weapon in the car in case you decide to use it in a driving incident

(15) Deliberately bumping or ramming another car in anger

(16) Trying to run another car off the road to punish the driver

(17) Getting out of the car and beating or battering someone as a result of a road exchange

(18) Trying to run someone down whose actions angered you

(19) Shooting at another car

(20) Killing someone

How far down did you go on the continuum? The checklist is divided into five unequal zones of intensity of aggressiveness.

Unfriendly Zone: Items 1 to 3—mental and verbal acts of unkindness toward other drivers.

Hositle Zone: Items 4 to 7—visibly communicating displeasure or resentment with the desire to punish or retaliate.

Violent Zone: Items 8 to 11—carrying out an act of hostility either in fantasy or in deed.

Lesser Mayhem Zone: Items 12 to 16—epic road rage contained within personal limits.

Major Mayhem Zone: Items 17 to 20—unrestrained epic road rage; the stuff of violent media headlines.

NOTES

1. Personal anecdotes quoted throughout this chapter were sent to us by e-mail correspondents.

2. American Driver and Traffic Safety Education Association [online], adtsea.iup.edu/adtsea [May 20, 2000].

3. Community Transportation Association (CCTA), "Dollars and Sense: The Economics of Public Transportation in America" [online], www.ctaa.org/pubs/dollars/section3.shtml [May 20, 2000].

4. "State of the Commute Report," 1998 [online], www.scag.ca.gov/major/soc98.htm [May 20, 2000].

5. "Urban Mobility Study," Texas Transportation Mobility Study, 1998 [online], mobility.tamu.edu [May 20, 2000].

6. Ibid.

7. Leon James and Diane Nahl, "Aggressiveness in Relation to Age, Gender, and Type of Car," DrDriving.org [online], www.aloha.net/~dyc/surveys/survey2/interpretations.html [May 20, 2000].

8. John Larson, *Steering Clear of Highway Madness: A Driver's Guide to Curbing Stress and Strain* (Wilsonville, Ore.: BookPartners, 1996).

9. Leon James and Diane Nahl, "Driver Personality Survey," DrDriving.org [online], www.aloha.net/~dyc/surveys/survey3/personality.html [May 20, 2000].

10. Redford Williams and Virginia Williams, *Anger Kills* (New York: Harper Perennial, 1993); Paul Pearsall, *The Pleasure Prescription: To Love, to Work, to Play— Life in the Balance* (Alameda, Calif.: Hunter House Publishers, 1996).

11. Williams and Williams, *Anger Kills*, pp. 30–60.

12. American Heart Association, "Older Men with Highest Levels of Anger May Have Tripled Risk of Heart Disease," November 1996 [online], www. smhrt.org/Whats_News/AHA_News_Releases/964473.html [June 2, 1997].

13. Pearsall, *The Pleasure Prescription*. A similar approach is taken by the Cuss Control Academy, online at www.cusscontrol.com; James V. O'Connor, *Cuss Control: The Complete Book on How to Curb Your Cursing* (Three Rivers, Mich.: Three Rivers Press, 2000).

14. Brad J. Bushman, Roy F. Baumeister, and Angela D. Stack, "Catharsis, Aggression and Persuasive Influence: Self-Fulfilling or Self-Defeating Prophecies?" *Journal of Personality and Social Psychology* 76, no. 3 (January 1999) [online], www.apa.org/journals/psp/psp763367.html [May 20, 2000].

THE ROAD RAGE SPECTRUM

JEKYLL-HYDE SYNDROME

It's been commonly observed that otherwise perfectly friendly, courteous, and neighborly citizens abruptly switch personality the moment they get behind the wheel. Their egos swell, and it seems that an inner beast emerges, takes control, and dictates a radically changed outlook on their fellow man. There is always a margin of error in any activity, and driving is no exception. Every driver is aware that mistakes are dangerous, but the reality is that we all will make mistakes, perhaps out of ignorance, perhaps inadvertently, perhaps from negligence or a momentary impulse to recklessness. When we're placed at risk by another driver's mistake, it's hard not to feel stressed and angry. We are also alert critics of bad driving. We tend to add a dose of self-righteous indignation to our disapproval. We personalize incidents to the point of confrontation:

This wasn't rush hour, but there were quite a few cars on the road. Since there were no bike lanes designated, we rode along the right-hand lane as the law states that we are to do. All of a sudden this lady in her car right behind us starts honking. She didn't honk just once. No—she honked three or four times. This really pissed me off. I scowled and told my sister to just keep going. Then when we pulled off the main street to make a turn, I glared at the woman as she passed by. She glared at me also and I really wished that I could just yank her out of her car and slap her silly. I wanted to say to her "Are you stupid? The law states that when there isn't a designated bike lane and ample room on the side of the road, bicyclists are to use the right-hand lane!"[1]

Anger plus self righteousness is the classic recipe for road rage. However, it's important to recognize that road rage is expressed in different ways by different drivers. Our research over the years has yielded a number of distinct road rage personalities. They range from aggressive moralists, to those obsessed with defeating the clock, to the passive-aggressive and the outright murderous. The lesson to be drawn from these types is that through our shared culture, we each may harbor some of these irrational mental habits.[2] Our research has uncovered three different types of road rage. Each type represents particular emotional challenges.

PASSIVE-AGGRESSIVE ROAD RAGE

We define *passive-aggressive road rage* as a reactionary protest against feeling thwarted, coerced, mistreated, or repeatedly wronged, characterized by feelings of rancor and resentment against other drivers. It's a feeling of desperation that says, "You can't push me any farther!" Passive-aggressive road rage is a form of passive resistance that is expressed by ignoring others or by refusing to respond appropriately. The intent of passive-aggressive road rage is to be obstructionist and oppositional.

People commonly complain that drivers who prevent others from doing what they need to do are inconsiderate, especially those who insist on maintaining the speed limit in the fast lane. These motorists can infuriate others because they seem deliberately unaware of the explosive events taking shape around them. They fail to respond when prompted to move over, they keep people out, and they act oblivious to their environment. Passive-aggressive road rage is as dangerous as other types because you never know whether someone you are blocking is looking for a fight, wants to teach someone a lesson, or simply enjoys retaliating when obstructed.

Two researchers at Pennsylvania State University observed people leaving a shopping mall parking lot.[3] They noticed that departing drivers (both men and women) took eleven seconds longer to vacate a spot when someone else was waiting for the space than when no one was there. Even the implication of "pressure" by just waiting can evoke resistance. Instead of hurrying up, they tend to take longer. This power-based behavior is counterproductive because it takes longer for them to leave and engenders hostile reactions. So why do people do it? The researchers investigated the issue further by sending in cars driven by a student who honked at the departing driver. Drivers who were honked at took even longer to depart than drivers who were not honked at. The researchers attribute this "territorial behavior" to people's desire to proclaim rightful occupancy of a space. When this right is questioned by a hostile honking motorist, the tendency is to reaffirm rightful ownership, and this is accomplished by taking even longer to vacate the place because the power struggle is the focus.

Passive-aggressive road rage can be directed toward pedestrians, cyclists, and passengers:

> She always bugged me whenever I gave her a ride home up the hill. It's a winding road with lots of switchbacks, and she'd always brace herself by slamming her hand on the dashboard at every turn, as if she would fall over. Why couldn't she just hold the door handle like everyone else? Why did she have to make a scene on every turn? I couldn't stand driving her because of that. She never said anything, and neither did I, but I silently resented her during our rides, so I wasn't really outwardly nice either, I just acted like I was in a bad mood.

Putting on a bad mood to protest a passenger's reaction is a form of passive-aggressive road rage that has long-term consequences for physical and mental health.

Left-Lane Bandit

Left-lane bandits can be motivated by contrariness, stubbornness, and even the perverse enjoyment of dominating others by forcing them to line up behind. The most common complaint we hear is about those who insist on driving slower than is considered normal for a given area. The nicest term applied to them is "inconsiderate drivers." People who provoke others by claiming the right to obstruct the faster traffic flow: "If I'm moving faster than the prevailing traffic, I'm neither legally nor morally required to move over. It's that simple." This receives a furious response from the highway vigilantes:

> *Wrong.* As a considerate human being (there are so few of them left anymore), you should be prepared to move over as soon as it is safe to do so. This may require speeding up a bit to clear traffic, or slowing a bit to drop into an open space. But whenever a faster car comes up behind

you, *get out of the way*. A few times bozos like that have made it obvious (one-finger salute, brake lights, and so on) that they'll be darned if they're going to give up their inherent right to be in the left lane, doing any speed they please to move, so I've made it obvious to them that they'll get run off the road if they don't move over. The cops sure aren't going to do anything about it, so we might as well.

There's a better way to move aside the idiots who clog up the interstate's passing lane; however, driving a snowplow with the wing blade down at 80 MPH is not for everyone. As an alternative, turn on your headlights and make sure the high beam switch is activated. Then turn them off. As you approach one of the "turtle-type" drivers (I call them turtles because they are always traveling slow and have their heads up their shell), simply flash your headlights at them a couple of times. Many of these jerks do not mind getting out of your way but they fail to ever notice you until you have, out of necessity, become one of "those tailgating fools." This type of driver almost always believes it is his sacred duty to "punish" tailgaters by not getting out of the way.

As long as there are people who don't understand "left lane fast, right lane slow," I'm gonna pass these pompous idiots on the inside. I used to wait for them to move over, but I've learned that 90 percent of drivers who are driving 2 MPH above the speed limit in the supposedly "fast" lane really don't care about any other car's desire to drive faster than they are, and some even derive some sort of perverse pleasure in preventing me from getting two car lengths ahead.

But it's not always that clear-cut:

My problem is being victimized by the road rage of others. I can tell you a very good reason why slower moving traffic "cannot" keep to the right. Because of a left exit—the city I live in is *full* of them. I have found that if I wait too long to get into the left lane when traffic is heavy, no one will let me in and I miss my exit. Another problem in my area is that people will not move out of the right lane to let you enter the highway.

People in this predicament cannot rightfully be called left-lane bandits, And they have the right to enter an exit lane in time to safely make the exit. They are not inconsiderate, they simply must decelerate in the passing lane because of highway design. Nevertheless, many drivers slow down passive-aggressively in an effort to hold others back by enforcing either posted or idealized speed limits.

How are we to deal with passive-aggressive challenges? We've already seen that the vigilante response of punishment and retaliation is unhealthy, unsafe, illegal, and hardly moral. Moreover, the bullying response is ineffective in changing the behavior of the left-lane bandit. **87**

ROAD RAGE AND AGGRESSIVE DRIVING

The emotionally intelligent way to cope is to go around the blocking vehicle without tailgating, without revving the engine, without giving the look of disapproval (or worse), and without bad-mouthing the offensive driver mentally or aloud.

Aggressive thinking is emotionally challenging because its biased logic too often leads to a desire to punish and retaliate against the driver who acts in an unexpected manner. But you have a choice to opt for more emotionally intelligent alternatives.

> I've often wondered what makes these people drive in the left lane and refuse to move over when I come up behind them. Mostly I just got furious at them and called them all sorts of names. Sometimes I would cut back into the left lane just a little close to let them know I'm displeased. That made me feel better for a few seconds, but I kept thinking about afterwards and I realized this whole drama is my own. I had to admit that there could be several reasons why that man drives in the left lane. I tried to list them: he is unaware that I'm behind; he is old and is afraid to cross lanes, sort of stuck there; he doesn't realize the commotion he is creating, it just doesn't enter his mind; he is lost and thinks he's going to make a left turn; the passenger is holding a gun on him and forcing him to stay there. I had to laugh at this last one. Anyway, my earlier certainty that he was perverse and enjoyed making me feel bad was no longer such a certainty. In fact, next time this happened I was able to see the whole thing in advance and I do what I usually do: wait, then pass, then switch back into the left lane, but without the venting stuff. I feel much better. More in control. Proud of myself.

CHECKLIST: YOUR PASSIVE AGGRESSIVE ROAD RAGE TENDENCY

Check each example of passive resistance that pertains to you.

1. ___ I insist on driving at the speed limit in the passing lane because it's the law.
2. ___ I hold up a long line of drivers on a one-lane road.
3. ___ I ignore drivers who attempt to enter my lane, closing the gap.
4. ___ I ignore yield signs.
5. ___ I don't bother giving proper signals.
6. ___ I am slow to get going when traffic lights turn green.
7. ___ I show insufficient alertness or consideration to drivers and conditions.
8. ___ I repeatedly tap the brakes or slow way down to retaliate against a tailgater.

9. ___ I take my time entering and leaving parking spaces, especially when someone is waiting for me.
10. ___ I make gestures and facial expressions to myself to show my disapproval of pushy drivers.

VERBAL ROAD RAGE

We define *verbal road rage* as the habit of constantly complaining about the traffic, keeping up a stream of mental or spoken attacks against drivers, passengers, law enforcement officials, road workers, pedestrians, speed limits, and road signs. Undoubtedly the most common form of road rage, the purpose of verbal road rage is to denounce, ridicule, condemn, or castigate a rule, an engineer, or another driver. We found such negative expressions frequently used in electronic discussion groups: morons, stupid idiots, louts, unbelievable fools, crazy jackasses, damn maniacs, criminals, creeps, selfish freaks, and dunderheads—among many others.

Have you listened in on yourself behind the wheel? Drivers have a tendency to chatter to themselves about what's going on. It's natural. Everybody does it, and not just in traffic. But it's not common to listen in to our mental broadcasts. Listening to yourself thinking behind the wheel informs you of the kind of driving persona you maintain. Some of this self-talk comes out as swearing, cursing, or complaining. But these overt verbalizations are merely the tip of the iceberg. Deeper within your mind reside cultural habits of reasoning and reacting emotionally. It's possible to become aware of these automatic mental habits by using the methods outlined in chapter 6.

Some drivers revealed that they carry a noise-making toy on the seat and use it to "zap" offending drivers with various optional settings befitting their crime: pistol, machine gun, grenade, flame thrower, tank. The sense of satisfaction lies in calibrating the right amount of punishment. We discovered that comic-book images, fantasies, or visualizations are routine for most drivers, though they vary in frequency and degree of gory detail.

Verbal road rage that's directed against the self is often an integral part of a driver's inner dialogue. Some drivers maintain a continuous stream of negative thoughts:

> I was in the far left lane when another car decided to come into my lane. It entered the freeway from the grassy area on the side. It wasn't as if there were a lot of cars on the freeway behind me. It could've waited, but no. I had to come to almost a complete stop. I was furious. I had tears streaming down my face. I was scared and very angry. I nearly hit that

car. The driver did not seem concerned. He had a giggly smirk on his face and was trying to get from one side of the freeway to the exit right across. I pressed hard on my brakes and blew my horn in an angry way. I was not about to let this idiot get away with what he did. I wanted him to know just how angry I was at him for foolishly coming on to the freeway, knowing just how fast I was going and him going at a turtle-like speed. There were actually three people in the car, but that didn't intimidate me. I stuck my finger at them in anger and rolled down my window with my fist out. I wanted them to come out of their car so that I could punch their faces in. Nothing would've stopped me at this point. They just ignored me.

I know I was not acting like a lady but I also know they were being like idiots!! I kept driving down the freeway with tears in my eyes. I was overwhelmed by the whole incident. I felt destitute, scared, and hopeless. From the expression on the driver's face I could tell that he wasn't terrified or even a bit remorseful. He was rather arrogant and seemed amused at the whole thing.

Verbal road rage is a form of short-term relief for some frustrated drivers, but it injures their self-esteem and promotes an alienated culture of discontent. Much verbal road rage is so habitual that we are unaware of it:

I was beginning to wonder if the driver was doing it on purpose. I then got more frustrated and muttered some "not-so-nice" things and even a few swear words. After I muttered them, my reaction was one of disappointment and mild shock. I never thought of "Jennifer the Driver" as being one who reacted by cursing out others. I mean, yes, I do swear here and there, but it usually isn't personal. If it is, it's usually serious. That's why I was shocked at my reactions. I began to wonder if I took minor happenings on the road and blew them out of proportion by letting them get the better of me. No longer was I simply disappointed, I began to really worry about how well I actually knew myself.

Even a simple trip to the shopping mall can be upsetting when one is emotionally unprepared to handle crowded conditions:

On a Saturday afternoon during a sale at the mall, I arrived at the parking structure. Glancing at all the cars circling round and round looking for parking made me cringe. I knew I was doomed. As usual, I started off in my calm, cool, and collective manner. However, after circling around fifteen times looking for parking, my blood pressure began to rise.

After circling a few more times, my patience ran very thin and once again I became angry and hostile. I felt like eliminating all the people in sight. I kept thinking: "Why does everyone have to shop at this mall at this particular time?" It frustrated me that I couldn't start shopping until my car was properly parked, but there were no spaces available. Every time I saw people walking to their car, it was located behind me. Or else they would just drop off their packages and head back for another round of purchasing. My two famous quotes for the occasion: "This is *crazy!*" and "I hate these people!" I was wasting my time looking for parking space when in fact I could've been looking for a nice pair of jeans.

This driver was obsessed by the idea that she was wasting time finding a parking space rather than making purchases. Unfortunately, her mind has set up a no-win situation that is torturous. She separated the act of the purchase from the act of parking, and this illogical distinction only allowed her to torment herself. Verbal road rage seldom works to achieve goals and increases strife.

CHECKLIST: YOUR VERBAL ROAD RAGE TENDENCY

The following statements were taken from self-witnessing reports of drivers. Check each statement that could be something you say to yourself.

1. ___ Hey fool, get out of the way!
2. ___ What's wrong with this driver? I can't believe how slow he's going!
3. ___ Nope, I won't let you sneak into my lane.
4. ___ Hey, what's the big rush? Don't be so pushy!
5. ___ I'd like to see you squirm, you pushy geek.
6. ___ Did that scare you? Good. I hope it teaches you a lesson.
7. ___ I'm tailgating you now. Pay you back. So who's the smart one, huh?
8. ___ Figures, it's a woman. Women can't drive for #%*! (also works for different social class, orientation, ethnic identity, and age groups)
9. ___ I hope you break your neck!
10. ___ Who do you think you are, creep?
11. ___ Get a life!
12. ___ Look, that airhead left his blinker on!

EPIC ROAD RAGE

We define *epic road rage* as: the habit of fantasizing comic-book roles and extreme punitive measures against another driver, such as chasing, beating up, ramming, dragging, shooting, and killing, sometimes to the point of acting on it.

In a 1950s Disney cartoon, Goofy played a Jekyll-and-Hyde role portraying nerdy but calm Mr. Walker who, every time he started his car, became fire-breathing maniac Mr. Wheeler. We define epic road rage as the product of fantasizing comic-book roles like the Avenger, the Punisher, and the Destroyer, and sometimes acting on these fantasies by taking extreme punitive measures against another driver. Epic aggression is confrontational and combative, harsh and defiant, with righteous fury, seeking revenge and punishment. Whether or not it is openly expressed and acted on depends on circumstances. Giving chase, for instance, involves all the feelings of epic road rage, although it doesn't always result in physical contact:

> One night, after I closed the store where I was working as a manager, I was leaving the parking lot when a car came up behind me and hit my rear bumper. The driver then tried to push me out into the oncoming traffic as I held down tight on my brakes. I was pretty scared and as soon as the traffic cleared I shot out onto the road.
>
> As I pulled away I made an obscene gesture at the car. Suddenly we were side-by-side on the freeway. The car got closer and bumped into me, as if trying to run me off the road. I looked at the gun on my seat, which I carried with me because of the bankroll from the store. I felt it was time to defend myself. Before I knew it, the gun was in my hand. The car kept coming. I held the steering wheel with my left hand and pointed the gun at the car. At this point we were traveling pretty fast so I slowed down in order not to lose control of the wheel when I fired.
>
> The car also slowed down and moved closer. This is what I wanted: to see that passenger's face when she saw the gun. I was furious now, and I wanted to kill them. It seemed as if I was viewing a movie scene. I was watching other cars moving down the road from a distance. The adrenaline was surging and I felt like I was on a high. The woman saw the gun pointing at her face. The hunter became the hunted! The car suddenly braked real hard. I braked also. She suddenly sped away. I wanted to pursue her but I decided to control myself after all.

Are these ordinary people, or out-of-control wackos? Our studies reveal that these feelings and responses are far more common than we'd like to believe. In many cases, verbal road rage gave way to epic road rage:

> As the traffic slowly progressed, I would become violent to a high degree—pounding my steering wheel, stomping on the floor, and talking out loud to myself. . . . Although my actions resorted to hitting and kicking objects, they were very mild in comparison to my thoughts.

Glaring at the stream of cars ahead of me, one thought would constantly run through my mind: "What the hell is taking so long?!"

Off of this question branched many abhorrent, detestable thoughts about the construction workers and the motorists around me. Anything that hindered me from my final destination was cussed and cursed at repeatedly. No longer was I the passive, nice person. I was now an aggressive, competitive road maniac! I would never let a person cut in front of me, and instead of stopping in time, I blocked intersections when my light turned red. When I needed to change lanes, I would eagerly butt my way in. The drivers had no choice but to let me in or collide with me. As I drove in this state my thoughts gradually became worse. All the harsh thoughts would then become vocal. If words could kill, everyone around me would have been dead. Finally, I did it, I chased a woman who cut me off into a parking lot, got out and beat on her window, screaming at her. I tried to open her door, but it was locked. She was terrified, and people were watching, so I quit after a few minutes.

Traffic obsessions are exaggerated by mental isolation in heavy traffic when drivers can avoid normal social relations. Air conditioning with closed and tinted windows contributes to a sense of detachment. The artificial social isolation of driving creates a psychological condition that can foster irrational thoughts, feelings of paranoia and insane impulses—"I chased her . . . got out and beat on her window, screaming at her . . . tried to open her door. . . ."

For some drivers, an epic road rage mentality can transform driving into a fantasy ride filled with the thrill of winning mythical races against "bad guys" in fast cars. They get a high from the adrenaline rush during risky maneuvers and dangerous incidents. Their self-esteem depends on being ahead of everyone. In this state of mind, drivers are obsessed with racing metaphors—getting ahead, getting there first, keeping others back, catching a lucky break, seizing the advantage, winning: "Out of my way, 'cause here I come!"

There is slow-moving traffic in the right-hand lane and people are moving so slow to pass them. I'm anxious to get home. I tail the person in front of me. It's a woman driver. They cannot drive. She obviously does not get the hint. Come on! Move it! Hey, there's an opening. I cut right and accelerate. I maneuver through the oncoming traffic to make up for the lost time that the woman caused me. Heh, heh, 75 MPH and climbing. Eighty-five MPH . . . this is about right. If it weren't for the speedometer I would not know how fast I was driving.

I'm scanning the area in front, to the side, the rear. Checking for chasers, cops, and potential dangers. It's difficult to drive at 85 MPH for prolonged periods of time. You can't have a lapse in your concentration. This is very serious business. A little miscalculation or error in judgment can have serious consequences. You've got to be a responsible individual to do this. I'm passing this red 1990 two-door Accord. He is speeding also. I think he saw me closing in on him and he's trying to accelerate to catch me. I knew it! A race.

He's trying to catch me, but I have the momentum and the power. I put more power on the accelerator. 100 MPH . . . I don't know, it feels like I'm going faster than I should. I can't let fear overcome me now. I've got to concentrate more. At this speed the car is a lot more unstable. The Accord can only chase me but he can't gain on me. Wow, I'm passing cars at an unbelievable rate. I don't know . . . a sudden lane change by a driver could mean disaster. OK, I'm slowing down. The overpass is coming up and that's where the speed trap is. Fifty MPH . . . I'm continuing to slow down. Speed limit here is 35. Hey, the Accord is passing me. How about giving chase buddy? Nah, better not. Wow, look at that cop with the radar gun over there. I hardly believe this. He got in his car and is chasing the Accord.

Yup, there he is, blue lights go on, he's stopping him. Chuckle, chuckle. This guy was probably not speeding as bad as I was, but he's the one receiving the citation instead of me. I feel victorious and giddy. I broke the law and got away with it.

Extreme speeding and racing gives this driver a sense of accomplishment. He gets a rush from "probing the limits of my vehicle, and surviving." His elation comes from his epic accomplishment: "I broke the law and got away with it."

A random sampling of recent reports on the Internet of epic road rage incidents reveals a striking pattern of escalating violence on roads across the country. Take this series from a city famous for orderliness and restraint, Salt Lake City, Utah. Utahans once were incredulous over reports of freeway shootings in places like New York or Los Angeles. Now, road rage reports commonly have a Salt Lake City dateline. In 1999 there were a dozen freeway shootings there, these among them:

In February, a forty-nine-year-old father of five was shot to death by another motorist on the 7200 South on-ramp. Hours later, police arrested a twenty-year-old man, who they say sideswiped the victim's car before shooting him. He has been charged with capital homicide.

In March, a man fired shots into another car traveling on Interstate 15, striking two occupants in the hands. That same man was charged with brandishing a weapon a few days later at another motorist after a minor altercation in a parking lot.

In April, a Salt Lake County woman was sentenced to fifteen years in prison in the March 1996 death of a second woman. After a fender-bender, the second woman got out of her car to talk to the first woman, but the first woman started to drive away. The second woman then stepped in front of the other's 1966 Lincoln Continental. The first woman gunned the engine and hit her, pinning her body under the car and dragging her along 3900 South.

A South Jordan man escaped without injury in April after another motorist on Interstate 15 fired shots into his car. The South Jordan man had honked at another car, driving in a closed-off lane, who passed him. As both cars exited at 1300 South, occupants of a blue sports car shot two rounds at the South Jordan man's car.

A middle-aged motorist honked at an elderly man's car because it was stopped in the middle of 1300 West. That honk led to an altercation that has left the middle aged man partly disabled and the elderly man with a criminal conviction on his otherwise clean record.

A seventy-five-year-old driver, peeved that the driver honked at him for blocking traffic, followed him when he pulled off the road, hurled his prescription bottle at him, and then smashed his knees with his '92 Mercury.[4]

In Texas:

In February, delivery van driven by a thirty-three-year-old man collided with a pickup driven by a forty-two-year old man. A side mirror was broken in the minor collision. The delivery driver got out of the van and argued with the pickup driver. The delivery man started punching the older man as he sat in his truck. The man in the truck pulled out his licensed, concealed .40-caliber handgun and shot the puncher in the chest. Police charged the shooter with murder, but a grand jury refused to indict him, clearing him in the road rage killing.[5]

Meanwhile, in Boston:

A motorist confronted a Boston school bus driver who allegedly cut him off. After spitting in the bus driver's face, the motorist returned to his car. Angered, the bus driver left his vehicle to confront the motorist, only to receive a thrashing in the street.[6]

The regional coordinator with the Ohio School Bus Safety Program in Circleville recalled an incident in which a bus driver pulled over after being signaled by the driver of a trash-hauling truck:

The trucker didn't look upset, so, not thinking, the driver opened the door. He thought the guy was going to tell him there might be something wrong with the bus. Next thing he knew, the guy went back to one of the teenagers and punched him, bloodying his nose, and said "thank

95

you," and on his way he went. Turns out the kids had tossed a soda can at the trash hauler and had followed that with a obscene hand gesture.[7]

In a similar case in Toledo, Ohio, troopers handled a crash involving a vehicle that intentionally rammed a car carrying a mother and father and their three kids. The reckless driver, who was eventually charged with felonious assault and driving under the influence, told troopers he ran into the other car because one of the children gave him an "obscene finger gesture." Another incident of a provocative gesture led to a violent outcome:

> Milwaukee police said Wednesday the death of twenty-two-year-old John Sentowski, who was stabbed repeatedly by another motorist Saturday in the 4400 block of West Sumac Place, was likely a case of "road rage." Sentowski was stabbed with an unknown instrument by the driver of another car after a traffic disagreement escalated from obscene gestures to violence.[8]

In Philadelphia:

> In early August, an argument between the occupants of two cars on Allegheny Avenue erupted into gunfire. A nineteen-year-old woman was shot in the head. On August 12, the driver of a sport-utility vehicle tried to run a van driver off the road in Upper Darby. After a collision, the first driver stabbed the second in the leg.[9]

In Milwaukee:

> A college professor pulled a gun on a federal drug agent and the agent punched him, ending a dispute that started on Interstate 43 near downtown Milwaukee, according to police. The agent told police the professor cut him off, while the professor's attorney says the agent turned his high beams on the professor's car.[10]

In Colorado Springs:

> A fifty-five-year-old man persuaded a seventeen-year-old boy who had been tailgating him to pull over, and decided that rather than merely scold the lad, he would shoot him. And he did. Fatally—after the youth threatened him.[11]

It's not only drivers who feel free to express their anger on the roads:

> A bicyclist, enraged at being knocked off his bike by a car outside Washington, D.C., got up, pulled out a handgun and shot the driver to

death, police said. The bicyclist killed a nineteen-year-old college student with a single shot in the head. He ran off on foot but was caught ten minutes later.[12]

The road rage legend suggests that it's mostly confined to men. Not so. In Ohio, a young mother of two was jockeying for position on a highway with a pregnant woman. She ended up slamming on her brakes on purpose to show her rage, and the pregnant woman hit a parked truck and went flying. She lost the baby. The mother of two was sentenced to over a year in prison for vehicular manslaughter of the fetus. (See the analysis of this road rage tragedy in chapter 5.)

CHECKLIST: YOUR EPIC ROAD RAGE TENDENCY

The following statements were taken from self-witnessing reports of drivers. Check each statement that may apply to you behind the wheel.

1. ___ I have had occasion to give someone a brake job.
2. ___ I carry a weapon in my vehicle to defend myself and my family from anyone on the road who tries to hurt them.
3. ___ I have chased someone down, pulled over, and confronted the person.
4. ___ I have physically attacked someone for interfering with me on the road.
5. ___ I often imagine myself doing extreme violence to pay back some stupid driver.
6. ___ I'm gonna get you for this, madman!
7. ___ I would run someone off the road if I thought they deserved it.
8. ___ I'm gonna kill you now bud, annihilate you! *Zoom vrooom*, you're gone!
9. ___ Honk at me at your own risk.
10. ___ Anyone who cuts me off is fair game.
11. ___ Wouldn't it be nice to have a zap gun right now, or maybe a fireman's hose to sweep them all aside!

AUTOMOTIVE VIGILANTE

This automotive bully aggresses against other motorists, chosen at random or for some specific reason, with a constant stream of verbal abuse, offensive gestures, and threatening maneuvers with the vehicle, sometimes going to extreme of physical violence. When engaged in a dispute or when confronted by the law, the vigilante motorist will typically deny responsibility and counterattack, feigning victimhood to evade accountability, often with success. We received this note in 1999:

> You wrote that according to Dr. Brenner, "If someone cuts you off, don't do battle with them. If you give in, you win." What a crock. If you give in, you are reinforcing their attitude to do it again and again. The person learns *nothing* from this event, except they got away with it once, and they will do it again and again! There have to be consequences for wrong behavior. If reinforced, it is likely to repeat! I say chase the bastard down and give them an earful. They may still be too stupid to learn from the incident but a few times of this should give them the message!

Retaliation is often rationalized as a mission for the public good. Drivers who take on the role of highway vigilante love to ferret out, isolate, and punish certain drivers in the name of law and order. They see themselves as self-appointed cops, and often, as judge, jury, and executioner. Their sense of righteousness and moral superiority ignites road rage. A female driver argues:

> I don't think one should move out of the way of tailgaters. That encourages this very unsafe practice. If we continue to bow down to such overly aggressive and dangerous behavior, then driving will turn into a free-for-all, with the survival of the most aggressive driver.

A man describes how he opposes tailgaters:

> Sometimes when I don't use the turn signal, I realize that I'm choosing not to use it because a driver behind me made me mad. I guess it's a good way to get back at them. The drivers deserve it. Who do they think they are, tailgating me like that? I can't tolerate someone bullying me into something I don't want to do. They're messing with the wrong person because I won't let that happen, and I feel ecstatic when I can prevent them from pushing me around. My plan is to teach them a lesson: Trying to intimidate others will get them nowhere because they aren't getting past me. If they're going to be so obnoxious, I'm going to give them a dose of their own medicine—or should I say, their own poison. I understand that what I'm doing is a little evil, but I must do it so they won't get the best of me.

For some, it feels good to retaliate:

> I'm driving on the highway at night. Someone is approaching ahead with high beams on, and they don't lower the lights for me. My reaction is to lower mine and then raise them again when the car gets closer so I

can shine it right in the driver's eyes. I do this to retaliate against his not lowering his beams for me. I feel glad that I paid him back.

In an electronic discussion group on how to repay tailgaters:

Rig up a very bright halogen headlight on your back window. If you are being tailgated badly just turn it on and blind the sucker. I know it isn't legal but neither are a lot of things we do.

This response prompted a slew of fantasies:

Even better, though, is installing a few tear gas grenades under the rear bumper, complete with solenoids (controlled by switches on your dash, for example) to pull their pins. . . . Even truly minimal amounts of tear gas will render the driver of the car behind you almost completely blind instantly.

These drivers see themselves as "just having fun" with these fantasies (some make us laugh), but they may be underestimating the danger of a powerful psychological mechanism, because cruel fantasies permit people to accelerate their anger whenever they feel justified.

CHECKLIST: ARE YOU AN AUTOMOTIVE VIGILANTE?

Check each statement that reflects your attitude.

1. ___ Getting out of a tailgater's way only encourages that behavior.
2. ___ You need to retaliate against aggressive drivers in order to maintain law and order on highways.
3. ___ It's justified to resist bad drivers by scaring them a little so they don't think others are unaware or powerless.
4. ___ If you see a driver making what you think is a stupid, dangerous mistake, it's your right and duty to teach that driver a lesson.
5. ___ The situation on the road is so competitive and aggressive that sometimes I think of some bad things I can do to some of the idiot drivers that endanger everybody's lives by being too aggressive. Of course I don't do anything about it. It's just a harmless little fantasy.
6. ___ Some drivers are so foolish and selfish that they need to be taught a lesson by vigilante drivers who look out for the public good by punishing these selfish drivers.
7. ___ Aggressive driving cannot be cured. It's part of human nature in

a competitive and dangerous situation. We need to teach drivers how to be aggressive and safe at the same time.

8. ___ Driver A was justified in expressing his anger when driver B was blocking his way in the passing lane.

9. ___ Driver A was justified in cutting off driver B to let him know that he should not block the passing lane.

10. ___ I would use tailgating only as a last resort, when a stubborn or selfish driver simply refuses to let me pass when I'm in a hurry and can't afford to lose more time.

RUSHING MANIAC

Rushing mania is one of the most common driving obsessions, yet its connection to road rage is often not noticed or understood:

> My mind is focused on getting to my destination in a certain amount of time, and I don't seem to care how I do it as long as I don't crash. Even if I don't have to get somewhere by a certain time, I'm always in a hurry.

This dysfunctional driving style has two complementary elements. One is an extraordinary need to avoid slowing down. The other is the consequent anger against anyone who causes a slow down. In this mental state we are perpetually anxious on the road, berating ourselves for being slow, being late, being behind others. We get into a habit of lane hopping, always trying to figure out which lane is faster. This mental attitude creates impulsive driving that is unpredictable and difficult for other drivers to read. We become the victims of our own fantasies about beating traffic or avoiding congestion.

> When I'm driving in really heavy traffic and I'm in a hurry (which is almost always), I get really irritated if I get in a slow-moving lane. If cars are passing me by in the other lane, I'll really bully my way in if nobody brakes a little to acknowledge my turn signal. When the tables are turned, however, and I'm in the fast lane and another motorist wants to get out of the slow moving lane and into the fast lane, I speed up even closer to the car in front of me to ensure that person's car won't have the time and space to slip into the fast lane in front of me. I drive aggressively enough to intimidate the person wanting to change lanes to wait for an easier opportunity and not get in front of me. (Young man)

When motorists are frantic about traffic, their mood can deteriorate dramatically:

The Road Rage Spectrum

When I'm late, I turn into an angry, hostile, lane-changing daredevil. The longer the delay I have to endure, the more hostile I become toward others who may try to cut in front of me. I tend to lose sight of my belief that we all have a right to use the road.

Running red lights and ignoring stop or yield signs are the most frequent causes of urban crashes. Traffic police often hear the "I'm late for . . ." excuse from drivers who are pulled over for speeding, and as they hand them a citation, they are likely to answer, "So, leave a little earlier next time." Being late is not a legal reason to drive aggressively. Drivers give these typical reasons and justifications for rushing all the time:

- Being late for work, an appointment or an important interview when traffic is slow
- Leaving home too late to make it on time
- Busy schedule makes them rush while multitasking
- Avoiding wasting time on the road

It's true that the traffic environment is uncomfortable for many reasons. People are often late and traffic is often slower and heavier than we expect it to be. Coming home from work during rush hour is stressful. We're hot or cold, upset, edgy, thirsty, and hungry. Our driving style naturally reflects our inner commotion. We rush to a stop light, we corner faster, we sort-of-slow-down-but-don't-quite-stop at the sign, we switch lanes to avoid the feeling of being in a hopelessly slow lane, and we treat other motorists as obstacles, as if we have more of a right than they do.

Many motorists say that rushing helps them get there faster, but what real difference does rushing make? We clocked ourselves on different trips under various conditions and were amazed that the time ranges were so small. For instance, during rush hour it takes between forty and fifty minutes to go seventeen miles from home to work through dense traffic. That's a maximum difference of ten minutes, but the average difference is only eight minutes. At low-traffic times, the trip takes between twenty-four and thirty-five minutes, a maximum difference of eleven minutes, but an average of only four minutes longer. Similar results were obtained by others who tried this experiment. It seems counterintuitive, but rushing doesn't actually save much time. It's common to see a car that whizzed past you waiting at the next traffic light. And yet drivers still rush. There are deeper psychological pressures to rush that may not be consciously understood:

I find these self-reports of my driving behavior disturbing enough to really want to change. It seems that the first thing I try to do is to avoid

101

construction zones at all costs. I really hate it that much and feel so uncomfortable sitting in traffic that I'd go out of my way to avoid them. I carry flash cards with lecture notes when I think I might hit traffic jams. At least this way I won't feel like I'm wasting my time sitting in traffic. I also make lists in my head about what I need to do that day. I think the exasperating feeling of wasting time, even when I'm not late, circles back to my hard driving personality and a chronic sense of time urgency.

So my method of behavior self-modification is to try and make the time feel used rather than wasted. I also keep a plastic bag in the car so I can clean up candy wrappers and stuff lying around. I would also keep new photos I've picked up but haven't had a chance to look through in my glove box in case I'm desperate to make my time useful rather than rageful.

Rushing mania behind the wheel could be a manifestation of what author James Gleick calls "hurry sickness" in his 1999 book, *Faster*.[13] Gleick bemoans the cultural obsession with saving time, not wasting time, doing more things simultaneously to get more things done:

> It is possible, after all, to tie shoes and watch television, to eat and read, to shave and talk with the children. These days it is possible to drive, eat, listen to a book, and talk on the phone, all at once, if you dare.... "Attention! Multitaskers," says an advertisement for an AT&T wireless telephone service. "Demo all these exciting features"—namely, e-mail, voice telephone, and pocket organizer. Pay attention if you can. We have always multitasked ... but never so intensely or so self-consciously as now. If haste is the gas pedal, multitasking is overdrive. We are multitasking connoisseurs-experts in crowding, pressing, packing, and overlapping distinct activities in our all-too-finite moments.[14]

CHECKLIST: ARE YOU A RUSHING MANIAC?

Check each statement that applies to you.

1. ___ I make it my primary goal to get to my destination in the shortest possible time and spend as little time as possible on the road.
2. ___ I feel really good when I get somewhere fast, beating my own record.
3. ___ One of my worst nightmares is sitting in traffic, wasting my time.
4. ___ My schedule makes me rush in traffic—I have to rush to make all my stops.
5. ___ I see other cars as obstacles in my way that I need to get around.
6. ___ I find the fastest lanes—that is my most satisfying achievement in traffic.

7. ___ I think that missing a light is usually my fault for not hurrying up.
8. ___ I've learned to constantly look over my shoulder for cops.
9. ___ I like to leave as late as possible and time things close to the minute.
10. ___ I have to work in my car while driving under time pressure.

AGGRESSIVE COMPETITOR

Competition is seen as a good thing in America, but on the road it is lethal and dangerous, risking the lives of others and ourselves. Some drivers are so competitive that they need to be in the lead at all times, and feel a sense of loss and rising anxiety if another car passes them. There are those who, when they make a mistake, are deeply embarrassed and worry about what other drivers might think; but when other drivers make a mistake, it's their turn to ridicule them. We do this automatically, by cultural habit and childhood upbringing. Getting a parking space brings a sense of victory and superiority, while missing one can leave us with a sharp sense of personal defeat. It's not unusual for someone to get depressed over losing a parking space to a competitor shopper. But we pay a high price for this type of gaming. Compulsive competitiveness is an ego-centered orientation that shreds everyone's nerves, and by provoking a simplistic game of winners and losers, it contributes significantly to driver rage.

In this example of macho competition we see how zealous, redblooded adolescent drag-racing evolves into a form of win-at-all-costs road rage:

> I'm driving down the hill and merging with the rest of the traffic. I anticipate the traffic ahead at the intersection and decide to move into the far right lane because there is no one there and I can cut in front of this Nissan Sentra. As I roll to the right I sense that he doesn't want to let me in. He revs his engine to cut me off. The light turns green and he does what I anticipated he would do. He accelerates hard into the intersection, but I also do the same. Since I have the momentum going into the light and my car has more horsepower, I just jump out in front of him and cut him off. Yeah, I did it! We are both accelerating hard up to the next intersection. It's a red light and I brake hard. I'm going to make a left turn here. I race my engine to beat the oncoming traffic. He's right behind me. The light is going to turn red. I'm making my move. The light is now red but I'm completing my turn. I'm in the intersection making my turn at full throttle. Yes, sir! I've completed my turn. The light just turned green. The Sentra is stuck. I feel a sense of joy, elation,

accomplishment. Right on! I'm shaking from the adrenaline. What an adventure. I feel good.

One might think there is nothing wrong with this type of harmless fun. The idea of "just having fun" in cars has extended itself to "cruising," resulting in cruiser crackdowns in Los Angeles and anticruising traffic signs in Florida. These law enforcement activities lead to bitter complaints by young cruisers who speak as though they're being discriminated against by police for not being allowed to have fun. Demanding the right to use public roads for dangerous social practices needs to be countered with instruction in emotional intelligence. A crucial step is to break through people's natural denial of their excessive competitiveness. All drivers must be informed of how their behavior influences other users on the road. Self-witnessing of one's competitive behavior behind the wheel looks at the emotions, the thoughts, and the acts we perform when we behave as if driving is a competitive game.

CHECKLIST: ARE YOU AN AGGRESSIVE COMPETITOR?

Check each statement that applies to you.

1. ___ I really hate it when traffic is congested and I can't get ahead of others because I feel like I'm losing.
2. ___ I've discovered that I can force my way into any lane by being pushy.
3. ___ I believe the law that prevails on the road is the law of the jungle—we might as well face it: The most aggressive drivers end up getting what they want.
4. ___ I'm driving in the left lane in heavy traffic and trying to switch to the right lane to make a right turn at the next intersection. The driver in the car next to me sees my signal and closes the gap, preventing me from entering the lane. I miss my turn as a result. This proves that he purposely kept me out.
5. ___ I love it when I pass a long line of waiting cars, then when I cut in at the front of the line. Victory! Only losers wait in line.
6. ___ A lot of drivers can see that I'm in a hurry. So what do they do? They intentionally try to slow me down or block my way. That's how they get their kicks.
7. ___ I need lots of space between me and everyone behind me. I'm a natural leader, so I feel best when I'm way out in front.
8. ___ When traffic is heavy, drivers have to compete against each other

or else one gets left behind. The better you can compete on the road, the better you can do your job, and the more useful you are to society.

9. ___ It's necessary to drive in a competitive manner because the other drivers are very competitive. I'm expected to be competitive on the road.

10. ___ As the streets are getting more crowded, drivers make each other angry. It's a competitive situation and I can't afford to worry too much about how my driving makes others angry because we all make each other angry.

SCOFFLAW

A notable feature of the culture of cynicism on the highways is the tendency we have to automatically disregard certain traffic laws, regulations, and signs. We act as if we're entitled to break regulations whenever we feel like it. Some drivers are compulsively rebellious—for them a stop sign means reduce speed slightly, yield means grab the opportunity when you can, slow means reduce speed only if cops are around, yellow means hurry up and try to make it through, do not pass is really for the weak-hearted, and, of course, 35 MPH means 55. We assume we are above the law.

> I guess there must be a special reason for that sign and I'll find out one day when I get a ticket for not stopping. I feel that this stop sign just slows me down. I don't stop, but even yielding to it takes some time, too. I get mad at the city for positioning stop signs at places where it's not necessary. Stop signs are almost as irritating as speed bumps. They're everywhere. When I see a car make a full stop at some stop signs, I laugh to myself and say, "What a fool." I do that because I have more power on the road when I don't stop. I feel that if I can get away with it, I won't ever have to stop at those useless signs. I feel daring and rebellious. I love it.

Stopping at legal signs or even touching the brakes is commonly considered "weak." The aggressive driving culture promotes cynicism about the agencies and officials who make the road regulations, from the legislators who formulate them and the judges and county officials who administer them, to the cops and troopers who enforce them and the engineers who advise them. Nowhere is this attitude more striking than on the issue of speeding tickets:

> Speed enforcement in this country is a mockery. Police work has evolved to the point where the cops and everyone else in the system prefer that you speed. It makes their job easier.[15]

ROAD RAGE AND AGGRESSIVE DRIVING

"Cops are hypocrites," writes a former trooper, "because they themselves tend to break the speed limit when driving off-duty, and because they lower or raise their tolerance level to meet their daily quota of tickets."[16] The implication is that transportation officials want the public to keep speeding so that they can issue more tickets. If the volume of speeding were to dramatically decline, an entire army of civil servants would be negatively affected, according to this argument: officers, supervisors, court clerks, accountants, judges, secretaries, stenographers, bailiffs, computer operators, and programmers. Whether or not this cynicism is well-founded, it's still wrong to speed to your heart's delight, because it affects innocent others. Every driver has a choice of orientation: Either focus exclusively on yourself and do whatever you can get away with or see yourself as part of a community and do what's intelligent and safe for everyone. The first pattern is illegal, antisocial, and profoundly negative. The second is appropriate, socially responsible, and positive.

CHECKLIST: ARE YOU A SCOFFLAW?

Check each statement that you agree with.

1. ___ There are too many traffic lights and stop signs.
2. ___ I feel that a yield sign is an iffy thing.
3. ___ Often it's too much trouble to signal a lane change.
4. ___ I avoid making full stops when my friends are with me because they wouldn't tolerate such wimpy behavior.
5. ___ I regard speeding tickets and fines as nothing but an illegitimate method for many towns to obtain extra income from hapless motorists passing through.
6. ___ I think all highways and streets would be safer without speed limits of any kind.
7. ___ I don't always wear my seatbelt. Sometimes I just don't feel like putting it on.
8. ___ It's always safer to drive over the speed limit than under, because if you drive under the speed limit, other drivers get annoyed at you and they start creating hazardous conditions as they try to pass you.
9. ___ Ideally I don't want to break the speed limit or switch lanes without signaling, but I feel forced to go the same speed as everyone else. What else can I do?
10. ___ I think it's OK to let small children sit in adults' laps if they don't want to be strapped into a child seat.

REAL-WORLD DRIVING TIPS

What can we do when another driver rages at us? People everywhere feel at risk from road rage because it can erupt at any time, beyond our control. But how unpredictable is it?

Safety experts studying road rage breakouts and violent incidents between drivers have found a common pattern. One driver is annoyed at another driver and shows it. Now comes the critical point: How does the target driver respond? This is the moment of decision when road rage can be contained. The target driver has the power either to fan the first driver's angry flames or to help put them out. Challenging an angry driver is dangerous because there's a high risk that the situation will escalate out of control. Yet it's increasingly common to see drivers overtly expressing disagreement or contempt. One driver interviewed on the *Oprah* show described how he honked at a truck driver who was partially blocking the street from a driveway. The truck driver immediately pursued him, repeatedly bumping him until the driver stopped. The truck driver then dragged him out of the car and severely beat him.

Numerous Web sites offer driving tips. Some of the ideas that are frequently mentioned give a snapshot of the nation's collective wisdom on how to handle aggressive drivers and avoid road rage.[17]

1. Avoid eye contact with an aggressive driver.
2. Don't take your eyes off the road.
3. Consider the effect of your driving on others.
4. If you are followed, either drive to the nearest police station or call police dispatch at 911 on your cell phone.
5. If you are tempted to drive angrily, ask yourself: "Is it worth being killed? Is it worth going to jail?"
6. Keep away from erratic drivers.
7. Understand that you can't control the traffic, only your reaction to it.
8. Stay cool—turn on your air conditioner.
9. Driving is transportation, not competition. Want to compete? Find a racetrack.
10. Never assume that an apparently aggressive act was intended.
11. Pretend other drivers are people you know.
12. Take it easy; why drive yourself crazy? Keep peace in the car and on the road.
13. Go with the flow, no matter how slow.
14. Do not slam on your brakes if a car is tailgating you.

ROAD RAGE AND AGGRESSIVE DRIVING

The nation's collective wisdom, expressed in these principles of driving, stands in sharp contrast to our individual actions as drivers (remember that millions are injured every year in collisions). Immersed in a deeply ingrained conflict mentality, few of us behave according to these principles, many of us regularly ignore them in our actions, and some of us defend aggressiveness, rejecting the collective wisdom on philosophical grounds. The individual rejection of what we all know to be true creates the spectrum of road rage in its frightening variety. We may feel helpless in the age of cynicism, afraid that human nature cannot change. But this is demonstrably wrong, because civilized society provides an adequate remedy. We have the means to put the advice from the collective wisdom into practice for the common good. The tools of emotional intelligence are effective in addressing the entire range of aggressive driving and road rage.

NOTES

1. Personal anecdotes quoted throughout this chapter were sent to us by e-mail correspondents.

2. UK National Workplace Bullying Advice Line, "Bullying in Schools" [online], www.successunlimited.co.uk/school.htm [May 20, 2000].

3. R. Barry Buback, "Territorial Defense in Parking Lots: Retaliation against Waiting Drivers," *Journal of Applied Social Psychology* 27, no. 9 (May 1997): 821.

4. Yahoo! Road Rage Coverage, 1999 [online], headlines.yahoo.com/Full_Coverage/US/Road_Rage [May 20, 2000].

5. Ibid.

6. Ibid.

7. Ibid.

8. Ibid.

9. Ibid.

10. Ibid.

11. Ibid.

12. Ibid.

13. James Gleick, *Faster: The Acceleration of Just About Everything* (New York: Pantheon Books, 1999).

14. James Gleick, "Attention! Multitaskers" [online], www.faster-book.com/cgi-bin/faster/fchapter.pl?22 [May 20, 2000].

15. James Eagan, *A Speeder's Guide to Avoiding Tickets* (New York: Avon Books, 1990), p. i.

16. Ibid., pp. 2–12.

17. Leon James and Diane Nahl, "Cage the Rage: Arrive Alive. DrDriving's Rage Tips from Various Web Sources," DrDriving.org [online], www.aloha.net/~dyc/tips.html [May 20, 2000].

DRIVING PSYCHOLOGY

PART 2

EMOTIONAL INTELLIGENCE FOR DRIVERS

5

INNER POWER TOOLS

Hostile expression occurs frequently in both family and workplace settings. Anger intensifies aggressiveness and judgment becomes impaired accordingly. Venting is the mental mechanism for justifying aggression and amplifying it to epic proportions, creating "proofs" and "criminal" charges against the other. The more one is convinced of these mental fabrications, the less one is capable of backing out of the coming showdown. The inevitable, angry aggression accelerates and explodes into impulsive and sometimes violent action. Depending on the aggressive action, one suffers deep regret, embarrassment, financial loss, depression, injury, or death.

The acceleration effect is clear if you place aggressive acts in order of their severity:

- denigrating thoughts about the other
- verbal abuse (including offensive gestures and harsh facial expressions)

ROAD RAGE AND AGGRESSIVE DRIVING

- grabbing
- shaking
- shoving
- slapping
- scratching and biting
- punching
- choking
- battering and stabbing
- strangling and shooting

This violence continuum shows the natural escalation of angry aggression when unchecked. Cases show that a trivial event can easily end in gruesome violence. Many aggressive driving exchanges begin with a reaction to endangerment. Threat and danger produce excitement in the body and anticipation in the mind. But this is only a momentary reaction that quickly dissipates, unless fanned by the fires of venting for condemnation or vengeance. When we get emotionally upset and physically agitated we tend to lose some ability to see alternative explanations for a situation—unless we teach ourselves greater emotional intelligence.

The best protection against the ravages of aggressiveness and rage is to inhibit venting and let the excitatory endangerment response dissipate. So we need to understand why we have difficulty in *not venting* when we experience a flare of anger in the face of endangerment. To be effective in inhibiting the venting response, your anger management techniques must involve two components: (a) relaxation techniques to reduce physical arousal, and (b) mental reappraisal of the situation. Emotional self-control consists in monitoring both these components, such as consciously breathing slowly and relaxing your grip a bit (a), and systematically observing your thinking (b). Inner power tools provide the techniques to restructure your assessment of the situation. Driving psychology provides the knowledge to manage our "driving personality" in an increasingly complex transportation environment that makes legal, economic, social, behavioral, and ethical demands on drivers. Inner power tools are techniques smart drivers learn to use to overhaul their old driving personality by retraining their emotional intelligence with exercises behind the wheel.

OVERCOMING EMOTIONAL HIJACKING

In his popular 1995 book, *Emotional Intelligence*, Daniel Goleman reviews neural and behavioral research showing that emotional explosions are literally "neural hijackings" because intense feelings are accompanied by detectable neural discharges in the brain, especially in a little organ known as the *amygdala*, which has been nicknamed "the seat of passion."[1] The driver who blows up at someone is experiencing a "neural takeover" in the limbic brain, also known as the "emotional brain." Ordinarily, information from the emotional brain is filtered through the neocortex regions of the brain that are related to rational thinking or assessing the importance and significance of the emotional information. There is ordinarily a harmonizing balance between the emotional and the rational brain functions, between what the heart feels like and how the head disposes of it.

However, neuroscientists have shown that this balance breaks down when the intensity and quality of the emotion overloads the neural circuitry and interrupts normal thinking. When drivers vent their anger, feeling self-righteous indignation for being wronged, the power of the emotion alters normal thinking and judgment. They now give different interpretations to signs and events, influencing their perceptions. Rational thinking, which is objective, balanced, and accurate, changes into emotional thinking, which is subjective, biased, and inaccurate. Thus the thinking corresponds to the feeling.

Research reviewed by Goleman has uncovered six components of emotional intelligence that can be learned with appropriate practice:

- How to reappraise a situation and look for alternative explanations
- How to self-regulate negative mood shifts
- How to empathize with "the other side"
- How to persist in a plan despite distracting frustrations
- How to control or neutralize one's aggressive impulses
- How to think with positive outcomes[2]

Anger is one of the most difficult human emotions to control. Not only is it explosive, but it gives you the sensation of being energized: heart pounding, head shaking, face scowling, hands tightly gripping the wheel, especially while venting. In the "rage rush," the rational mind becomes irrational, and is placed in the service of calculated anger, breathing vengeance and, through self-righteous indignation, justifying punishment or mayhem. The sense of outrage is especially persuasive when our safety is threatened by what seems to us like someone's inconsiderate behavior. Another common occasion is the feeling of having been insulted or symbolically attacked and demeaned.

Road rage is especially intense and hostile when both factors are present—endangerment and insult. For example, suppose you start **113**

ROAD RAGE AND AGGRESSIVE DRIVING

switching lanes when a car behind suddenly overtakes your car, forcing you to swerve back into your lane. You feel endangered, your heart begins to pound, and you make a great effort to control your impulse to yell. To top it off, as the car passes you, the driver honks and throws you an obscene gesture. You're still not recovered from the feeling of being placed in danger, you feel insulted and provoked. This is the moment of greatest challenge, as your emotional systems seem to be short-circuiting, adrenaline pumping through your blood, emergency hormones quickly spreading throughout your muscles, readying you for aggression. It's the road rage rush. How do you handle it?

Psychologists have shown that a practical way of reducing anger is by reappraisal of the situation. Despite the seductive persuasiveness of self-righteous justification, you can compel yourself to reframe the anger-pro-voking event. Emotional intelligence provides you with an understanding of how anger escalates, how venting keeps it going, and how to deflate it through rational counterarguments. Negative emotions slowly dissipate as you force yourself to think positively and expect positive outcomes. The power of positive thinking lies in its ability to attract positive emotions such as empathy and forgiveness. These interpersonal and coopera-tive emotions in turn facilitate reappraisal of the anger-provoking event.

Road rage thinking is biased and less intelligent, inflexible and selec-tive, jumping to conclusions and presuming hostility where there may not be any. It's difficult for drivers to avoid this trap given a culture in which it's common to witness displays of physical and verbal aggres-siveness at every level of society. Most drivers bring to the wheel an emo-tional vulnerability to being coerced or provoked by a stranger in a public place. Motoring in traffic is perceived as a test of wills, "I'm not going to let you walk all over me," or "You can't stop me from doing what I want," or "You shouldn't have done that to me. Now I must punish you."

Daniel Goleman argues for an expanded school curriculum that includes "emotional literacy" or "self-science," which involves self-awareness and self-management skills regarding our emotions, using the vocabulary of emotions, and knowing their distinctions:

- Understanding the causes of our feelings
- Recognizing the difference between thoughts, feelings, and acts
- Being able to tolerate frustration or provocation without becoming hostile or aggressive
- Using techniques to deflate anger when aroused
- Using positive and cooperative thinking to counteract negative and combative thinking
- Valuing supportive, community-building exchanges
- Practicing self-calming techniques

- Being more democratic about the rights of all
- Accepting the legitimacy of diversity and pluralism[3]

Goleman advocates educational programs that teach people to better manage their feelings. People need to realize that they have many more choices than either "fight" or "flight." This emphasis has long been discussed as "affective education" in public schools and playgrounds. Where these programs have been implemented, the results are impressive:

- Fewer fights and verbal put downs
- Greater emotional self-awareness
- Better frustration tolerance
- Greater skills in conflict resolution
- Better anger management[4]

Our research has led us to develop classified inventories of feelings, emotions, and intentions in various daily settings—at home or in the workplace, while shopping, studying, following a diet, and so on. In each case we found the same result: Record keeping reveals the pattern of *habitual* emotions and thoughts, and enables you to modify them. Drivers who used the inner power tools described in this book were able to "shrink" their emotional territory behind the wheel, feeling less inclined to go to battle, more aware of the awful risk involved, and more motivated to modify a suspicious defensive style that turns into an retaliatory offensive style at the slightest provocation.

Traditional driver education is brief and limited, and not designed to reverse a cultural habit ingrained from fifteen years of childhood spent witnessing and absorbing the behavior of aggressive drivers (see chapter 7). We believe that in order to prepare young people for their long careers as drivers, traffic emotions education should be part of a driving-psychology school curriculum for grades K–12. Emotional intelligence as a driver doesn't come automatically with basic driver's education in high school or with a driver's license. Driving in the fast-moving, congested age has fundamentally changed to something very complex, and the time has come to reframe driver training as a continuing or lifelong learning process rather than a single, one-time course. There's a critical need to protect the future of our children by teaching them, and modeling for them, new roles behind the wheel, supportive and peaceful rather than aggressive and hostile. Emotional literacy for drivers starts in childhood, and the best way to instill positive models is to create a K–12 curriculum for driving psychology (see chapter 9).

Drivers need access to training in self-modification techniques that help them diagnose breakdowns in their thinking and emotions, enabling **115** them to overhaul unintelligent reaction patterns. One thing we've learned in the last few years is that road rage is not an individual problem like, say, fear of heights. It's a universal problem that cannot fully be solved by external methods of law enforcement and safety engineering. Neither can defensive driving do the job, for it can harden and intensify oppositional attitudes and suspicions of motorists toward each other. Training in emotional intelligence gives drivers the tools to manage their social relations in a driving environment that routinely presents serious emotional challenges.

The three types of road rage—passive-aggressive, verbal, and epic—manifest themselves differently, but the remedy is the same. Everyone has the power to change, to improve, and feel better. Psychologists have shown that self-directed change is possible by following a systematic self-modification plan.[5] A regular practice of witnessing yourself in traffic opens a window to the deeper motives and emotional reactions that are part of driving. This new self-awareness is a tool for developing better self-control and frees motorists from the captivity of constant negative emotions and their toll on health and driving enjoyment.

Motorists discover that negative feelings and thoughts about others don't make them feel better after all. They begin to understand that the driver's emotional state has the power to influence others—motorists, passengers, cyclists, and pedestrians. Our research has produced several strategies for road rage containment, resulting in a new paradigm for life-long driver education and training:

- Practice in self-witnessing behind the wheel
- Retraining the "automatic" driving self and its faulty habits
- Learning emotional intelligence techniques for "shrinking" your emotional territory
- Acquiring facility in "acting as if" by maintaining civil conduct when you feel like aggressing
- Working with a designated driving buddy or passenger who is allowed to give feedback on your driving (Partnership Driving—see chapter 8)
- Participating in a family, neighborhood, or workplace Quality Driving Circle (QDC—see chapter 9)
- Participating in the Children Against Road Rage (CARR) exercises with your own children (see chapter 7)
- Practicing the new paradigm of Lifelong Driver Self-Improvement
- Adopting supportive driving styles and promoting new roles for the next generation

The exercises in this book will help you and your family to get started.

THREE LEVELS OF EMOTIONAL INTELLIGENCE

Table 5.1 helps to track your growth in emotional fitness as you try to identify the various elements of your driving style and philosophy. For a complete picture, keep track of your feelings, thoughts, and actions as a driver. Driving more intelligently is the result of positive feelings and right thoughts coming together in effective actions.

Table 5.1
Levels of Emotional Intelligence

Emotional Intelligence Level	State of Feelings	Sequence of Thoughts	Type of Actions
1	oppositional	irrational	selfish, reckless, impulsive, and hostile; constantly expresses criticism; feels insulted and insecure
2	defensive	logical	suspicious, wary, and competitive, but prudent and restrained; expresses worries and complaints
3	supportive	prosocial	helpful and friendly; gives others the benefit of the doubt; expresses enjoyment and optimism

Level One—Oppositional Driving

At level one we're unfit to handle road exchanges because our feelings are oppositional and negative, made worse by irrational thought patterns. The result of this deadly combination is an impulsive, reckless, and hostile driving style. Most drivers operate their vehicles at this lowest level of emotional intelligence some of the time, and many drivers are in it most of the time. In this precarious mental state, it's easy to interpret a traffic incident as a personal insult that encourages a bad mood and produces other negative consequences. Being intolerant goes along with thinking irrationally about other drivers because in any incident: *they* are always at fault while *we* excuse our own mistakes. A self-serving bias interferes with the ability to be objective and logical. Our surveys show that one in three motorists are oppositional drivers on a daily basis. Two-thirds are oppositional to a lesser degree, and rare is the driver who claims to be peaceful, tolerant, rational, and law abiding all the time, or even most of the time.[6] It's useful to discover the elements of one's oppositional thinking.

117

ROAD RAGE AND AGGRESSIVE DRIVING

Level Two—Defensive Driving

Defensive driving teaches motorists to concentrate on the safety of the vehicle, driver, and passengers. This preparedness philosophy helps reduce irrational decisions and encourages more logical thought patterns, such as, "What would happen if . . ." and "If I do this they'll respond with that. . . ." As a result, actions are more prudent than in level one. However, a level-two orientation has disadvantages because it encourages a competitive environment on the road. As defensive drivers we can still measure success competitively in terms of how fast we get there, how many cars we leave behind, or how long we can coast without having to touch the brakes. Driving defensively does not provide immunity to negative thoughts or to impatience and intolerance of the faults of other drivers. While defensive driving is more mindful than oppositional driving, it leaves us in a state of competition or suspicion.

Level Three—Supportive Driving

Level-three driving overcomes the disadvantages inherent in oppositional and defensive driving orientations. Supportive driving is a mental orientation that enables drivers to manage other motorists and the traffic using a positive approach that avoids the built-in negativity of oppositional and defensive driving styles. The key to acquiring a supportive driving mentality is to practice *prosocial thought patterns* that promote helpful actions and a benign demeanor. Oppositional driving incorporates antisocial thought patterns, while defensive driving incorporates negativity as a normal part of driving. Supportive driving styles encourage us to be prudent and safe as well as tolerant and friendly by focusing on the enjoyment of driving while remaining unfazed by its hassles. Supportive driving is a mental orientation that emphasizes the *positive* bias, opposite to the automotive vigilante mentality. Instead of finding fault with the other driver, find an excuse (for example, "Look at that airhead forgetting his blinkers on. Oh, I take it back. Maybe he's really preoccupied, or confused. We all make mistakes, including me."). The key to maintaining a supportive driving orientation is witnessing your antisocial statements and immediately neutralizing them with prosocial statements. Do this consistently and you become a supportive driver.

People who decide to become supportive drivers carefully and consistently observe their own behavior on the road, and they keep a record of the thoughts and the emotions that accompany their actions. When they figure out what motivates their actions, they are often surprised to discover that it wasn't what they assumed, so they create a plan for change. Follow this driver's reasoning process as he evolves from the oppositional level-one driving style to a level-three supportive style:

> If there was a bus on the right of me and I saw that it was trying to get in, I would speed up and try not to give it the opportunity to cut me off. I asked myself why I did such a thing. My response was that they always cut me off so that is why I react to them in that manner. They think that just by them giving you a wave they have the right to cut you off.
>
> What I did next was a new beginning for me and great progress in my driving personality makeover. I started to ask myself why I thought the bus drivers usually forced themselves into traffic. I started trying to see things from their perspective and I think I may have struck something. Maybe, I thought, bus drivers force themselves into traffic by cutting people off because motorists almost always give them a hard time about getting in.
>
> This realization blew me away. If more people were to be kind enough to allow the bus to cut in front of them in traffic—they, too, have a schedule to keep—then maybe they would not have to force themselves in as often. Then, if they didn't cut people off as much as they do, people would not be speeding up and preventing them from entering traffic. It works both ways. I just had to realize it.[7]

Being a friendly driver is contagious. When you're nice to others, they're nice to someone else and it spreads. Seeing the lighter side of incidents accentuates the positive and neutralizes the negative. Driving incidents become opportunities for minirelationships lasting seconds when friendly rituals such as making room, giving way, waiting, getting out of the way, signaling ahead, maintaining safe following distance, and courtesy waving or smiling thanks become a source of personal satisfaction, security, and community pride. Focusing on the organic nature of driving can make you a traffic lover, like Australian pianist David Helfgott:

> I love traffic. I love traffic. Traffic is very important, and it shouldn't be ignored. You have to be alert because there's a pattern in the traffic and it helps you to concentrate and relax. It's very important to enjoy the journey.[8]

This is what we've lost since aggressive driving practices have become predominant on the roads. And yet there is not merely hope for a better day but even an opportunity to use this downturn as an occasion to create a renewed sense of highway community. We have the means to turn ourselves toward the philosophy of supportive driving, but it requires both intellectual and emotional effort. It is crucial to teach ourselves how to analyze driving incidents in a rational way, following emotionally intelligent principles. The following section presents a scenario analysis of a real road rage incident between two young mothers that ended in death. This scenario analysis presents what happened along with emotionally intelligent alternatives that could have prevented this tragedy.

ANATOMY OF AN EPIC ROAD RAGE TRAGEDY

Road rage exchanges often begin as verbal road rage, with an explosion of invectives and accusations, silent or aloud, reaching a rapid peak that lasts a few seconds, then lessens with a temporary feeling of relief from the pent-up pressure of frustration or fear. What happens next depends on circumstances. In many minor-though-annoying events, hostile exchanges die down after a few moments, as soon as the hormonal symptoms of anger or fear dissipate in the blood stream, while in the mind they recede into the subconscious, asleep, but ready to awaken at the next opportunity, maybe only a minute or two later. The cycle of anger can be rekindled just by seeing the other car, or it can die down if the target driver avoids eye contact, verbal replies, and other forms of provocation. This is why safety officials always advise us to "avoid eye contact" with an outraged motorist. Avoiding contact gives you more power in determining what happens, hopefully nothing. Responding in any way weakens your control over the situation since it strengthens the other's motive to escalate the duel.

Sometimes you suddenly find yourself involved in an aggressive driving exchange without being conscious of having done anything. The provocation may reside entirely in the mind of the outraged person. It's easy to let this personal innocence lead to feelings of indignation, and from there to overt expressions of protest. Since you haven't done anything to deserve the other's hostility, you feel indignant. But consider the effect of your gesture or eye contact: Does it protect you from turning a minor incident into a dangerous feud? The answer is no, and in fact may increase the likelihood of further trouble. By avoiding making any sign of disapproval, you adhere to the driver's prime directive: retain maximum control over the situation. To some extent you can influence the other's rage, amplifying or diminishing it by how you behave.

Often the two drivers amplify and recycle their combative emotions, transforming their verbal rage into epic proportions. The more the cycle of hostility turns, the more intense it becomes until the individuals are less inclined to back down. This is because the intensity of road rage is determined by rationalizations and self-righteous justifications, and the more "rounds" the antagonists go with each other, the more reasons they

Table 5.2
Anatomy of a Road Rage Tragedy

Sequence of road rage steps	Emotional Intelligence (EI) choice points
Step 1: A 24-year-old mother of two, driving alone in a Grand Am, is following a VW driven by a pregnant woman. In front of them are several cars behind a truck going 35 MPH. The Grand Am pulls into the left lane in order to pass, and speeds up to 55 MPH.	Overtaking a line of vehicles is always risky. You must expect that other drivers in the line also want to break away, so don't speed up excessively. *EI Choice 1*: Pull into the lane and speed moderately in case someone pulls out in front of you. This requires restraining yourself and accommodating others' movements.
Step 2: The VW suddenly pulls out into the left lane, in front of the Grand Am, going 20 MPH slower and forcing the Grand Am driver to apply the brakes suddenly.	This provocative maneuver suddenly creates a dangerous incident. Trial records show that this was done deliberately to annoy the Grand Am driver for tailgating. It's an aggressive act, in direct opposition to another driver already engaged in a lane change maneuver. *EI Choice 2*: Avoid engaging in power struggles with other drivers. This means backing down from a challenge, being less competitive, and intending to facilitate rather than oppose what other drivers want to do.
Step 3: The VW gradually overtakes the slow truck, passes it, and pulls back into the right lane.	This is a proper maneuver, but doesn't by itself defuse the power struggle that is in progress. *EI Choice 3*: Be prepared to pacify hurt feelings. This takes self-regulation to remain calm in the face of potential backlash. You can predict that the other driver will likely retaliate.
Step 4: The Grand Am, still in the left lane, now overtakes the VW, honks several times, makes obscene gestures, and flashes her lights as signs of outrage—"to let her know that she almost caused an accident just then."	One of the worst things a driver can do is openly duel with another driver. This driver has used all of the behaviors considered to be acts of war on the road. *EI Choice 4*: Retain self-control by refusing to fan the flames of your righteous indignation. Resist the temptation to teach other drivers a lesson. Valuing other motorists as fellow human beings gives you the inner power to resist the impulse to retaliate.
Step 5: The VW driver responds by flipping the bird and shaking her head.	The worst thing to do in a road rage power struggle is to continue the duel. By not defusing the situation, she is irresistibly drawn into the duel. *EI Choice 5*: Use every opportunity to "come out swinging positive" by appearing to be calm, like you're no longer taking a fighting stance. This means switching to a nonconfrontational posture and rationally predicting the consequences of road rage.
Step 6: The Grand Am now tries to pull ahead in the left lane in order to reenter the right lane, but the VW accelerates, blocking the way.	The die is cast for tragedy, with both drivers locking themselves into a pathological game. *EI Choice 6*: Desist. Recognize that you are in an insane power struggle that you instantly need to back out of. This takes self-witnessing to help you realize how far gone you are in your emotional hijacking.
Step 7: The Grand Am slows down and pulls in behind the VW, keeping up the pressure by tailgating dangerously.	Having no choice, the driver is forced to back off momentarily, but hasn't calmed down. She escalates the fight. *EI Choice 7*: Use a lull in the fight to calm down and pacify the other driver by not appearing hostile. Train yourself to be able to back out of a fight by practicing "an attitude of latitude" or forgiveness.
Step 8: Now the Grand Am suddenly pulls out into the left lane again, overtaking and cutting off the VW, then gives her a "brake job," slamming on the brakes to punish her.	The driver uses her experience to wage war. She's no longer just getting even. She started out by getting upset that the VW driver almost caused an accident, but then ended up creating a major battle herself. *EI Choice 8*: Realize that the law of escalation exacts tragedy. This takes an overhaul of the aggressive driver's personality and driving philosophy.
Step 9: The VW driver applies her brakes suddenly and they lock, causing her to veer sideways to the right, where she hits a truck parked on the shoulder. She is thrown from the car and is taken to the hospital, where she recovers from surgery; her unborn child dies.	The driver started out nearly causing a crash by pulling out in front of the Grand Am. Instead of pacifying the other driver, she flipped her the bird, and ended up losing her baby. *EI Choice 9*: It's too late to do anything. It's gone too far.
Step 10: The Grand Am driver continues on to her office, where she tells her supervisor that she's been in an accident, that "the other driver had it coming," and that she "wasn't going to take #%@* from no one." Later, she is arrested and charged with vehicular homicide for causing the death of the unborn child.	Not only did the driver have no remorse, but she was proud of what she had done and bragged about it. This came back to haunt her when it was brought out in the trial in her supervisor's testimony. *EI Choice 10*: She needs a complete driving personality makeover, which could take years and will involve examining and changing her self-image, her ego relationship to cars, her values about human rights, and her anger management.

ROAD RAGE AND AGGRESSIVE DRIVING

fabricate to continue and escalate the feud. Understanding your own road rage requires the ability to analyze a road rage incident and see its natural steps of development or escalation. Each step provides drivers with a choice point: to continue the conflict or to back out of it.

To help you see these steps, we analyzed a road rage feud that involved two aggressive women drivers whose mutual provocations ended in tragedy.[9] We reconstructed this incident in ten road rage steps with accompanying emotional intelligence choice points in Table 5.2.

The 1997 trial took place in Cincinnati. The jury found the driver of the Grand Am guilty of both aggravated vehicular homicide and aggravated vehicular assault, and she was sentenced to an eighteen-month prison term.[10]

EXERCISE: NEGATIVE VERSUS POSITIVE DRIVING

Review the contrasts between antisocial and prosocial driver orientations in Table 5.3, and explain the difference in each example. Show how they differ in terms of the focus. For example, consider the first example: "They're boneheads!" versus "I'm feeling very impatient today." The latter statement is a positive orientation because it accurately focuses on me and my feeling impatient today. The negative focus is antisocial because it always wants to blame, punish, and retaliate. The positive focus is prosocial because it is rational and objective and stays away from aggressing against another. Try come up with an explanation for each of the other items: Why one is subjective, false, and injurious while the other is objective, true, and peaceful?

The transformation from negative and aggressive driving to positive and supportive driving is illustrated by the driver competence skills in Table 5.3. The oppositional driving mode is a negative mental quagmire, while the positive driving mode is emotionally intelligent because motorists exert rational self-control. The actual words in these examples may not fit your own style of thinking, but try to figure out what each example stands for and think of the words you would use in that frame of mind.

SHRINKING YOUR EMOTIONAL TERRITORY

Emotional reactions are selective. We care about some things more than others, sometimes even to the point of passion or conflict. Our emotional territory consists of all the things we value or believe strongly, and all the

Table 5.3
Positive and Negative Driver Competence Skills

Driver competence skills	Negative Driving	Positive Driving	Your driving
Focus on positive roles vs. negative roles	Emotionally challenged	Emotionally intelligent	Add your own words
1. Focus on self vs. blaming others or the situation	"This traffic is impossibly slow! What's wrong with these fools? They're driving like nutcases!"	"I'm feeling very impatient today. Everything seems to tick me off."	
2. Understanding how feelings and thoughts act together	"I'm angry, scared, outraged! How can they do this to me?"	"I feel angry, scared, and outraged when I think about what could have happened."	
3. Realizing that anger is something we choose vs. giving in to an impulse	"They make me so mad when they do that!"	"I make myself so mad when they do that."	
4. Being concerned about consequences vs. giving in to an impulse	"I just want to give this driver a piece of my mind! I just want him to know how I feel!"	"If I respond to this provocation, I lose control over the situation. It's not worth it."	
5. Showing respect for others vs. thinking only of oneself	"They'd better stay out of my way—I'm in no mood for putting up with them! Out of the way, folks!"	"I wish there was no traffic, but it's not up to me. These people have to get to their destinations too."	
6. Accepting traffic as collective team work vs. seeing it as individual competition	"Driving is about getting ahead. I get a jolt out of beating a red light or finding the fastest lane. It's me versus everyone else."	"I try to keep pace with the traffic, realizing that my movements can slow others down—like switching lanes to get ahead."	
7. Recognizing the diversity of drivers and their needs and styles vs. blaming them for what they choose to do	"How can she be so stupid? She's talking on the phone instead of paying attention to the road!"	"I need to be extra careful around drivers using handheld cellular phones, since they may be distracted."	
8. Practicing positive role models vs. negative ones	"Come on, buddy, speed up or I'll be on your tail! Go, go! What's wrong with you? There's no one ahead!"	"This driver is going slower than I'd like. Now I can practice the art of patience and respect for the next few minutes."	
9. Learning to inhibit the impulse to criticize by developing a sense of driving humor vs. giving in to impulse	"I can't stand all these bozos on the road! They slow down when they should speed up! They gawk, they crawl; anything but drive!"	"I'm angry. I'm mad. Therefore I'll act calm. I'll smile and not compete. Already I feel better. Be my guest; enter ahead."	
10. Taking driving seriously by becoming aware of mistakes and correcting them vs. being uncritical of self	"I'm an excellent driver; assertive and competent, with a clean accident record and hardly any tickets."	"I monitor myself as a driver and keep a driving log of my mistakes. I think it's important to include thoughts and feelings, not just the overt."	

things we would fight for if challenged. Some are "big" things like religion and country, others are "smaller" things like how someone pronounces a certain word or whether someone keeps his car clean. Large or small, our sensitivities and emotions are involved and we feel protective and *territorial* about them.

When we begin forming driving habits, the "automatic self" has a natural tendency to be overcritical, blaming and ridiculing other motorists. We behave as though we have to personally care about everything that's going on around us. This makes our emotional territory very large, so that it encompasses everything that we can notice about others. Any little thing can bother us because we take things personally and are intolerant of deviation and plurality. For instance, think about your reaction to a driver in front of you who inexplicably slows down to well below speed limit. You strain to see ahead, looking for some logical explanation, and finding none, you are puzzled. Soon puzzlement turns into annoyance, and finally you get angry, fanning this anger by criticizing, ridiculing and blaming the "thoughtless driver" who obviously is behaving erratically for no good reason. You might feel justified in taking charge by tailgating, honking, yelling, or gesturing. In a moment of thoughtless passion, you could become embroiled in an incident whose outcome you no longer control, because of an overextended emotional territory. When a driver slows your progress, it becomes a personal affront. You step through a series of escalating emotions: puzzlement, annoyance, anger, and desire for vengeance. These negative emotions increase the likelihood that you will defy the driver's prime directive.

Yet it's still possible to back pedal, to regain self-control, to steer the interaction in a new direction before it slides deeper into the road rage danger zone. Use inner power tools; for instance, giving yourself a territorial pep talk, reminding yourself what's really going on. Use "self-prompts" to help focus on and further examine emotions of displeasure and annoyance. For example, prompt yourself with a question, "Why am I so annoyed by this?" or "Exactly what is it that I object to?" or "What's most important here?" Self-questioning reduces the intensity of the emotion and provides an opportunity to redraw the boundaries of your emotional territory. What is it that you really care about? What would be worth a fight or an unpleasant exchange that haunts the mind for minutes, hours, or days? This kind of self-talk helps shrink your emotional territory.

Often you can trace the intensity of your emotion to pet peeves and irrational driving rules that lurk unexamined in the background, influencing your emotions. Take this reaction for example, "There is no excuse for this behavior. But the driver is a dolt, so what can you expect?" This

124   reasoning is actually a psychological mechanism for enlarging emotional territory. By making another driver's action your personal business, you set yourself up to become enraged, to punish and retaliate. You still have the choice of reframing emotional territory by redefining your role in the situation:

> Is it really up to me to enforce the laws of logic on other drivers? Wouldn't it be easier and safer to concentrate on how to avoid them or compensate for their mistakes? Beyond that, am I really justified in retaliating? I might just as well be more philosophical in accepting a less-than-perfect road environment. The main thing is to get somewhere without mishaps.

Focusing on the driver's prime directive shrinks territorial defense lines. Say that after giving yourself a territorial pep talk, another car ahead slows down inexplicably. You're puzzled for a moment, then take action to pass the car. You were able to shrink your emotional territory by taking an objective attitude: "Well, whatever it is that this driver is doing doesn't matter. I'll just pass." You didn't lose your cool because you were prepared with a rational priority and a simple technique. The situation is similar, though more challenging, when you cannot pass due to road conditions. You can find the best thing to say to yourself to promote emotional intelligence habits that increase self-control and enjoyment.

The choice of shrinking or enlarging emotional territory can arise at any moment. Appointing ourselves highway watchdogs or driving critics automatically extends our emotional territory. In this mental state we drive with the proverbial chip on the shoulder. The eyes and thoughts are automatically pressed into servicing these unwritten rules: a mistake or infraction must not go unnoticed, a blunder deserves ridicule, a reckless act ought to be punished, other drivers' bad behavior must not be rewarded by condoning (ignoring) it nor by acquiescing (giving in) to it. These obsessive tasks occupy the mind and rev up emotional levels of stress, resistance, and conflict. We are unhappy, dissatisfied, combative, flirting with disaster, never knowing when we'll come up against a road warrior who will pursue, scare, or injure us. We have lost control over the situation and every driving trip becomes a dangerous event.

Fortunately, the same mechanism that automatically enlarges emotional territory can be used to reduce and shrink it. All that's needed is a role switch from despotic judge to tolerant professional. Abdicating the role of critic or competitor limits the conditions for emotional involvement. Putting limits on what you care enough about to get upset over, works to retain control over the situation. For instance, suppose you notice that a car behind switches to the left lane and passes briskly. In the role of a competitor you would take it personally ("He's mad 'cause I'm driving too slow for him."). In a professional role you can dismiss the earlier thought by following it up with: "Actually, who knows what he's thinking or doing. It's probably not about me and it really doesn't matter to me. Happy motoring!" In one case, emotional territory is large, the other driver easily steps on it, and you're not happy. In the second case, you compact your territory so your self-esteem cannot be threatened by the actions of a stranger. You retain power over your destiny and keep negative emotions from spoiling driving enjoyment. To achieve this you need to keep a close watch on your emotional life behind the wheel and learn some useful techniques.

> I finally realized that the only thing I have control over on the road is my own behavior and feelings. I don't want to be responsible for creating trouble that leads to hard feelings, accidents, or violence. I have too much respect for human life to continue to drive aggressively. I've gained perspective and I'm committed to doing my part to make the roads safer and kinder. It won't take extra time because I'm already driving around. It won't cost money because I'm already paying for gas and maintenance. All it takes is my commitment to practice being a benign driver.

Reframing negative thoughts behind the wheel is an effective coping mechanism for the inherent frustrations and dangers we experience in congested driving surrounded by aggressive drivers. To do this we need to achieve a dual perception of ourselves. Part of us needs to observe the part that vents, rants, and raves. We call this *self-witnessing* because the rational self mentally stands aside, as it were, and observes the emotional self. In this "metanoid" perspective behind the wheel, the preoccupation with other drivers' faults ceases. Attention is refocused and this shift changes how you react. You can foresee consequences, reject the rage route, and restore order in your domain. Self-witnessing is the act of verbalizing thoughts and feelings aloud during driving, providing you with objective data on your "mental scripts" or habits of thinking. This awareness protects you from biased perceptions, as this driver realized about his tailgating habit:

> I later came to realize how it feels to be on the other end, when I am the tailgater. I have to have more empathy for others because I am just like them. It is just difficult to see two sides of the story when you are so biased. Whenever I am tailgated, I get so upset because I can't understand why people tailgate others. I think that it's so rude and it may only save you a few seconds on the road. It never dawns on me at that moment that I, too, tailgate others, until it is too late. What I must do is understand that I am exactly like the other tailgater who frustrates me

so much. The way I'm behaving is hypocritical and to realize that is to admit that I am wrong. It was amazing to me how frustrated I got when I was tailgated, and yet I still tailgated others.

Imagine driving in the left lane next to a pack of cars in the right. You see an opening and go for it, but the driver closes the gap when you try to squeeze in. Your reaction to this event depends on the meaning you attribute to the driver's behavior and the emotional significance you attach to it. If your orientation or mental state is objective and prosocial, you can professionally dismiss the event as an unimportant detail in a long series:

Who knows why this driver closed the gap on me? Maybe the driver felt loyal to the pack or didn't want to annoy the driver behind. Or perhaps it was an automatic reaction, something he did without thinking. Or whatever; it's unknowable and unimportant.

This person's reasoning reflects an objective feeling orientation that shrinks emotional territory by reducing oversensitivity and undue negativity. It removes us from the critic's role with its vast emotional territory: "What a nincompoop! Won't let me in. Hope someone does it to him." This reaction reflects a subjective feeling orientation that sets the stage for hostile and aggressive actions, like going to battle over the slightest issue: mentally criticizing drivers, verbally protesting, physically rubbernecking and seeking eye contact, and performing other acts of threat and displeasure. This type of activity enlarges emotional territory, setting up a negative role for the next unexpected occasion, endangering self and passengers, giving up control of the driving situation, spoiling the fun, and raising the stakes and the risks for everyone.

EXERCISE: ACTING AS IF

An effective exercise in shrinking emotional territory is to act like something doesn't matter to you, even if you feel upset. For instance, say something positive out loud even though you feel upset, or smile and look pleasant even though you feel the opposite. This exercise accomplishes three important results. First, you become vividly aware of your own impulsiveness. As the calm external mouth says something objective or positive, the agitated inner mind feels the opposite. Observing this conflict between the outer supportive act and the inner oppositional act creates a new awareness as a driver. Witnessing the contrast between these two dispositions gives us a choice to continue or to reverse. Second, the exercise creates an opportunity for discovering that driving in a supportive manner allows you to get there on time. You discover that obsessing about the time or about how someone drives just isn't necessary because it doesn't improve the situation. Third, you experience what it feels like to have friendlier exchanges with other motorists, perhaps discovering that you like and value this more positive relationship. Kinder, more humane traffic exchanges are rewarding, making it beneficial to adopt gentler ways on a permanent basis. It's the smarter choice.

To try this exercise, take a moment upon entering your vehicle to designate that trip as "special." The object is to pretend to be cool whenever you feel crazed by the traffic or some maddening incident. Commit yourself to performing this exercise for the duration of one entire trip. Study the two columns in Table 5.4 until they're familiar and you can translate each entry into something suitable to your experience.

Table 5.4
Inner Power Tool: Acting As If

Oppositional driving style	Supportive driving style
When you say or think this:	*Say or think this immediately after:*
"Nope, you can't come in here. We're all in a hurry, not just you. You'll just have to wait your turn."	"We're all in a hurry, but there's room for one more. Go ahead, be my guest. Sorry I can't let the whole line in."
"Look at that fool! Forgets to turn off the signal for miles! Where is his head, anyway?"	"Ooops! There's a boo-boo. You have to stay alert when you drive. Hope it won't cause an accident."
"Oh, great! Just what I wanted to do, sit in traffic and crawl inch-by-inch. Come on, airhead! The light is green! Move, go, go!"	"Slow today. Well, I can fidget or I can relax. Either way I'll get there the same time. Might as well cruise. How about some relaxing music?"
"Hurry up, idiot! Stop holding up traffic like that! I'm going to honk at him."	"I feel like honking, but it's not worth the trouble. Besides, honking might slow him down even more or startle him and cause a crash."
"I'm going to make that light. Come on, come on, get out of my way! Turning yellow . . . I can still make it if I step on it."	"All right, I'm not going to make this one. Slowing down gently. I can relax for a few moments."
"No way are you taking that parking place! What, are you serious? I've been waiting here! It's mine! Hey, bonehead, stop that! Stop! Hey!"	"Now that's not fair. I've been waiting here. Oh, well, it's not worth a fight. Don't be rude to the rude. Besides, it's possible she didn't see me. I'll get one soon. There's always someone leaving."

One driver who tried this exercise wrote:

> When I came up behind a slow-moving vehicle, I would say to myself out loud, "You are obviously not in a rush. That's OK, I'll simply get around you." I had to say that to keep my head from filling up with "Get the !@#* out of my way!" I used the "as if" approach, namely, forcing myself to act tolerant and accepting even though I felt like doing the opposite. By acting and talking in a tolerant way, I was hoping to end up feeling tolerant and accepting. I know this is what I'd like to truly feel rather than hostile and angry.

In some situations this worked fine, but as soon as he became anxious about the traffic, his patience and understanding of others literally went out the window. "If I hit heavy traffic or was running late, the whole world turned into fools who couldn't drive and shouldn't." Nevertheless, he persisted in his attempts and succeeded in regaining composure.

EXERCISE: SCENARIO ANALYSIS
TO MODIFY OPPOSITIONAL THINKING

In Table 5.5, read down the symptoms column and explain what is wrong in each statement. For example, in "being overcritical," a person might say or think, "Look at that idiot who forgot to turn off his signal." This statement has two parts: (1) He forgot to turn off the signal, and (2) he is an idiot because of that. The first portion is objective and true, but the second portion is subjective and not a true statement about the other driver. The statement that "he is an idiot" is not an explanation but a put-down. Its purpose is to insult or punish in retaliation. Go over each statement and try to isolate the objective part and the subjective part. Try to think of new items for each symptom.

For further clarification, consider the statements in symptom area 2, "righteous indignation." Why does a person say, "Nobody gives me the finger and gets away with it"? Because the individual feels insulted and wants to retaliate. The justification for the planned punishment is that you need to protect your self-worth which was attacked when the other driver insulted you. This is symbolic, unrealistic, and subjective thinking. Ignoring the insult doesn't mean the other is getting away with it. It only means that you choose not to respond in kind. This choice is more intelligent because it allows you to retain control over the situation. Once you respond to an insult in kind, you have given up control since you do not know how the other will respond to your insult.

When you have identified the hidden wrong assumptions in these

ROAD RAGE AND AGGRESSIVE DRIVING

Table 5.5
Driving with Emotional Intelligence:
Transforming Oppositional Symptoms into Intelligent Remedies

Oppositional symptoms	Statements used in traffic	Emotionally intelligent remedies
Obsessing about slow traffic	• "At this rate, we'll never get there!" • I feel like I'm going backward!" • "Now I'm stuck behind this slow driver." • "What a royal waste of time—I can't stand this waiting!"	• Leave earlier. • Give up getting there on time. • Distract yourself with calming talk radio or music. • Admire the scenery. • Practice deep breathing.
Feeling combative with self-righteous indignation	• "This fiend just cut me off! Gotta give him a piece of my mind!" • "I don't deserve to be pushed around!" • "Nobody gives me the finger and gets away with it!" • "Nobody messes with me and gets away with it!"	• Make funny animal sounds to yourself. • Make up some possible excuses for the driver's behavior. • Think about your parents and children, who might do the same thing. • Think about being an angel.
Feeling excessively competitive	• "Darn! That guy made the light and I didn't!" • "How come that lane is faster than this one?" • "Those pedestrians better watch out, 'cause I'm coming through!"	• Tell yourself it's just a habit from childhood to feel anxious about not winning, or being left behind. • Remind yourself it feels good to be civil and helpful.
Being overcritical	• "Look at that idiot who forgot to turn off his signal!" • "I can't stand the way he slows down and speeds up, slows down and speeds up!" • "He can't pay attention to the road if he's babbling on the phone."	• Tell yourself it's human to make mistakes. • Recall your own mistakes. • Remind yourself that patience is a virtue. • Try to maneuver away from the car.
Love of risk taking	• "I like to go fast, but I'm careful." • "I can make this light if I speed up." • "I can squeeze into that opening if I time it right." • "I can insult that driver 'cause I can drive away fast!" • "I feel the need for speed!"	• Think of how you would feel if you did something that hurt someone. • Think of how your loved ones would feel if something happened to you. • Tell yourself you prefer to be a mature and prudent person.

oppositional traffic statements, focus on the last column. Consider each remedy and explain where its positive benefit lies. For example, in "obsessing about slow traffic," if your anxiety is caused by the fear of being late, leaving earlier is a remedy. Similarly, when you tend to rush out of habit rather than necessity, distracting yourself with relaxing music or the scenery works. See how many new items you can add for each remedy.

EXERCISE: IDENTIFYING WRONG ASSUMPTIONS

As additional practice in debunking oppositional thinking, consider the following letter we received.

> Hello, I was arrested for DUI because I was sitting in a parked car in a parking lot when a public safety officer came up behind me and started blowing the horn at me. I was not in an actual parking space but pulled off to the side where I was not blocking traffic. People had been passing me for half an hour when this guy pulled directly behind me and started blowing the horn.
>
> I was not driving nor was I planning on it but was sitting in the driver's seat listening to a game with a friend. After I blew the horn back, he blew again. I then got out and asked him why the @#$* he was blowing the horn at me. He told me to move my car into a parking space. I got irate that he blew the horn to tell me, when he could have pulled beside me to ask me.
>
> After he told me to move the car, I did. He then realized I was drunk and I had him really mad by now asking him why he was blowing the horn instead of going around if I was not blocking traffic. He then called in five other public safety officers, who weren't even there when it happened. All they knew was that I was drunk. They tested me, handcuffed me, and took me to jail. I did lose my temper but I feel I was provoked. It has cost me $2000 and a company vehicle. I go to court next month. What do you think?

Now reread each paragraph and identify the wrong assumptions this young man makes. When you're finished, check to see if you noted these points.

In *paragraph one*, he ignores the crucial distinction a safety officer must make between someone parked in a designated parking space and someone who is not. He fails to empathize with the officer's duty and perspective, and considers only his own perspective. In *paragraph two*, he fails to note the significance of his "blowing the horn back" as a gesture of noncompliance. He then compounds the oppositional behavior by leaving his car and confronting the officer in a belligerent manner. His focus is egocentric ("he blew the horn to tell me, when he could have pulled beside me to ask me") and ignores the officer's official role and legitimate behavior. He focuses on style and symbolism, not substance and function. In *paragraph three*, he has not backed down and continues to escalate, failing to focus on his legal state of intoxication. Clearly, even as he wrote the letter he failed to come to terms with his oppositional thinking, its symptoms, and its consequences.

NOTES

1. Daniel Goleman, *Emotional Intelligence* (New York: Bantam Books, 1995), pp. 13–29.

2. Ibid., pp. 235–36.

3. Ibid., pp. 261–87.

4. Ibid.

5. David L. Watson and Roland G. Tharp, *Self-Directed Behavior: Self-Modification for Personal Adjustment* (Monterey, Calif.: Brooks/Cole, 1985).

6. Leon James and Diane Nahl, "Driver Personality Survey," DrDriving.org [online], www.aloha.net/~dyc/surveys/survey3/personality.html [May 20, 2000].

7. Personal anecdotes quoted throughout this chapter were sent to us by e-mail correspondents.

8. *Dateline*, NBC, March 21, 1997.

9. Leon James and Diane Nahl, "Aggressive Driving and Road Rage: Dealing with Emotionally Impaired Drivers," DrDriving.org [online], www.aloha.net/~dyc/testimony.html [May 20, 2000].

10. *Ohio* v. *Alfieri* [online], www.courttv.com/casefiles/verdicts/alfieri.html [May 20, 2000].

THREE-STEP DRIVER SELF-IMPROVEMENT PROGRAM

6

OBJECTIVE SELF-ASSESSMENT FOR DRIVERS

Road rage and aggressive driving exist on a single behavior continuum. Aggressive driving is not solely how someone operates a vehicle; it is also a mental state, a readiness to interpret the acts of others in a hostile way and a desire to respond in kind. In the mental state of aggressive driving we impulsively take more risks and stay on the verge of angry exchanges throughout the trip. At the extreme end of the aggressive driving spectrum assault and battery occur. Many are surprised to learn that the majority of drivers experience intense emotions in traffic that put them at risk of expressing road rage. Research with hundreds of drivers led us to formulate a three-step program to help drivers develop better emotional fitness on the road. The first step is to *acknowledge* that every driver, including you, needs traffic emotions education. The second step is to act as a *witness* to your actual behavior while driving, systematically observing your thoughts, feelings, and actions to identify the type and degree of aggressive driving and road rage you practice. The third step is to *modify* the behaviors you want to change, one thing at a time, continuing this process throughout your career as a driver. The three-step program must be continuously recycled. There are thousands of habits and skills to manage as a driver, including constantly developing new ones. Each habit or skill must be separately acknowledged, witnessed, and modified or improved.

The goal of self-assessment is to identify problematic tendencies and habits that either produce emotional rage in the self or provoke it in others. The symptoms of road rage may be obvious to everyone except to the road rager. Part of the problem of road rage is that though most feel it, few admit it. The basis for an objective self-assessment is the ability to see yourself as others see you. For instance, listen to yourself when you tell driving stories. Which party is always blamed for an incident—you or the other motorist? Who is denigrated? There's a strong tendency to adopt a self-serving bias when we represent ourselves as victimized drivers, so it's always the other motorist who started it or is at fault. But what about our own contribution? A self-serving bias clouds our understanding of why we get angry, so it can appear to aggressors that they are the victims, while true victims are seen as victimizers. This inverted view reflects a lack of objectivity and makes for dramatic stories of retaliation.

The following exercise engages drivers in comparing their own estimation of their driving skills with the perspectives of their passengers.

EXERCISE: ASSESSING MYSELF AS A DRIVER

Step 1: Think about your driving over the past few weeks. Make a list of your best traits and another list of your worst traits as a driver. Use an additional sheet of paper, if necessary.

My Best Driving Traits According to Myself	My Worst Driving Traits According to Myself
1.	1.
2.	2.
3.	3.
4.	4.
5.	5.
6.	6.

Three-Step Driver Self-Improvement Program

Step 2: Talk to people who have driven with you recently. Ask them to tell you what they consider to be your best and worst qualities as a driver. Record the passengers' comments exactly as they were intended, without reinterpreting, sugarcoating, exaggerating, or judging. It's useful to repeat this step with several passengers to get a variety of perspectives on your driving personality.

My Best Driving Traits According to My Passenger	My Worst Driving Traits According to My Passenger
1.	1.
2.	2.
3.	3.
4.	4.
5.	5.
6.	6.

Step 3: Compare your lists of best and worst driving behaviors with those of your passenger(s). How do your perceptions differ from those of your passenger(s)?

A—ACKNOWLEDGE

Developing emotional intelligence as a driver begins by acknowledging that you need a better understanding of the road rage syndrome. We're born into a car culture where rushing, traffic congestion, noise, fumes, and irate drivers are the norm. Though our society loves cars, we don't necessarily love the motorists who drive them. This older man's acknowledgment statement reveals the common threads of discord among drivers:

I acknowledge that:

(1) I'm not in full control of my emotions all of the time. This is dangerous.
(2) I harbor resentment against some drivers who tick me off. This is not how I want to be.
(3) I become hostile when a passenger tells me what to do. This is unfriendly.
(4) I don't mind threatening pedestrians with my vehicle if they're too slow to move. This is illegal and uncivilized.

(5) I often fantasize I have a gun and I am spraying bullets. This is inhuman.
(6) I often have violent impulses, like running a car off the road. This is horrific.[1]

The act of acknowledging is the most difficult step in changing undesirable habits. But you cannot change a single habit without first acknowledging that what you're doing is not healthy and that you need to quit. Driving consists of thousands of little habits that are candidates for change:

- Habits of feeling a certain way when something happens—our traffic emotions and attitudes
- Habits of thinking a certain way about a certain event or person—our emotional intelligence as a driver
- Habits of operating the vehicle—our automatic habits of alertness and vehicle manipulation.

These driving habits were acquired subconsciously and are maintained without awareness. It's typical to deny it when a terrified passenger complains that you're taking great risks or that you made a mistake. Most people rate themselves as an 8, 9, or 10 on a ten-point driving excellence scale even though in the same survey, 75 percent confess to aggressive driving such as regularly swearing at others, habitual speeding, or changing lanes without signaling.[2] Since these behaviors do not contribute to driving excellence, this is evidence of denial on a mass scale! In addition, it is difficult to change ingrained driving habits established and practiced since childhood. Nevertheless, change is feasible and self-help programs often begin with this step: *I acknowledge that I've got a problem I need to fix.*

It's absolutely essential that formal acknowledgment be made in each of the three areas of the driver's habits: emotions, thoughts, and overt actions. If you merely focus on overt behavior (for example, speeding, not signaling, tailgating), you may be puzzled as to why it's so hard to follow through on good resolutions. No matter how hard you try, you end up speeding, switching lanes without signaling, circumventing road work barriers, or chasing someone down. Why are you speeding, yelling, or not signaling? We need to face the possibilities: Perhaps I'm impatient. Perhaps I'm driving selfishly, not caring. Perhaps I'm being cynical, assuming everybody is just out to get ahead. Perhaps I'm a vigilante at heart and enjoy punishing wrongdoers. The point is that uncovering and acknowledging our driver character traits provide the information necessary to begin to implement successful self-directed changes.

Finally, acknowledging cannot be accomplished by a general resolution such as "I promise to improve," or "I should be more careful," or

"I'm going to be less aggressive." You need to be as specific as possible about which particular attitudes, intentions, feelings, beliefs, words, or acts of the eyes, face, hands, feet, or mouth that you need to modify. For example, *I will avoid looking directly at another driver when I think the person is doing wrong.* Systematic self-witnessing is required to achieve the necessary level of specificity about one's behaviors.

W—WITNESS

Witnessing or self-witnessing follows acknowledging. Self-observation or self-monitoring are equivalent terms for this step. Some overt acts of motorists are visible and measurable by third parties or instruments, for example:

- Vehicle speed
- Following distance
- Blood alcohol (BAC) level
- Running through red
- Crossing a double line
- Failure to yield
- Circumventing road work barriers
- Insulting or threatening gestures
- Yelling

Some of the small movements we perform while driving are not easily visible to others but can be measured with sensing equipment, for example:

- Amount of pressure applied to the brake pedal
- How hard we grip the steering wheel
- How we contract the abdomen under stress
- Rate of shallow breathing
- Moving the head due to pain
- Slight variations in how we maneuver around corners
- Slight variations in how fast we approach traffic signals or pedestrian crossings
- Mutterings about traffic and drivers
- Bobbing of the head of a sleepy driver about to fall asleep at the wheel

But no measuring instrument can detect what's going on in our thoughts and feelings, yet they determine our overt actions. This crucial information is available only through self-witnessing.

ROAD RAGE AND AGGRESSIVE DRIVING

Self-witnessing is the act of *verbalizing* thoughts and feelings *during* an activity in order to create a play-by-play description of *what's going on*. In other words, part of the self acts as a witness and thinks aloud what the other part is doing, thinking, and feeling. This makes it possible to capture material from thinking and feeling operations and put it into long-term memory so that one can reflect on it later. The ability to observe and verbalize our thoughts sets us apart from animals. Our awareness can be split into the doer and the watcher, the thinker and the observer, or the actor and the audience. Charles Cooley named this ability the "looking glass self," without which we lack the ability to change ourselves or manage our growth.[3]

We encourage drivers to use a voice-activated tape recorder while driving, to speak their thoughts aloud to capture their natural stream of consciousness. The play-by-play must be done from the perspective of a "driving witness" whose job is to bring out the events that are relevant to driving. The witness uses the language of description that's appropriate to particular driving events to gain self-knowledge:

- What is my mood or emotional state?
- Where am I looking?
- What am I noticing?
- How do I react to that?
- What kinds of things do I fantasize?
- What do I think or say to myself?
- What do I intend to do now?

It's not necessary to tape record yourself because merely pretending there is a recorder works as well. Objective driver awareness increases by the mere act of verbalizing the thoughts and emotions behind the wheel, since it allows you to "listen in," to be mentally online, as it were. When we began our research about three decades ago, this kind of private or inner information was not available in the professional literature on driving behavior. "Retrospective reports" or questionnaires from debriefing sessions after trips were available, but recollections of events are often inaccurate and distorted. Our self-witnessing research was the first to produce information on the thoughts and emotions of drivers behind the wheel.[4]

Self-witnessing reveals your driving personality, the "automatic self" who actually does most of the driving through the cluster of habits you have acquired over the years. One of the first things to notice is that the eyes, hands, and legs seem to operate on their own. This is ordinarily good because there isn't enough time to think things through during many routine tasks in driving. In a pack of cars traveling at 55 MPH or more, with a distance of one car length between them, you have a mere fraction of a second to apply the brakes when the car ahead of you does. Your leg automatically does the work in the split second that your eyes detect the red brake lights ahead. The automatic driving self accomplishes a lot, but you still have to remain alert. Your eyes can't safely wander off to fool with a cellular phone or the tape deck. Safe driving is a combination of automatic reflexes and alert monitoring of events.

Self-monitoring of these microactions during driving is a proven method for identifying errors in automatic habits and skills. Equally important is witnessing our thinking and feeling behind the wheel. For most drivers, mental acts of road rage occur routinely, though drivers may be unaware of the frequency and intensity before they systematically observe themselves in traffic. To accomplish this, it's necessary to assume the role of an observer and to act as a witness to yourself as a driver to find out how often you entertain critical, judgmental, or derogatory thoughts about other drivers, passengers, cyclists, or pedestrians. Use a convenient way to keep track, such as:

- Thinking out loud into a tape recorder or video camera while you drive
- Putting a coin or bead in a cup for each instance, or using a counter device
- Having a passenger count for you
- Dictating notes to a passenger
- Making notes in your driving diary or log after arriving at the destination

After keeping track for a few trips, listen to the recordings or review your notes and add up all the instances of negative feelings, thoughts, and actions. This is your "baseline list," or benchmark. As you continue to witness yourself behind the wheel in future trips, compare the changes over time. Sometimes merely becoming more aware of a specific behavior allows you to modify it at will. But often this fails, so you may need more powerful methods.

Because emotions and intentions precede overt driving acts and constrain them, it's important to focus on your "inner driver" or the subconscious mind, to become aware of these precipitating thoughts and feelings.

Examples of negative events to witness:

- Feeling claustrophobic in traffic
- Feeling insecurity behind the wheel

ROAD RAGE AND AGGRESSIVE DRIVING

- Often feeling rushed and time pressured, unable to drive calmly
- Taking excessive risks
- Criticizing, insulting, name calling, denigrating, or ridiculing others
- Complaining, feeling indignant, and disapproving of others
- Feeling happy about another's mishap or trouble
- Hating the road and feeling alienated from other drivers
- Stressing over police
- Fantasizing acts of violence or vengeance
- Shouting, gesturing, or shaking the head
- Provoking, threatening, retaliating, or punishing
- Using the vehicle to pressure, threaten, or attack

Examples of positive events to witness:

- Enjoying the idea and the feeling of showing kindness to another driver
- Being ready to return a favor or kindness
- Feeling good when someone waves thank you, feeling connected to the human family
- Feeling satisfied with precision driving (for example, being careful not to roll over the double line while making a turn)
- Enjoying facilitating the progress of all, not just your own
- Enjoying the drive, despite the congestion
- Driving connected, feeling part of the traffic flow and the highway community
- Feeling appreciative when spotting a patrol car and viewing it as protection
- Thinking compassionate or forgiving thoughts about another driver's mistakes or flaws
- Feeling responsible for everyone's safety

CHECKLIST: WITNESSING YOUR AGGRESSIVE DRIVING

Objective self-assessment is a skill that can be acquired with practice. The three behavior zones to observe are emotions, thoughts, and actions. This checklist of examples helps you focus on specific elements of your driving style, but in order to be objective you must observe yourself actually performing the actions, thinking the thoughts, and feeling the emotions. The purpose of the checklist is to alert you to the areas of the driving personality to be witnessed. The items represent common aggressive behaviors from the self-witnessing reports of many drivers. Since they are cultural norms, it's likely that we all have them to some extent.

Remember, it's one thing to check items but it's critical to actually observe them as they happen in driving. Experience proves that we can't wish these habits away with resolutions or declarations. It's necessary to begin by consciously observing them *as they're happening.* As a practical strategy, select one or two items to observe on each trip. Don't try to take on too many at once because you will be defeated. Use the checklist to mark when you've observed each item. It helps to keep notes on the circumstances during which the emotion, thought, or act occurred.

Witnessing Your Emotions:

1. ____ Getting angry when forced to brake by another motorist
2. ____ Feeling insulted and furious when a driver revs the engine in passing
3. ____ Feeling hostile when your progress is impeded by congestion
4. ____ Being suspicious when a driver doesn't let you change lanes
5. ____ Feeling justified in retaliating when another driver insults you
6. ____ Enjoying thoughts of revenge and torture
7. ____ Enjoying the role of being mean behind the wheel
8. ____ Feeling satisfaction when expressing hostility against other drivers
9. ____ Fantasizing racing other road warriors
10. ____ Enjoying stereotyping and ridiculing certain drivers
11. ____ Constantly feeling like rushing, even when you're not late
12. ____ Striving to get ahead of every car
13. ____ Being pleased when getting away with breaking traffic laws
14. ____ Enjoying the feeling of risk or danger when moving fast
15. ____ Other: _____
16. ____ Other: _____

Witnessing Your Thoughts:

1. ____ Justifying rejection of the law that every lane change must be signaled
2. ____ Thinking that it's up to you to choose which stop signs should be obeyed
3. ____ Thinking that there is no need for speed limits
4. ____ Being ignorant of safety rules and principles (e.g., who has the right of way)
5. ____ Thinking that it's not necessary to figure out the route before leaving, when it is

6. ____ Not leaving early enough; thinking you can make up time by driving faster
7. ____ Thinking that some drivers are fools, airheads, rejects, and so on
8. ____ Thinking that other drivers are out to get you
9. ____ Believing that passengers have fewer rights than drivers
10. ____ Thinking you can handle drinking and driving due to your special ability to hold your liquor
11. ____ Thinking that you can use in-car communication systems safely without having to train yourself
12. ____ Believing that pedestrians shouldn't have the right of way when jaywalking
13. ____ Believing it's OK not to a wear seat belt since you probably won't need it
14. ____ Thinking it's best to get ahead of others even if you cause them to slow down
15. ____ Other: _____
16. ____ Other: _____

Witnessing Your Actions:

1. ____ Not signaling when required by law
2. ____ Lane hopping to get ahead rather than going with the flow
3. ____ Following too close for the speed
4. ____ Gap closing to prevent someone from entering your lane
5. ____ Turning right from the middle or left lane
6. ____ Blocking the passing lane, not moving over as soon as possible
7. ____ Speeding faster than the flow of traffic
8. ____ Shining high beams to annoy a driver
9. ____ Honking to protest something when it's not an emergency
10. ____ Gesturing insultingly at another driver
11. ____ Speeding up suddenly to make it through a yellow light
12. ____ Making rolling stops when a full stop is required
13. ____ Threatening pedestrians by approaching them quickly
14. ____ Illegally parking in a marked handicap space
15. ____ Parking or double-parking where it's illegal
16. ____ Playing the radio loudly enough to be heard by other drivers
17. ____ Taking a parking space unfairly or opportunistically
18. ____ Driving under the influence of alcohol or medication
19. ____ Bad mouthing other drivers when kids are in the vehicle
20. ____ Ignoring the comfort of passengers or verbally assaulting them when they complain about your driving

21. ____ Failing to yield

22. _____ Other: _____
23. _____ Other: _____

M—MODIFY

There are some things that don't change simply because you want them to. Modifying your driving personality can be an overwhelming task unless it is broken into small steps, working on one target behavior at a time. Permanently changing lifelong driving habits requires systematically mapping your emotions, thoughts, and deeds behind the wheel. Drivers are more successful in their self-retraining efforts when they focus on one specific habit at a time, for example:

- Leaving home fifteen minutes earlier than usual (actions)
- Increasing the following distance (actions)
- Signaling sooner before changing lanes (actions)
- Driving less frequently in the passing lanes (actions)
- Reducing cruising speed by 5 to 10 MPH (actions)
- Contradicting yourself each time you think that some drivers are fools, airheads, and so on. (thoughts)
- Reinforcing the idea that your passengers have their rights (thoughts)
- Repeating to yourself that pedestrians always have the right of way, even when jaywalking (thoughts)
- Contradicting your belief that it's OK not to wear a seat belt because you probably won't need it (thoughts)
- Avoiding getting angry when forced to brake by another motorist (emotions)
- Avoiding feeling hostile when your progress is impeded by congestion (emotions)
- Avoiding retaliation when another driver insults you (emotions)
- Not letting yourself enjoy thoughts of revenge and torture (emotions)

One young male driver drew up a plan to modify five specific target behaviors, one per trip, then recycled this strategy for as many weeks as necessary to automate the new behaviors:

- Mostly stay in the right lane rather than the left. (action)
- Leave a minimum of four car lengths when traveling in a fast-moving pack, rather than the usual two. (action)

- When you see pedestrians, repeat to yourself they always have the right of way. (thoughts)
- Avoid looking at a driver who is mad or indignant, reminding yourself it's best to stay out of fights. (action and thoughts)
- Not letting myself slide into a bad mood when traffic gets congested. (emotions)

The practice of witnessing your actions, thoughts, and feelings while driving creates objective self-knowledge. You become a spectator to your own driving personality traits, seeing yourself as an impartial observer might see you. This is objectivity. The driver above wrote at the start of his self-modification project:

> I find it hard to judge my driving because I feel I'm a good driver. For the sake of objectivity, I'm going to break the problem down into several categories such as alertness, speed, safety, driving record, decisiveness, and interaction style. After looking at all these areas, I'll be able to make a prognosis about what I need to do to make my driving better.

Objective self-assessment demands a detailed inventory of real life in real traffic, the kind of person you actually are—your emotions, judgments, and actions—observed over time under a variety of road conditions. You can't rely on your accident record, on your memory, on your reputation, or on one or two quick observations. At the start of his driving personality makeover program, this driver considered himself to be a safe driver and named the strategies he practices. At the same time he recognized that he had a speeding problem. He was faced with having to reconcile two conflicting beliefs about himself: "I'm a good driver" and "I'm a speeder."

Overhauling automated and subconscious driving habits is not only a smart thing to do, it gives you a healthy sense of competence and self-confidence. The effort you make in driver self-improvement will extend your effectiveness in other daily situations in the workplace and the family. However, attempts to modify unwanted behavior often encounter resistance.

RESISTANCE TO CHANGE

Drivers initially resist changing their driving style. This resistance gradually dissipates in the process of discovering that driving without automatic inner pressures is safer and more enjoyable. Our data show that driving stress stems from inner reactions to external events, not from congestion or the actions of others. Untrained emotions in traffic create a noxious inner atmosphere, polluting the mind with disapproval, hostility, dissatisfaction, fear, and alienation. For many, this insight is a turning point. Suddenly they are free to experience the benefits of a more relaxed, less competitive, and more supportive driving style, one that does not depend on criticizing and correcting others' behavior.

In traffic we have no choice but to be affected by the actions of others. We don't like it when we're subjected to hostile driving. Yet under certain conditions, most of us are ready and willing to display hostility toward others on the road. This usually happens when someone crosses a line we've defined as unacceptable behavior that arouses our ire, indignation, even outrage. A sense of self-righteousness coupled with a sense of entitlement builds strong feelings of resistance to changing our own behavior, even focusing on it. When drivers do something you despise, think of how difficult it is to resist giving a disapproving look or, as we say in Hawaii, "giving stink eye." It's tempting to stare, to punish, to make sure the other driver knows we're displeased. Maybe we hope they'll feel guilty or stupid. What a satisfying thought! According to Dr. Arnold Nerenberg, aggressive driving becomes road rage when you feel compelled to let the other driver know that you're displeased and mad. He estimates that in 1999 there were two billion unrecorded hostile exchanges between motorists in the United States.[5] We believe the actual number is closer to four hundred billion.[6]

One useful technique for modifying unwanted behavior is mentally switching roles with the other driver, or empathizing. Ask yourself, "How might he or she be feeling?" and "What if that were my grandma (kid, spouse, pastor)?" If you approach it positively, this can shift your perspective and increase motivation to stop a negative behavior. For instance, try thinking about how bad the victim of your disapproving stare might feel. Ask yourself if you really want to be the kind of person who makes someone feel awful, who chooses to be an unkind or vindictive person. Consider one shaken driver's story:

> I was driving on the Pali Highway toward Waikiki and a person tailed me from the intersection of Kamehameha Highway all the way to the tunnel and then gave me the stink eye. I was really scared, so I had to pull over to just kind of rest for a while before I continued. I tried to ignore what he was doing, but it was hard. I didn't know how.

You might think a stare is just a harmless little thing, a mere look: "Sticks and stones. . . ." But clearly, this driver was emotionally affected by the implied threat in a "stare." Being worried that she was followed heightened the threat of the man's look. Perhaps she was only imagining being followed or even being stared at, but perhaps not. How could she be sure? In any case, impressions activate fear and fear has real consequences. This realization calls for a new sense of social responsibility about how we look at other drivers, the expressions on our face, and the impressions we give off. Civility behind the wheel has disappeared for an entire generation, but we can get it back with systematic efforts like the three-step program for lifelong driver self-improvement.

To not stare—mission impossible? It seems so at first to this middle-aged man:

> This week I was working on modifying my compulsion to stare and give people the evil eye. For the first three days I just tried to observe where I was doing it. I wasn't trying to make myself stop. I noticed that I looked at drivers that were going too slow (in my opinion). As I passed them on the left I felt my head turning sideways and staring. Then I noticed that I would invariably spin some derogatory story about that person. Like, "Oh, figures. It's an old guy. He probably can't even see." Or "Maybe he's too scared to drive normally." I decided to alternate days between staring and not staring so I could see what it felt like.
>
> On the fourth day I told myself this was going to be a "no staring" day. I noticed that I had to consciously warn myself as I was passing, "Don't look. Don't look. You promised you're not going to look. Don't move your head. Just keep going." It's as if I had to talk to myself throughout the time I was passing, so I didn't trip up and stare.
>
> I was very impressed at how difficult it was for me not to look. I heard this little voice whining in the back of my head: "Oh, No. It's not fair. I want to look. I want to see who it is. I need to know. Is it an old guy again? Is it a woman? Are there any passengers? Oh no, I didn't see. Now I just have to wonder." I'm amazed at how silly I can be. Must be my inner child that is trying to assert itself, I guess.
>
> When I was waiting at red lights my head would automatically sort of turn left and right to examine the other cars. I did not realize how much I was using traffic stops for entertainment. I was treating other cars like they were on a television screen for me to look at. My inner child was very upset when I denied it the privilege of this entertainment. It was crying and whining and feeling deprived. I had to give myself pep talks, bring out my big superego guns to make it feel guilty, to silence it into shame: "Now, now, it's not nice to stare at people. Just because you can doesn't mean you have to. Besides, it'll be good for you. Don't you want be the kind of person that you can trust not to stare at other people? Respects their privacy, their right to be left alone. Also, if you stare, you might slow down and that will affect the others."

It's important to realize that you can use powerful inner tools to help regulate behavior by talking differently to yourself. To be effective, the new form of talking to the self must occur *during* self-witnessing and it must be very specific. Concentrating on one small driving behavior at a time is essential to bringing about systematic change in the long run. This middle-aged woman successfully used the technique known as "thought stopping" by replacing troublesome thoughts with those that help to regulate physical activity:

> While working on modifying my unconscious driving behavior, I found that I was doing it when the radio was on. Turning off the radio helped when singing to the music was the cause of the unconscious behavior. My observations showed me that when I have a lot on my mind and the radio is on, then my thoughts start to wander. One technique I used is "thought stopping." I would think out loud and remind myself that I am driving. This would bring my thoughts and attention back to the road. In order to objectively assess my success I continued with my observations. I am learning to increase my awareness of when I lapse into unconscious driving. Knowing when and under what conditions I start driving without staying conscious of it helps me keep it from happening.
>
> So far I have identified three conditions during which I have to be alert: when I am preoccupied with something, when I turn the radio on to my favorite music, and when I drive a lot. I found that I need to fill my mind with what goes on in traffic to prevent my other thoughts from taking over. So I think about the turn I have to take and when I should be turning on the signal. I think about other drivers and make sure I don't follow too close so I don't upset them.
>
> My first week of systematic self-observation has shown me that I have many undesirable driving routines. Through this experience I have learned that I can modify my driving behavior, but I need to know first what the behavior is that needs to be changed, and then it's not going to be easy or fast. I feel that I have a better driving persona since I started this self-modification effort. I am more aware of when I lapse into automatic pilot and have learned the means to prevent it.

At this stage she has confidence in her ability to take control of her unconscious driving behavior for the sake of safety and well-being. Self-witnessing fosters objective self-awareness, so it's required to make changes in your driving personality. Consciously reflecting on your driving behavior is essential to following a strategic plan for transformation. Since everyone experiences road rage, aggressive driving habits are deeply ingrained, covering all aspects of driving—whether you're a chronic critic, yeller, honker, bird flipper, lane hopper, gap filler, tailgater, speed fiend, or all of these. Changing the driving personality requires the help of inner power tools for accurately assessing and observing your characteristics of feeling and thinking as a driver.

> I would like to learn how to stop my road rage and aggressive driving. I'm just tired of dealing with people on the road. I just want to get off the road and out of my vehicle.

ROAD RAGE AND AGGRESSIVE DRIVING

DRIVER'S DIARY

One witness did a self-assessment of her behavior at a particular stop-light where she makes a right turn daily. She was concerned about the fact that she often failed to make complete stops. She recorded herself over a two-week period, speaking her thoughts into a tape recorder and driving according to her usual pattern without trying to do anything different. This provided her with an objective *baseline* of her typical behavior. On each of ten trips she observed her feelings, thoughts, and specific actions at this one particular intersection where she usually makes a right turn. She listened to her tapes and wrote a summary analysis of the circumstances and the specific ways she negotiated that right turn:

> *Day 1.* I was in a good mood as I arrived at the intersection. I was intent on getting to my destination in time. I didn't come to a complete stop because I didn't see any cars.
> *Day 2.* I felt very tired as I left the parking lot. All I thought about was getting home and going to sleep. I didn't stop completely at the red light. I slowly rolled around the corner and quickly sped away.
> *Day 3.* I was feeling angry as I left my workplace. I felt used. I thought of all the work I did which was not acknowledged by my supervisor. I approached the red light, hardly slowing down, and veered right, speeding up, all in one smooth action. I enjoyed the feeling of not stopping. I avoided looking at other drivers. Who knows what they were thinking about me?
> *Day 4.* I felt happy and in a good mood as I left home for work. I was a few minutes earlier than usual. No need to rush. I was enjoying the sunrise and the after effects of my good breakfast. I came to a complete stop at the red light, looked around, and stepped on the accelerator slowly, enjoying the feeling.
> *Day 5.* I wasn't feeling very well as I left the office building. My mind was jumping around on all sorts of topics. I saw the police car as I was approaching the intersection. I thought of getting a ticket if I wasn't being careful. I made a complete stop, then slowly turned right. I felt self-conscious, like people were watching me. I hate that feeling.
> *Day 6.* I was on my way to the shopping center. I was hungry. I thought of all sorts of foods I can eat. I thought of different restaurants. I slowly made a right-hand turn at the red stoplight, but I didn't make a complete stop.
> *Day 7.* I was on my way home when I saw this other car getting a ticket. I was nervous. I better be real careful. I heard the sound of a police car, then I saw a police car chase another car. It's a good thing it wasn't me! I came to a complete stop at the intersection before turning right on red.

Three-Step Driver Self-Improvement Program

Day 8. I left home too late and I was feeling scared. I didn't want to get scolded by my supervisor. I did not come to a complete stop while making a right turn at this red light.

Day 9. I was on my way back from a party with good friends. I was feeling very happy and was in a joyous mood. I came to a complete stop and enjoyed it. I was doing the right thing. I wasn't sneaking.

Day 10. The car behind me was so close. I didn't dare make a complete stop even though I wanted to. I didn't want to get hit. I just wanted to get away. I hardly slowed down as I made the right turn on red. The car behind me then abruptly passed me on left like he was really displeased with me.

It's clear that a driver's actions at the same spot can vary considerably from trip to trip, influenced by what's happening on the road as well as what's going on inside the driver's private world of feelings, thoughts, and moods. This driver gained important insight into her reasoning and the hidden assumptions governing her external behavior that gave the solution for some positive change:

I discovered that I had the tendency to turn the corner while looking to see if there were any cars approaching the intersection from the green right-of-way. It was as if I literally understood the red *stop*light to mean the same thing as a *yield* sign. I didn't come to a complete stop when I was nervous, tired, frustrated, or angry. I did come to a complete stop when I was happy, when I saw a policeman, or when I was scared. My actions in driving were apparently based on how I felt at the time and what I was thinking. I realized how my attitude affected my driving errors.

Armed with this new information about her attitudes and reasoning process, she planned a strategy to change her typical pattern:

I made a new rule for myself about stopping at the light. It's because I decided that I don't want to be at the whim of my own changing feelings or forced by the pressures of other drivers, even cops. I want to keep in control of my vehicle at all times, so this rule is an important part of that. I still keep track of when I don't want to follow the rule and when I really don't follow it, but it's less and less. I feel much clearer on what kind of driver I want to be, and I feel that I can accomplish my goal of stopping at the light every time without feeling bad.

ROAD RAGE AND AGGRESSIVE DRIVING

CHECKLIST: IDENTIFYING YOUR IRRATIONAL DRIVING RULES

We're vulnerable to the unexamined rules in our heads, like the one about having to make all the lights. Many assumptions about driving are simply irrational rules that add to stress. If you don't recognize these, it's possible that you're not conscious of the background assumptions affecting your thoughts, feelings, and actions.

1. ___ I must make all the lights.
2. ___ I mustn't brake unless absolutely necessary.
3. ___ I must go as fast as possible in any traffic condition.
4. ___ I must strive to get ahead of everyone.
5. ___ If someone passes me, I'm probably going too slow.
6. ___ If I don't see any other cars around, I don't have to signal.
7. ___ When drivers honk near me or at me, they're insulting or punishing me.
8. ___ When the light turns yellow, I must speed up to make it through the intersection.
9. ___ It's always better to make a light than to stop.
10. ___ Drivers should keep out of my way, otherwise they hinder my progress.

NOTES

1. Personal anecdotes quoted throughout this chapter were sent to us by e-mail correspondents.

2. Leon James and Diane Nahl, "Aggressiveness in Relation to Age, Gender, and Type of Car," DrDriving.org [online], www.aloha.net/~dyc/surveys/survey2/interpretations.html [May 20, 2000].

3. Edward C. Jandy, *Charles Horton Cooley, His Life and His Social Theory* (New York: Octagon Books, 1969).

4. Leon James, "Musings of a Traffic Psychologist," DrDriving.org [online], www.aloha.net/~dyc/ch14.html [May 20, 2000]

5. Arnold Nerenberg, personal communication with the authors, 1998.

6. Here's the way we figure it: 125 million (drivers on the road daily) X 1,000 (mini-exchanges between drivers during two commutes per day) X .01 (1 percent are hostile or stressed exchanges) X 365 (days per year) = about 400 billion stressful or aggressive exchanges per year in the United States.

CHILDREN AND ROAD RAGE

ROAD RAGE NURSERY

Road rage is a feeling of hostility that is inherited through the culture of disrespect condoned on highways. Motorists don't try to hide it because they are often proud of their aggressiveness, so it's common for children to hear parents and other adults swearing and demeaning other drivers:

> While backing out of the parking space I heard a screech and felt a little bump when a woman and little girl in a Camaro appeared in my rearview. We all got out and I apologized, though I knew full well that she had been far away and had sped up to try to outrun me, instead of waiting for me to leave the space. I felt miserable when her little girl started screaming at me, obviously repeating what she had heard her mother say about me in the car to excuse her own dangerous behavior, "Stupid lady! She's a stupid lady, mommy! Why don't you watch where you're going, stupid lady? You have to pay for this, stupid lady!"[1]

ROAD RAGE AND AGGRESSIVE DRIVING

Kids do whatever their parents do, they say the things they hear older kids and adults saying, and their emotional reactions are shaped by mimicking adult feelings. Children soak up the norms of behavior in their environment, and that's how the road rage tradition is passed on to the next generation.

The following dialogue took place in a car between a middle-aged man and his two very young children during a conflict over a parking space with two young men in another car. The father gave the young men the finger and yelled an obscenity. One of the young men got out of the car and ran toward the car with the kids. One of the most shocking parts of the transcript is this:

Little boy:	Look Daddy, one of the guys in the green car is running toward us!
Father:	They can't do anything to us. Lock your door. Let's just get out of here.
Little boy:	No, let's get them first!
Little girl:	Get them, Daddy, get them!
Little boy:	Run him down, Daddy! Faster, Daddy, c'mon get him!

The two children, aged five and three, were caught up in the hostility that their father generated when he chose to assume a comic-book persona to aggressively compete for a parking space. He modeled this combative persona for his children, teaching them how to deal with challenges on the road with opportunism, hostility, and threats of violence. Years before they get behind the wheel of a car, children absorb and imitate the values of their parents and other authority figures. Clearly, we need to focus attention on how children learn to interact with drivers on the road while they're still very young passengers.

How can drivers deal with uncontrollable kids? Is this the one area where drivers need more control and can't get it? We need to help children develop emotional intelligence as future drivers by modeling appropriate behaviors in the car, and holding them responsible for being safe passengers. Show them what kind of passenger behavior you value and what the community values, and reward them for learning it and practicing it. Children can be taught to learn good passenger skills, and they will love it. All it takes is rewarding them for doing what you want, instead of merely punishing them for doing what you don't like. For example, if they won't wear seat belts, don't leave unless they are buckled in and/or remove a privilege. Give them something nice after each successful trip, but don't give it to them when they break the rule. Rewards can be small, like positive comments about their good behavior, some special time alone with you, a colorful sticker, a small notebook or purse, a certain privilege, a special food, time on the computer, or special TV time. Rewarding kids for becoming good passengers is a useful idea because it helps them learn to value doing a good job as a passenger.

The power of this strategy is in frequent but small rewards that help shape the child's behavior into a desire to do a good job of being the best possible passenger. Without backseat management techniques, driving kids is a major headache because your emotional territory is constantly breached.

> Carpooling the kids is horrendous. These three kids drive me totally bonkers. Thank God I only do it every other day so I can recover in between. I cannot get them to do what they should. I get so distracted trying to settle their fights and answer their incessant questions. They won't stay put or wear seat belts. If I ask before we leave if they have seat belts on they say, "Yes Mrs. P!" But then a few minutes later they take them off when I don't know. I can't keep checking them and drive, too. They make so much noise I swear I can't hear ambulance sirens. It's a wonder we get there in one piece. They're not my kids, so what can I do about it? They must know I'm helpless so they take advantage.

To avoid this dangerous chaos, adult drivers must teach their kids emotional intelligence from the earliest age possible. Children experience their first "driving lessons" as infants and toddlers in their parents' and caretakers' cars. Children learn how to feel, think, and act as passengers and as drivers from the adult drivers. It's good sense to make these early driving lessons deliberately educational. Help them to learn how to behave in the car by setting a good example for them. If you're a hotheaded driver, they will value that. If you let them behave unsafely in the car, they will value that. If you wear your seatbelt, they will value that, too. If you respect other drivers, they will value others.

VERBAL REWARDS FOR GOOD PASSENGERS

Children need lots of frequent positive reinforcement for doing the right thing inside the car. The rewards can include charts of their progress, badges, certificates and awards of merit for safe riding, verbal compliments and commendations, and earned privileges. Some ideas for verbal rewards include:

- "Thank you for being a very good passenger today."
- "I was so glad that you helped me concentrate on where I was going."
- "You wore your seat belt the entire trip, so I felt you were safe."
- "You helped us have a peaceful ride because you didn't fight with your brother in the car today."

ROAD RAGE AND AGGRESSIVE DRIVING

- "You were very good, ignoring the kids in that other car who were jumping around and yelling at you."
- "Thank you for telling the other kids to be quiet while we were driving to the market. You really helped them calm down and be safe in the car."
- "Thank you for reminding us to wear our seatbelts. I'm glad you care about us being safe in the car."
- "I was so happy that you didn't stand up while the car was moving today."
- "I was so proud of you today for teaching your friend how to behave and be safe in the car."
- "You did a good job of cleaning up your mess in the car. Thanks, I really appreciate it."

Affirming statements like these give kids messages about what adults value, and since they want to please their parents, they will adopt these values. Parents can help children internalize these values by acknowledging good passenger conduct. Kids need acknowledgment for being good in any situation, but moving vehicles are extremely perilous environments, where it's of the utmost importance that kids learn to become mindful riders. Acknowledging their contribution to a successful driving trip will instill in them a desire to become safe and kind drivers later in life. In addition, they will become more discerning of others' driving behavior and be able to decide when not to ride with someone who is rash.

Encourage children to practice witnessing their own behavior as passengers. They will enjoy keeping a trip log of what happens inside and outside of the car, especially when they're rewarded for it verbally. When focused, children are wonderful observers and take pride in making complete records of their own and others' driving behavior. Let the kids tell you about your own driving, and take their cautionary advice to show them that their input is appreciated. Help them do their own riding personality make-over along with your driving personality make-over. Taking an interest in their growth and improvement in this area will stimulate your own evolution into a more peaceful and emotionally intelligent driver.

CHILDREN'S ROAD RAGE

It's frightening to think that some drivers harbor violent feelings toward children walking down the street. While driving, normally nice people can feel provoked by what they perceive to be the intentionally bad behavior of children using "the driver's" streets:

Children and Road Rage

I shouldn't be this way, but I hate it when kids walking pile up at an intersection. I guess I did that when I was a kid, but I still hate their little games because they obviously just love to do everything to keep me from going. They jostle against each other, making a spectacle of themselves. They walk incredibly slow on purpose, stop in the middle of the crosswalk to look in each other's purses or backpacks, put on makeup, play video games, or start a mock fight. It's like a stage play for them. They're just trying to get attention. They act like they own the road and they always get to the other side after the light has changed, trying to force us cars to wait before we can enter the intersection, and then you're lucky if you make it through the light at all. I feel like speeding up and scaring the living daylights out of them. Sometimes I drive up to them to force them to run, but they usually slow down more and they even give me the evil eye—as if a kid can play chicken with a car. They're nuts. They really make me mad and I have to keep myself from trying to hurt them. I have to work on this—why am I contemplating mayhem with kids crossing the street?

Even though we all know that we have to behave responsibly in the presence of children, the urge to teach them a hard lesson is strong. Children and adolescents alike have a history of provoking drivers, and that can lead to devastating consequences.

Children are perhaps the most vulnerable as pedestrians because of their size, and because they have limited knowledge and experience in risky traffic situations. Schools typically use crossing guards and Junior Police Officers (JPOs) to ensure the safety of their students. But just beyond the school, many children are on their own. It's not uncommon to see kids taunting passing motorists. A journalist in Honolulu complained in his column about children who express their road rage by walking into the path of oncoming cars, defying them:

What bugs me is a growing trend among teenagers in Hawaii to walk deliberately slow across streets, stopping cars in their tracks. It apparently is the cool thing to do these days. These rebels without a crosswalk are idiots waiting for a disaster to happen. They are maniacs who don't have the survival instinct of your basic road-crossing chicken.

In fact, children are fully capable of every kind of road rage, especially fantasy road rage where they pretend to be violent, and drivers often resort to aggressive tactics to make them behave.

I wanted to scare some naughty kids who were pretending to shoot people in cars with their toy guns. They were taking aim, making loud shooting noises, and hooting after they blew someone away. I have very dark windows so they couldn't see me too well—I hoped the car would look scary to them so they would think twice about pretending to fire a gun at a motorist. I was really afraid they might get shot themselves playing dangerous games like that, so I sped up to them and slammed on my brakes, screeching to a halt, then I blasted them with my horn—they ran and I was glad.

These little kids were playing this dangerous game of throwing small rocks at cars. I felt pangs of danger! Danger! My heart started beating very fast. I honked loudly at them and glared as I screamed, "Stop that!" when I drove by. They kept throwing rocks as I passed by. I was angry that their parents could let them do that. I decided to talk it over with my own kids that night to ask them what they would do if their friends wanted them to throw things at cars. I really believe that kids who think it's OK to do little violent acts will later think it's OK to do more violence. It shows that they don't value life and property, which I want my kids to value.

This cute little boy standing on the sidewalk smiled so sweetly as I drove by, so I smiled back and waved. Then, I looked in my rearview mirror at him only to discover that he was flipping the bird at me. I felt so embarrassed myself and sorry for him at the same time. I wanted to ask him, "Why? Why me?" I wished I could talk to his mother. I considered going around the block to confront him. Next time I might.

Teaching children to value road safety rules is the key to helping them develop good habits as pedestrians, and eventually as drivers. Families can work together to instill good traffic safety attitudes throughout a child's life, from infancy to young adulthood. If children begin their traffic education at an early age, by the time they're old enough for driver education, they will have developed emotionally intelligent habits and an orientation that embraces protecting self and others from harm. This is the best antidote to growing up and becoming infected with the habitual road rage around them.

Children are quite capable of witnessing their own pedestrian behavior, and this helps them to make informed and safe decisions around traffic. Even before they become automobile drivers, children need to learn how to develop appropriate traffic attitudes, understand how to be safe around traffic, and act safely near traffic. To avoid becoming involved in road rage incidents, kids have to learn a complex set of rules and skills:

- Keeping safe walking distance from roadways
- Understanding and following traffic signals
- Knowing and obeying the traffic laws governing pedestrian behavior
- Valuing road safety rules

- Being familiar with procedures for crossing various types of roads
- Valuing alertness by paying close attention to street conditions, and to what's happening around them
- Refraining from yelling, gesturing, or throwing things at vehicles
- Respecting the rights of everyone using the roads
- Taking responsibility for their own safety near roads
- Caring about the safety of other people near roads
- Understanding the special safety needs of animals near roads
- Keeping pets on leashes and away from the roadside

CHILDREN AGAINST ROAD RAGE

Children Against Road Rage (CARR) was founded in 1997, when we created the CARR Workbook as an interactive Web site for collecting and promoting a driving psychology learning curriculum for children. Parents and teachers can find a variety of anti–road rage awareness activities to keep children from becoming the next generation of aggressive drivers.[2] CARR is a driving-psychology curriculum designed to contain and reverse the road rage epidemic. Its main goal is to involve children in training for emotional intelligence as future drivers. Through various exercises and activities, children are encouraged to produce self-witnessing reports that detail their feelings, thoughts, and actions while on the road as pedestrians, cyclists, or passengers in cars and buses. Preschoolers can use tape recorders and video cameras operated by a helpful adult who takes care of the technical stuff. Older children use whatever technology they can handle, including writing, video, and multimedia Internet presentations.

These activities help children to become more aware passengers by focusing their attention on when and where they're being exposed to aggressive driving. As passengers in cars and buses, children are at risk of absorbing the hostile attitudes of their adult drivers. This unconscious cultural transmission is injurious to children now—and later, when they inevitably become aggressive drivers. Increased children's awareness of aggressive driving can prevent the unconscious absorption of aggressive traits. When children are taught supportive driving attitudes, concepts, and actions and they become more aware of the behaviors and attitudes they're exposed to, they have the choice to reject hostility toward other road users.

These exercises and activities will be welcomed by all who love children enough to want to protect them against the attitudes of road rage. Parents can use these activities as a fun and valuable learning exchange with their children, instructing them in good driving concepts. Tell them that supportive driving is your ideal, and what it has to do with char-

157

acter, responsibility, teamwork, fair play, and human rights. Tell them that even though you fail at times, as they have no doubt witnessed, you still maintain the ideal as a worthwhile goal to strive for. It's crucial to keep striving for this ideal and to uphold it to ourselves and to children. They depend on the development of an intact driving conscience to avoid becoming road ragers themselves. These activities with your children also double as a countermeasure to your own aggressive driving and road rage. Teachers also will find these materials helpful in planning lessons and activities on traffic safety, proper road behavior, and good passenger behavior and attitudes.

EXERCISE: RECOGNIZING AGGRESSION ON THE ROAD

Educational Objectives:

(1) To help children define the concept of aggressiveness in public places
(2) To sensitize children to their own aggressive experiences in public places

1. Think of the kids you see every day. How aggressive are they as far you can tell? Examples of aggressive behaviors include hitting, throwing, attacking, threatening, blocking the way, refusing to return something, yelling and cursing at someone, and doing other things that are mean, scary, or unfriendly. Circle one of the numbers to show how aggressive the kids that you know are.

NOT AGGRESSIVE   1   2   3   4   5   VERY AGGRESSIVE

2. Think of comic books and TV cartoons. Many of them show things that are aggressive, like hitting, shooting, attacking, breaking, hurting, yelling, throwing, insulting, doing bad things to other people. All of these things are aggressive. How aggressive are your own favorite comic books or TV cartoons? Circle one of the numbers to show how aggressive some of your favorite characters are.

NOT AGGRESSIVE   1   2   3   4   5   VERY AGGRESSIVE

3. You may have heard a driver get mad at another driver while riding as a passenger. Think about the last few times you were a passenger in someone's car, van, SUV, or bus. How mad do the drivers sometimes get? Circle one of the numbers to show how mad you've seen people get while driving.

A LITTLE MAD   1   2   3   4   5   VERY MAD

4. Try to remember: Do *you* sometimes get mad at drivers on the road when you ride in a car or bus? Circle one of the numbers to show how mad you sometimes get at those drivers.

A LITTLE MAD   1   2   3   4   5   VERY MAD

5. Think about this: You're being driven somewhere and you're anxious because you don't want to get there late. There is a car ahead that's going pretty slow, and there is no way to pass it. Do you think it's all right to tailgate the car? (This means to follow very close behind so the driver will be scared and speed up.) Circle what you think is the right answer:

A. No, you must never tailgate someone.
B. Yes, it's all right to tailgate someone who is going too slow.
C. Yes, you can tailgate someone who is going too slow when you are in a hurry and it's not your fault that you're late.

6. Think about this: You're being driven somewhere, and you're anxious because you don't want to get there late. Is it all right to cheat a little and break some of the rules, like going through a red light instead of waiting until it turns green? Circle the letter that you think gives the right answer:

A. Yes, you can break some of the driving rules if you're very careful not to hit other cars or pedestrians.
B. No, you must never break the driving rules, because they make the roads safer for everyone.
C. It depends on whether you're a good enough driver. If you're not a terrific driver you should not break the rules, even if you're in a hurry; but it's OK if you really know what you're doing, as long as you watch out for other cars, and as long as you don't do it all the time.

7. In your opinion, who is a really good driver? Circle the one you think would be the best:

A. A driver who gets there in less time than other drivers.
B. A driver who gets there without taking any chances and is always safe, even if it takes a little longer to get there.
C. A race car driver.

8. What do you think about seat belts? Who cares most about wearing seat belts in your family? Circle one:

ROAD RAGE AND AGGRESSIVE DRIVING

A. Me
B. Mom
C. Dad
D. None of us cares about seat belts

There are obvious benefits to parents and teachers engaging children in topics having to do with driving, drivers, and passengers. Younger children carry immature conceptions about the rights of others in public places. Since they're inevitably exposed to aggressive and hostile interactions, both in real life and on TV, they need to be resensitized to the implications and consequences of aggressiveness and disrespect for regulations. Giving children the opportunity to answer these questions enhances their awareness. At the same time it gives the adult an opportunity to explain the rationality of the preferred solution and to model a more supportive driving philosophy. But discussion is not the only approach needed to ensure that children develop supportive and respectful styles of conduct in public places. Parents and other adults who transport children have a special opportunity to help them focus on the driver's world.

EXERCISE: APPROPRIATE AND INAPPROPRIATE PASSENGER BEHAVIORS

Educational Objectives:

(1) To help children focus on passenger etiquette and safety.

(2) To sensitize children to bad behaviors in cars.

1. First, read the instructions. Then get the OK from your parents and other adults who drive you. *Be sure they agree before you start.*
2. Copy the passenger observation form below and bring it with you in the car. *Be sure to show this to the driver before you enter the car.*
3. Put a check mark on the list *every time you do one of the items listed.* This way, you can later count the number of check marks to see how many times you did something. Some items are about bad behavior as a passenger and some are about good behavior as passenger.
4. After the ride, add up the check marks for each item.
5. Discuss the results with the driver, your parents, or other adults.

It's important to fill out this form on more than just one trip. Compare several trips to see if they are similar and how they differ. On your next trip, see how many of the bad behaviors you can stop doing, and how many of the good behaviors you can do more. Don't throw away your record sheets. Save them to look at from time to time to see if there's a change over time. Compare your record sheets with those of your family members or friends. Who deserves a reward?

Passenger Observation Form

Date: _____ Time: _____ Destination: _____

PASSENGERS BEHAVING BADLY	PASSENGERS BEHAVING WELL
____ making noise, being loud, yelling	____ sitting quietly, acting calm
____ poking, pinching, pushing	____ wearing your seat belt
____ fighting, hair pulling, hitting	____ not distracting the driver
____ not wearing seat belts	____ helping the driver read road signs
____ throwing things out the window	____ learning the route
____ sticking hand out the window	____ talking calmly to the driver
____ making faces at other cars	____ observing the driver's actions
____ urging the driver to go faster	____ observing road conditions
____ complaining about the traffic	____ thanking the driver for being safe
____ other: _____	____ other: _____
____ other: _____	____ other: _____

Time at end of trip:_____ Total time for the ride: _____ minutes.

EXERCISE: OBSERVING DRIVING

Educational Objectives:

(1) To help children focus on driving etiquette and safety
(2) To sensitize them to aggressive behaviors in public places
(3) To help children realize the bad consequences of dangerous driving
(4) To help them learn the positive logic of emotional intelligence for drivers

1. First, read the instructions. Then get the OK from your parents and other adults who drive you. *Be sure they agree before you start.*
2. Copy the driving observation form below and take it and a pen or pencil with you in the car. *Be sure to show this to the driver before you enter the car.*
3. Put a check mark on the list *every time you see one of the items happen.* This way, you can later count the number of check marks to see how

many times something happened. Some items are about the driver and some are about you.

4. After the ride, add up the check marks for each item.
5. Discuss the results with the driver, your parents, or other adults.

It's important to fill out this form on more than just one trip. Compare several trips to see if they are similar and how they differ. Don't throw away your record sheets. Save them to look at from time to time to see if there's a change over time. Who deserves a reward?

Driving Observation Form
Date: _____ Time: _____ Destination: _____

                                                                    Totals

(1) The driver yells or uses bad language.   _____
(2) You get scared by how the person drives   _____
(3) You wish the driver would hurry up and go faster.   _____
(4) The driver talks bad about another driver.   _____
(5) You feel scared about the driver being too aggressive.   _____
(6) The driver yells or gets mad at you or at another passenger.   _____
(7) The driver waves or smiles to thank another driver.   _____
(8) The driver is helpful to another driver.   _____
(9) The driver makes a turn without signaling.   _____
(10) The driver is going over the posted speed limit.   _____
(11) The driver is going through red.   _____
(12) The driver switches lanes without signaling.   _____
(13) Other: Use the back or a second sheet.   _____

Time at end of trip: _____   Total time: _____ minutes.

EXERCISE: DRIVERS BEHAVING BADLY (DBB) RATINGS

Before they become drivers, children are exposed to thousands of scenes on television that depict drivers behaving badly. It's important to make children more aware of this passive exposure to driving lessons by discussing it with them. Parents and teachers can use specific examples that are familiar to their children. Discuss some of the programs with your children and encourage them to keep a DBB diary or notebook in which they can write their own observations while watching TV. Teachers can use this activity as homework or class discussion. Here are three examples and additional ones can be found at the DrDriving.org Web site.[3]

Tiny Toon Adventures:

This one-minute clip shows several of the Tiny Toon characters jumping into a fire truck to get to a school which is going up in flames. This short driving clip shows lots of reckless and dangerous driving without any care for others around them, including: speeding; driving fast on curvy roads, bumpy hills, and public roadways; the driver took sharp U-turns without slowing down, letting the back of the fire truck to go off the road and hit things on the sidewalks; and weaving in and out of cars on busy public highways.

The Dukes of Hazzard:

A couple of thugs kidnap Daisy, a cousin of the Duke brothers. The brothers jump in their car and pursue the kidnappers. They're going at high speeds, jumping hay barrels, and making wild turns and spins. Other police cars join in the pursuit. All of them are going at high speeds. One of the police cars tries to make a jump over a dirt ramp and ends up in a tree. In the show no one is hurt and they even make it look funny.

101 Dalmatians

In one particular scene toward the end of the movie, Cruella De Vil is chasing a big truck filled with the 101 dalmatians and goes around winding turns on a hill side. Cruella, driving a high-powered limousine, was trying to run the truck off of the cliff by sideswiping, tailgating, and ramming the truck from behind. She was chasing the truck down a hill at high speed. In her violent rage, she tailgated and rammed the truck from behind.

When you discuss TV programs and commercials in a group or family setting, have everyone contribute examples of DBB. Discuss each one in terms of its risks and its potential for influencing the behavior of drivers. You can watch TV together and point out scenes of DBB. Discuss their potential for lulling us into a false sense of security about taking unrealistic risks, minimizing risk and injury, and giving us a distorted image of danger, consequences, and the seriousness of injuries. Use this list to point out things that happen frequently, and to identify and record DBB scenes.

(1) Taking eyes off the road—count the seconds and point out consequences of doing that in real life.
(2) Hitting a parked car or object and not stopping to investigate or lend assistance (illegal and callous behavior).
(3) Giving chase and how that endangers the lives of innocent people and damages their property.
(4) Riding up a rocky mountain or river bed with large boulders—that it's made with video editing tricks.

163

(5) Jumping out of the car while it's still in motion and not falling or getting hurt.

(6) Yelling at passengers, other drivers, or pedestrians—that's road rage and it's illegal and rude.

(7) Driving and drinking or taking drugs—you can't get away with that if you're really driving.

(8) Driving in a confused mental state and making it to one's destination—not likely in real life.

(9) Speeding through red light at busy intersections and not crashing—unlikely in real life.

(10) Passengers fighting or partying—dangerous and illegal.

(11) Passengers urging the driver to speed and take risks—emphasize that drivers should always stay in control.

(12) Children behind the wheel, driving—illegal, dangerous, untrue.

(13) Trying to outrun a police car with sirens going—insane behavior that puts others in danger and for which you would go to jail.

(14) Chasing an ambulance or emergency vehicle—selfish, foolish, illegal.

(15) Driving off in anger, burning rubber—not admirable and shows weak character.

(16) Driving through traffic in a reckless manner—irresponsible, illegal, dangerous.

(17) Joking about running over someone—callous, lowers the tolerance for aggressive behavior and violence.

(18) Deliberately running over someone and laughing about it—inhuman, sick.

(19) Other: _____

Encourage children to keep a DBB TV log, writing down the date, the program or commercial, and the event. Take time to discuss with them the implications of uncritically watching thousands of such events before you become a driver.

Additional activities may include:

(1) Have children of all ages create drawings or posters of drivers behaving badly scenes and have them discuss the consequences of watching these scenes uncritically.

(2) Have children create posters of drivers behaving well and have them discuss the consequences of practicing courteous driving behavior.

(3) Participate in the annual National Critical Viewing Day sponsored jointly by the National Parent Teachers Association (NPTA) and the National Cable Television Association (NCTA).[4]

(4) Ask children these questions to "prompt" them to discuss their road rage experiences:

- What was happening?
- What were you thinking?
- What was it like?
- How did it feel?
- What were you afraid of?
- Did you think about it later?
- Did this happen before?
- Did you mention it to anyone?
- Do you think it's a bad thing? Why?
- What do you think they should do instead?
- Have you seen a thing like this before? Where? Tell me about it.
- What would you do if it was up to you?

Children grow up in an automobile society where they witness routine aggressive behaviors of drivers—in their family car, on school buses, in parking lots, on streets, and in films, cartoons, television shows, and commercials. Children's prolonged exposure to adult road rage puts them in double jeopardy. They're directly at risk from being injured as passengers, cyclists, and pedestrians as they navigate in a dangerous environment made worse by aggressive driving and parents who ignore safety rules with car seats and seat belts. Furthermore, children automatically absorb norms of aggression and roles of hostility as future drivers, learning how to inflame their own verbal road rage with a biased perception that justifies retaliating with righteous indignation. This negative socialization produces a new generation of road ragers and continues the cycle of violent crashes and deaths on the road.

NOTES

1. Personal anecdotes quoted throughout this chapter were sent to us by e-mail correspondents.

2. Leon James and Diane Nahl, "Children Against Road Rage: CARR Workbook," DrDriving.org [online], CARRworkbook.com [May 20, 2000].

3. DrDriving.org Web site [online], DrDriving.org [May 20, 2000].

4. National PTA, "National Critical Viewing Day" [online], www.pta.org/programs/critview/index.htm [May 20, 2000]. For the latest findings about the link between aggressiveness and media exposure, consult American Psychological Association, "Violence on Television: What Do Children Learn? What Can Parents Do?" APA Public Communications [online], www.apa.org/pubinfo/

violence.html [May 24, 2000]; Fumie Yokota and Kimberly M. Thompson, "Violence in G-Rated Animated Films," *JAMA Medicine and the Media* 283, no. 20 (May 24/31, 2000) [online], jama.ama-assn.org/issues/v283n20/full/jtv90009.html [May 24, 2000].

SUPPORTIVE DRIVING

BENEFITS OF SUPPORTIVE DRIVING

Supportive driving is an accommodating style that emphasizes adjusting to the great diversity of highway users and steering clear of the emotional entrapments of road rage thinking. Since intolerance and stereotypic thinking produce the road rage culture with its law of retaliation, tolerance is the antidote. Recognizing and accepting a diversity of drivers and styles is adaptive as well as supportive:

- Local drivers versus visitors
- Large vehicles versus smaller ones
- Healthy, able-bodied drivers versus those who are challenged, ill, in pain, or emotionally upset
- Sober drivers versus those under the influence of alcohol, drugs, or medication
- Young drivers with excellent vision and quick reflexes versus those who are older, slower, and less capable

ROAD RAGE AND AGGRESSIVE DRIVING

- Skilled drivers who maneuver quickly and skillfully versus less skilled or inexperienced who are less efficient and more unpredictable
- Drivers in a hurry versus excessively slow drivers
- Cool drivers in control of their emotions versus road ragers
- Self-confident drivers versus drivers who lack self-confidence

Not all drivers can be treated alike. Visitors are slower to recognize signs that are familiar to locals and break the pace of traffic flow. Supportive drivers accommodate them by accepting the reality of unfamiliar drivers and adjusting their driving to suit the situation. Ignoring this reality leads to feelings of resentment against "these inconsiderate drivers," accompanied by unrealistic and unjust thoughts:

> They should be more prepared and know where they're going. They shouldn't be so inconsiderate. They're jerks who don't care who they inconvenience. At least I should let them know I'm mad![1]

Adaptive thinking allows us to perceive that a driver who is slow or less alert may be ill or in pain. Less experienced drivers make more mistakes and can be less predictable. Drivers may be experienced but lack self-confidence, so they react unexpectedly. There exist two methods to deal with highway pluralism and diversity. The common approach is to oppose driver pluralism, to denounce it, and to strive to ban diversity ("Get these incompetent people off the road!" or "Don't give bad drivers a license!"). The more democratic approach accommodates to the diversity of driver needs and purposes.

Psychologists have long understood that human beings long to feel accepted and respected. In Hawaii, the "Aloha spirit" symbolizes an attitude of mutual acceptance. How do you feel when a courteous driver anticipates what you want to do and makes room or yields? You're likely to be filled with gratitude. When others are helpful to us it puts a smile in our heart. For example, the courtesy wave is a ritual that connects us as peaceful strangers. This simple act can restore some of the dignity lost when hostile drivers show disrespect by yelling or making obscene gestures. When someone waves thanks, we feel less isolated, we feel acknowledged, we feel validated. When we wave thanks to someone who does us a favor, though we are physically apart, we make a human connection by sharing good will.

To these emotional benefits, add the mental advantages. People who practiced the three-step program over a period of weeks and months have reported gradually changing their negative feelings and thoughts about drivers (see chapter 6). In many cases, while criticizing the errors of other drivers, they wrongly assumed that they didn't make the same mistakes. Once they began observing their own mistakes, their tendency to blame other drivers decreased. No blame was assigned because it was replaced by an "attitude of latitude." Driving is an inherently dangerous activity performed by fallible people, so it's reasonable to expect incidents and near misses. It's natural to react to incidents by blaming, exaggerating, and coming to inappropriate conclusions. But this is an initial reaction we can get past. It's possible to learn smarter choices and begin to practice tolerance and mutual support. Developing a new philosophy creates a new feeling orientation, which in turn promotes new thinking, resulting in new actions.

For example, when we asked people what they thought was the worst part of being tailgated, they said it's the feeling that a stranger is trying to force us to do what we don't want to do. On the other hand, why do we get infuriated when someone who cuts in front of us suddenly slows down for no apparent reason, forcing us to suddenly apply the brakes? Because someone is forcing us to brake. It's the element of arbitrary coercion that irritates us and pushes our emotions into high gear. On the other hand, few people get mad when everybody slows down because of an ambulance speeding by.

Each driver defines the emotional boundaries of what's considered reasonable given the circumstances versus what's considered arbitrary and hostile. The more latitude we build into our definition of what we're willing to tolerate, the less coerced we'll feel in routine traffic exchanges. Cultivating an attitude of latitude toward other drivers:

- Helps contain road rage
- Reduces stress
- Boosts the immune system
- Fosters community spirit
- Protects from emotional or physical injury
- Protects from financial liability

It's one thing to get off the road rage bandwagon yourself, and quite another to face drivers who indulge in road rage. But self-witnessing enables you to identify the occasions you use as excuses for ranting and raving against other drivers. You can also apply this self-knowledge to others, because what ticks you off is often what ticks others off. The focus of supportive drivers is to facilitate safe passage for everyone on the road by, for example, slowing down slightly to avoid tailgating, making room for a vehicle to enter the lane, or traveling with the flow. These cooperative acts are emotionally intelligent because they enable the pace to move more easily, anticipate potential problems, and create positive connections between drivers. Instead of calming traffic emotions, an aggressive driving philosophy may aggravate stereotypes and intolerance of the diversity of drivers:

> Every time I see articles on road rage, I wonder why they never mention that the primary cause of it is idiots who think that putting on lipstick, talking on their cell phone, and taking care of their child in a car seat in the back at the same time, is appropriate fast-lane behavior while driving 55 MPH with four cars backed up behind them. And they call "flashing high beams" aggressive behavior in all those articles.

Defensive driving does not reduce intolerance and stereotyped perceptions, while supportive driving helps build a new coalition of the diversity of drivers. People may not realize that defensive thinking limits their capacity to give emotionally intelligent explanations for driver behaviors that are outside local norms. For instance, if you see a driver hesitate, slow down for no apparent reason, then speed up again, you might feel annoyed because you're forced to brake and slow down. Or you could say, "Maybe he's unfamiliar with the road and got confused," or "Perhaps she's in pain and trying to manage it." We don't know in each case why motorists act unpredictably, but it's compelling to think that giving people the benefit of the doubt just reinforces their misbehavior. But a tolerant orientation focuses on the driver's prime directive: to remain in control of the vehicle and of the situation, to keep the flow going, avoiding conflicts, slow downs, and crashes. A driver describes his change of heart:

> What started to scare me was that I didn't have anything nice to say about other motorists. I really have got to change if I don't want to die a lonely, bitter man. This vision of my future is what will help me keep this under self-control. I have to understand that it's very wrong to stereotype a person I don't know. Even though it seems harmless because I'm keeping it to myself, I have to put myself in their shoes. I certainly wouldn't like it if someone was judging me based on the car I drive, what I was wearing, or what I was doing. Like they say, treat others as you wish to be treated. It really scared me when I looked at the list of people I observed in traffic and I couldn't find any positive comments. I believe that I'm a good person who is considerate of others' feelings and I couldn't believe how cold and cruel it made me sound. Just that alone was enough to make me cut out those mean observations in traffic.

Raising the emotional intelligence of drivers is consistent with society's ideals of increased safety and full participation for the skilled as well as the less confident, the less experienced, the less healthy, the less able. Road rage cannot thrive where drivers live the ideal of a diversified highway community.

MOTORIST-TO-MOTORIST COMMUNICATION

Drivers must constantly keep track of each other in order to avoid collisions. They have to hit the brake pedal within a second of each other to avoid running out of maneuvering space. At busy four-way stops, drivers are expected to monitor who gets to the curb before whom to determine who goes next. Waving someone on is common but no longer recommended since in recent litigation, courts have assigned partial responsibility to the individual who waved when an accident results. The formal car signaling system is still primitive, but pressure for expanded communication systems has increased in the past decade as the aggressive driving epidemic has spread. Several proposals have been put forth by both individuals and organizations. In the late 1980s, the National Motorists Association proposed seven new motorist signals:

(1) *Apology:* In a brief lapse of attention or judgment, you unintentionally inconvenience, irritate, or endanger another motorist. Hold two fingers in a *V* position, palm out.

(2) *Slow Down, Danger Ahead:* You see an obstacle in the road and would like to alert other motorists to the potential danger. Turn your headlights off and on. To alert traffic approaching from the rear, activate your brake lights or extend your left arm and motion downward. If you see the "slow down" signal from another motorist, heed the warning.

(3) *Lane Courtesy (Please Yield Left Lane):* While traveling on a multi-lane highway, you wish to pass another vehicle that is in the left "passing" lane. The "lane courtesy" signal will alert the other motorist of your intention. Turn the left directional light on and off, 4 to 6 blinks at a time. If the slower vehicle does not respond to the left turn signal, briefly flash your headlights to gain the attention of the other driver. If you see the "lane courtesy" signal from the motorist behind you, check the adjacent right lane, pull over when it is safe to do so, and let the faster vehicle pass.

(4) *Pull Over for Problem:* You come across a vehicle about to have a flat, or lose luggage from an outside rack, or litter the highway with skis, bicycles, or furniture. First, point in the direction of the problem (up for loose roof rack, back for trailer problem, and so

forth), then signal "thumbs down." If you receive this signal from another motorist, pull over and check your vehicle.

5. *Light Problem (Check Your Lights):* The directional lights on another vehicle have been unknowingly left on, or you see a vehicle with a burned out headlight or taillight. You would like to alert the other driver of the problem. Open and close your hand touching the thumb and fingertips together.

6. *Need Assistance:* You are pulled over to the side of the road and need help. Most passersby are unsure what help, if any, is needed. You need to signal for help without conveying panic. Make the sign of a *T* by crossing one hand above the other. If you see the "need assistance" signal, you must make a decision whether you will stop, phone for help, or ignore the appeal.

7. *I Understand (Thank You):* To acknowledge another motorist's signal or to thank another driver for courtesy, use the well-understood "thumbs up" or "OK." [2]

Civility remains a desirable objective, whatever gestural language is eventually adopted to improve communication between drivers. In a more complex and crowded road environment, it makes sense to teach drivers a universal motorists' sign language if it reduces ambiguity that can lead to injury and death. We need initiatives like this one in England:

> Britons drive on the left side of the road, but they have the right idea about roadway courtesy, at least for one day. Friday was a national day of courtesy, sponsored by the Royal Automobile Club and a group called "The Polite Society." According to surveys, normally polite Britons tend to be aggressive and discourteous when they get behind the wheel. And that, say experts, can lead to road rage, which leads to accidents. Sponsors are urging everyone to be just a bit nicer.[3]

On the Youth Against Road Rage (YARR) Web site we promote the *V* victory sign:

> The V-sign is the letter *V* made with the second and third finger of either hand, palm turned toward to the other driver. . . . The YARR sign says, I support peace and civility among drivers . . . and stands for the sentiment this generation's youth share against road rage and aggressive driving . . . it can mean:
>
> > I'm sorry—it's my fault.
> > I meant no harm or insult.
> > I should be more alert—thanks.
> > I wasn't up to par—forgive me.[4]

Private companies have developed in-car vehicle courtesy systems such as Envoy, a foot-long light panel display that affixes to the rear window. It has a hand control with three buttons that activate a brightly lit display of HELP, THANKS, or SORRY.[5] We predict that intervehicle communication accessories will proliferate as people strive to achieve better motorist-to-motorist communication.

TRAINING FOR SUPPORTIVE DRIVING

Supportive driving focuses on facilitating other drivers' efforts to accomplish what they want instead of competing against them. For example, when you become aware of someone who's trying to pass you, keep your speed steady and avoid accelerating in order not to interfere. If you see someone just ahead of you wanting to enter your lane and if the driver behind you is not following too close, make more room by very slightly slowing down. Here the supportive driver may have a conflict of altruism: I want to let that person in but I'm afraid I'll upset the driver behind who might not appreciate it if I slow things down. You're still better off adjusting than feeling anxious about getting ahead and upset if you can't. One traffic engineer told us he loves traffic because it allows him to practice a form of driving he calls "eating up traffic waves."[6] He does this in dense traffic by keeping the gap ahead large enough to allow other cars to enter the lane without having to slow down much. If enough motorists do this, many traffic jams could be avoided.

If you adopt and practice a supportive driving style you're protected from the road rage of other drivers because you're committed to putting up the least sail in their angry wind. For example, knowing that people rage against anyone who blocks the passing lane, you look frequently in the rear and side mirrors and move out of there when you see a car coming up fast. In parking lots, you avoid people that rage against anyone who competes for a space. When traveling in other locales, you observe the driving norms practiced by local drivers.

We have had to learn these supportive driving lessons over the years with the Aloha spirit. If you're prepared to deal with challenging moments of choice because you've been practicing supportive driving, you can successfully direct your focus to sympathize with other drivers.

> That poor guy must be in the grip of something, furiously gesturing at me, obviously emotionally unfit to handle road exchanges. I feel nothing but sympathy, wishing him speedy recovery. I'll just continue on my way over here, enjoying the trip. He might be the nicest man for all I know. Driving can bring out the demon. I better watch out myself. I

wonder if my children or wife would do that to someone. It's probably illegal.

By this time, the moment of choice is past and you're out of danger of acting impulsively. It feels good to be smart and safe. Sympathy brings empathy and understanding, and deeper insights into self and others.

> I tried modifying my behavior of retaliating against people who follow too closely by letting tailgaters do whatever they pleased without getting myself involved. Whenever I was tailgated, I would pretend I didn't notice anything, but I moved into the other lane. When they overtook me, I just let them go without a fight. I didn't view this as a sign of weakness, but as a sign of strength, not only because a bigger person always gives in but because I understand where they are coming from. Who knows—maybe the driver wasn't even deliberately tailgating me, but just has an unconscious habit of driving too close to the car in front.
> I was assuming they were tailgating me on purpose without knowing their full intention, which isn't right. I had to keep reminding myself that when I look at them, it's like looking in a mirror at myself. So I hung a tiny picture of myself on my rearview mirror to remind me of it. For me the key to keeping this under self-control is to remember how I feel when I'm tailgated.

A key realization—"I was assuming they were tailgating me on purpose without knowing their full intention, which isn't right"—freed him from the compulsion to pick fights with motorists who followed him too closely. Recognizing this inherited self-subterfuge in his driving persona frees him to feel sympathetic and supportive. This new, positive feeling liberates him from the longtime captivity of angry emotions. There's no anger problem now because he lets it dissipate without fanning it. Rage doesn't build up because he refuses to justify it. He doesn't retaliate because he's not striving for control over others. He's content to stay out of trouble. In fact, he's happy, feeling lucky. With his new, positive orientation of supportive driving, he senses himself as part of the traffic flow, integrated with other drivers, not alienated or competitive but helpful and making a difference. He forgives others when they try to cross him, and those who share his positive orientation respond to him with pleasant smiles and courtesy waves, or simply as law-abiding strangers peacefully going their way. He discovers that a peaceful demeanor is contagious.

COME OUT SWINGING POSITIVE

With billions of angry interactions between motorists every year, it's smart to be prepared with positive strategies to handle them. Hostile tactics will not protect you, while positive strategies effectively disarm a potential aggressor. Being passive by merely ignoring the aggressor does not give you the same power over the outcome as taking charge by influencing the angry driver through positive and supportive acts. To understand this technique you need to contrast the three philosophies that determine how people drive.

Level One: Oppositional driving philosophy involves

- a culture of disrespect on highways ("They're either unfit or stupid, probably born that way.")
- the trigger theory of anger ("They made me do it; it's their fault.")
- oversensitivity to social pressure ("Everybody always gets mad at me")
- intolerance of driver diversity ("They shouldn't be allowed to drive.")
- an aggressive and hostile style ("Don't mess with me!")
- the desire to retaliate or be the enforcer ("You can't let them get away with it or they'll do it again.")
- rebelling against legitimate authority ("Cops just want to make their quotas.")
- feeling alienated ("It's everybody for themselves.")
- breeding the next generation of aggressive drivers ("I can't control myself in front of the kids.")

Level Two: Defensive driving philosophy involves

- treating all drivers the same way ("You must always be wary or suspicious.")
- maintaining a competitive attitude ("It's me against them.")
- stereotypes of drivers and cars ("They're just no good.")
- retaining discriminatory beliefs about the diversity of drivers ("They should be banned.")
- remaining vulnerable to anger and opposition ("They provoked me. I had to let them know.")
- feeling dislocated from the flow of traffic ("They're all in the way.")
- feeling dissatisfied, stressed, and resentful ("They're all selfish people.")

ROAD RAGE AND AGGRESSIVE DRIVING

Level Three: Supportive driving philosophy involves

- a supportive attitude toward other drivers ("Everybody makes mistakes sometimes.")
- tolerance of pluralism ("Everybody has to drive and I support democratic motoring.")
- accommodation to diversity ("They have the right to use the roads.")
- shrinking one's emotional territory ("I refuse to take it personally.")
- feeling integrated with the flow of traffic ("We all have to get through.")
- transforming frustrating traffic into a community-building opportunity ("OK, be my guest.")
- practicing lifelong driver self-improvement ("I use my QDC membership to train myself to safely use those new car gadgets in traffic.")

A man was severely beaten after honking at someone who caught up with him at the next light. It didn't have to happen that way: Realizing his mistake, the honking man could have taken some steps to contain the other driver's road rage. Our natural tendency when challenged is to defend ourselves. Imagine you're involved in a hostile and aggressive exchange with another driver. You yell at one another, acting agitated and combative. You mutually excite each other into an escalating frenzy of anger. You both are emotionally out of control. Now visualize practicing the "attitude of latitude." You know you've gone too far by honking and gesturing, you realize you've aggravated the situation and you want to *reverse the escalation of hostilities.* What do you need to do? Come out swinging positive. Don't deny, don't defend, don't make excuses, don't give reasons. These are all occasions the other can use to escalate the encounter. Instead, come out swinging positive. Adopt an empathetic frame of mind and be apologetic, specifically and loudly declaring your regret about whatever happened. The less you defend yourself and the more you defend the other's ego, the more control you can exercise to defuse the situation. It takes inner power to pull this off, and you can develop it by practicing during less challenging incidents.

A bicyclist bumped a car by mistake and avoided getting into a potential road rage incident by applying a successful de-escalating strategy

I made a bonehead mistake yesterday at a stoplight, trying to squeeze between a Jeep and the curb. Caught my pedal on the curb and fell against the Jeep, just the handle bar end touched and I have plastic ends.

So I thought, no big deal. Light changed and I went on my way. Well, the driver chased me down for a little "talk." I stayed calm told him I was sorry, that I had made a mistake and agreed that yes there was a scuff on his door. Said I believed the scuff would buff out, said I would stay if he wanted to call the police and fill out an accident report. Also informed him that I had no insurance. He calmed down said he wanted me to see what I had done. I said yes I see and I apologize. OK, he drove off. Close one! I felt great and experienced a rush of success with the positive approach.

This bicyclist made emotionally intelligent choices that neutralized a conflict, but another bicyclist sits in jail for being oppositional and giving in to his rage.

A bicyclist, enraged at being knocked off his bike by a car outside Washington, D.C., got up, pulled out a handgun, and shot the driver to death, police said. The bicyclist killed a nineteen-year-old woman, a college student, with a single shot in the head. He ran off on foot but was caught ten minutes later, a Maryland police statement said. "It was senseless. . . . He wasn't even hurt. He was just mad," said an eyewitness. . . . Police said the suspect, a twenty-six-year old man, had been charged with first-degree murder and remanded in custody. The victim's father said his daughter had been headed for class when she was killed. "She was such a peaceable person. . . . I just want to say, my baby is an angel. . . . It's unbelievable. Why, why, why?"[7]

Todd Berger, a psychotherapist specializing in helping people with driving fears and stress, argues that parents need to help plant a sense of highway community in their adolescent children by defining driving as a "social occasion."[8] One exercise he gives problem drivers who are hotheaded, aggressive, and oversensitive involves riding around at leisure practicing an attitude of respect toward fellow drivers. Its purpose is to develop more democratic feelings for others, greater sympathy as well as empathy and awareness. Berger's positive therapy heals the driver's mind from "egotism and the false notion of separateness," using the mind's "Zen power" for self-calming in traffic. In "Zen driving," says Berger, "we do not need a horn." To fight against our "conditioned automatic response patterns" we need to practice "moving meditation"—a Zen awareness that frees the mind from its "incessant inner prattle."[9] The yin and yang of driving, according to Berger, are the "acceptance that all drivers are interconnected and form one body," and the "assertion" of self-confidence in the "ability to maneuver any situation." Real change as a driver comes, according to Berger, when "we begin to feel compassion, the stuff of acceptance." The purpose of Zen driving is to achieve an "inner equilibrium" with the "car-driver-road ecosystem," giving us the ability to synchronize with each other's rhythm, "interconnected with the Whole without losing our individuality."[10] We think that Zen driving would be a good way to prepare oneself for becoming a supportive driver for life.

EXERCISE: RANDOM ACTS OF KINDNESS FOR DRIVERS

Random acts of kindness by drivers is a cultural technology for containing and reversing the habit of road rage and aggressive driving. Nonviolence is the new horizon for the future of driving. By performing random acts of kindness as drivers you're helping to usher in the new age of supportive driving. A sample of acts selected from Dear DrDriving letters in 1999:

> I was in the left lane in a long line of cars. A car in the right lane was stuck behind a slow truck. His blinkers were on but no one let him in. I made space for him by slowing down a little, and he went for it. I saw his wave through his rear window. I felt a warmth.

> I was in the right lane going at speed limit, which is how I like to travel. A car in the left lane was also going at speed limit. We were almost parallel, which makes me feel uncomfortable. The people behind in the left lane must have been upset. There was a long line backed up. So I felt like I shouldn't just ignore their plight. I broke my usual rule and sped up quickly. Those drivers were sure relieved that they could now pass that obstructing driver on the right behind me. I could tell by the way they were zooming past that car in a hurry, then switching back into the left lane. I was happy for them.

> A car was backing out of a parking stall just as I was driving by. I was furious for a second, and felt the impulse of speeding up to it and stopping suddenly to make my tires screech. That should scare him right! But then I calmed myself and approached gradually, staying far enough not to scare or provoke the driver. I felt like I was being good and rational. Nice feeling.

> I don't like to courtesy wave usually. I just can't be bothered when I'm in a bad mood. But today I waved at a man who let me in the fast lane from the middle lane. I noticed he slowed just enough to increase the space ahead of him. I'd been trying to get there for several minutes. I didn't feel like waving, but I made myself anyway. I saw his face in my rear view mirror. He was smiling and nodding in a benign way. It really touched me.[11]

Try the traditional exercise of performing a minimum of one random act of kindness on your next three trips. If you start the trip with this orientation or purpose, opportunities will present themselves. Some acts of kindness take care of urgent needs, such as making entry space for a car that has been ignored by a long line of drivers ahead of you. Other acts of kindness address the small things that make it more convenient or safer for others, like turning your left-hand signal on sooner when you see a car approaching from the opposite direction. And some acts of kindness are hardly remarkable yet have a contagious influence, like wearing a pleasant face when in view of other drivers, pedestrians, or passengers. Notice how you feel as a result of these acts of kindness. Spectacular or hardly visible, acts of kindness are a secret source of good feeling that are mightily effective against those old competitive or aggressive impulses we would rather not have to cope with on top of the traffic congestion.

CHECKLIST: SUPPORTIVE DRIVING AFFIRMATIONS

Though it's natural to experience irate reactions, it wears us down emotionally and physically. The power of positive or prosocial emotions is enormous in its ability to free us from inherited negativity. Each positive statement about your interaction with other drivers is an inner power tool that is effective against normal negativity. These fourteen affirmations are harmonious to a supportive driving style. Which ones appeal to you? Are you willing to make a commitment to adopt some? Are you willing to practice them on a regular basis? They have the power to radically transform your driving philosophy, your style, and your behavior, and hence your safety and enjoyment as a driver.

1. ___ I enjoy making room to let another car into my lane.
2. ___ It makes me happy to slow down so that the other car can merge more easily.
3. ___ I'm careful to leave enough following distance because I want to avoid giving the impression that I'm tailgating.
4. ___ To be more helpful, I like to signal long before I make a turn or switch lanes.
5. ___ To show my appreciation, I wave thanks when a motorist does something nice for me.
6. ___ I reward myself when my thoughts about other drivers are forgiving rather than hostile.
7. ___ I approach pedestrians very slowly in order not to worry them unnecessarily.

8. ___ When it's ambiguous who has the right of way, I wait since it is the polite and safe thing to do.

9. ___ In parking lots I avoid being pushy and aggressive, to give others more of a chance, in case they need the space more than I do. I tell myself, "Someone's always leaving, so I'll get one soon."

10. ___ I make myself care about my passengers when I notice them squirming in fear, and I adjust my driving style to accommodate their comfort level.

11. ___ Whenever I feel a negative emotion against someone in traffic, I immediately reject that attitude and substitute positive feelings and thoughts.

12. ___ When I'm behind the wheel, I keep reminding myself to maintain awareness of my relation to the overall traffic as a willing participant (not rebellious).

Many of us might like to claim, for the sake of our reputation, that we're compassionate and peaceful drivers. But this white-knight reputation is quickly tarnished when we begin systematic self-witnessing behind the wheel. When you think aloud in the car you can actually hear that you're being angry and harsh, more aggressive than you had thought. It's so automatic that we're hardly aware of it. Seeing ourselves in this new light is upsetting, and there's an immediate impulse to want to forget it or take refuge in the idea that everyone else is doing it. It could be dangerous to drive differently from everyone else, right? Yet we realize that our hostile driving persona is unattractive, dangerous, and denigrating. Many of us sense this from time to time, and we're disturbed by it. The happy news is that our traffic emotions are trainable but, like keeping physically fit, it requires discipline to change old habits.

ROAD RAGE AGAINST PASSENGERS

Passenger: "Gasp!"

Driver: "What's your problem?"

Passenger: "You almost hit that car on my side!"

Driver: "Nonsense, I did not."

Passenger: "You didn't even see the car, did you?"

Driver: "Look, I don't need this kind of attack. Just shut up. And thanks, but no thanks!"

Drivers in the grip of road rage wield undue power over their passengers. Some drivers verbally abuse passengers who show fear or discomfort, some simply ignore their passengers' concerns altogether, while others threaten passengers psychologically and physically by driving dangerously. Still others refuse to stop to let passengers get water or food, make phone calls, or use a restroom. And it's an accepted norm that passengers are not to make comments or complaints about how driving bothers, upsets, or scares them. This autocratic power allocation is a form of passenger terrorism, and we believe that it is a human rights violation. A number of desperate wives, girlfriends, and teens write to us about how their "loved ones" terrorize them inside the car. For many drivers it's easy to deny or ignore passengers' complaints about their discomfort—easy because it's a cultural norm we grow up with and imbibe as children, then practice as teenagers and transmit in adulthood.

Being a passenger can be a harrowing experience. Many people have passenger horror stories to tell, such as this from a young woman who was riding with her high school boyfriend:

> Secretly, my boyfriend picked me up early for school. My parents said we weren't supposed to see each other for a while, and he asked me if they said I could go to his birthday party. I told him they said no—they never change their minds. So, he flipped out and went into a rage in the car. Suddenly, he turned us into a cow pasture and went way too fast down the narrow dirt paths. I was terrified, screaming, begging him to slow down, but he kept going fast, cursing my parents. Then the VW Bug skidded and rolled over completely and my head hit the roof hard. I knew no one had seen us and I was afraid I was hurt and couldn't walk. Later, after it was all "taken care of," he didn't even apologize. He said it was my parents' fault and he was even madder at them because he had to repair the car and get me fixed up. I didn't tell my parents, but I should have. They never knew how dangerous he was. I broke up with him because he scared me so much that time. I consider myself lucky to be alive and lucky that he's out of my life, because I'm sure he will do something like that again.

When this young driver heard that he wouldn't get his way, he used his power at the wheel to threaten his passenger's life. How can this happen? Why did he go so far? Surely he "loved" her, but his rage was stronger, so he suspended his love for her when she told him what he didn't want to hear and delivered her a very strong punishment that could have ended in permanent injury or even death.

Drivers who ignore the physical needs of their passengers are more common than you might think. Apparently, many drivers experience a great sense of accomplishment by "making good time" on a trip. It's compelling in the mental driving economy to make a few more miles, to get to the next town, to do so many hours before stopping, to minimize stops for the sake of the clock. It's like a personal contest they need to win. But passengers seldom, if ever, conform to the schedule the driver has in mind. They need to drink, eat, get out and walk around, and go to the restroom much more often than competitive drivers want to allow.

> I started asking him to stop for the restroom about fifteen minutes before I actually felt like I had to go. I do that because my husband always ignores my first three requests. I've timed it and it's usually about a half hour before he stops for me. And I have to beg and plead with him or he ignores me longer. Once he went an hour so we could make Portland when he wanted to. I could barely walk out of the car. I was so afraid I wouldn't make it to the bathroom—I always am. I wonder if he knows I started asking early? I hope not!

The driver placed his desire to control the trip time above his passenger's basic needs and used coercive tactics to have his way. He showed no compassion for his wife, compromised her dignity, made her anxious and worried, humiliated her by forcing her to obey his unreasonable will, and caused her physical discomfort. Why does a person disregard another's need to eliminate? The car is a convenient prison—one can't just leave a moving vehicle. Since drivers control what passengers can do, they have a clear choice to be humane or to be manipulative.

Passengers have a reputation for bothering drivers. A young driver who felt bullied by passengers wrote:

> I think most backseat drivers are just on a control trip. These are passengers who have no physical control over the vehicle but want to assume that control. So they try to control the driver in order to control the vehicle. Backseat drivers always give instructions about where to go, how to drive, when to turn, switch lanes, speed up, brake, etc. They complain when driving is not done to their satisfaction, scold me for neglecting to follow their directions, and pretend that they are afraid of my driving habits. Basically they try to control the car without actually driving it.

It's common to believe that passengers who give instructions, complain, or act fearful should instead be quiet, sit back, relax, enjoy the ride, and be grateful for it. Drivers rarely realize that because of their aggressive driving style, this just isn't possible because their passengers' emotions are involved. Passengers who also drive can find it difficult to ride in a different lane than usual. Their body anticipates every move in traffic and they sometimes act like codrivers. How important is it to cater to a passenger's comforts, down to the lane you occupy or how far ahead to change lanes before an exit? How much power sharing is needed to make driving more democratic?

To be fair, we can't ignore the fact that there are passengers who rage against drivers, as this exchange shows:

> I can't believe you're trying to drive the speed limit, now of all times. It's your fault we left late, and now you don't care if I get to work late. You always do this. Who ever heard of driving the posted speed? This is an expressway, you know! Look at everyone else going 75. They think you're a fool. You should feel ashamed to block traffic. I'm even embarrassed to be seen with you poking along like this. That guy is giving you stink eye! I can't be moving this slow! You'd better speed up and get me there on time or I'll pay you back, and you know I will. This is unacceptable!

Without question, the driver has to be in charge, and passengers are out of line when they interfere with the operation of the vehicle. It may be better to distract unruly riders by helping them focus their attention on a different topic or activity, instead of arguing with them. Drivers who won't compromise in the face of ridicule or pressure to take risks from passengers maintain their integrity as drivers.

> I call myself a safe driver because I avoid unnecessary lane changes and use good judgment. For example, I will not cut someone off or pull out of my lane when I cannot see. I will also not drive fast with other people in the car. I'm committed to obeying all traffic laws even though it means getting grief from my friends. For example, I often get laughed at for refusing to make illegal U-turns. I insist on looking for a safe and legal spot to turn around. I'd also rather park a mile away than park somewhere illegal which could result in a ticket or towing.

The benefits she experiences include:

- Freedom from worry over getting caught making unlawful turns or parking illegally
- Freedom from fear of injuring someone by taking risks
- Freedom from the pressure of competitive driving, jostling for position, frequent lane changes, or running the obstacle course
- Freedom from frantic rushing all the time

Many drivers who have adopted this attitude have told us how delighted they were to discover these new freedoms.

ROAD RAGE AND AGGRESSIVE DRIVING

CHECKLIST: DO YOU SUPPORT PASSENGER RIGHTS IN YOUR CAR?

This checklist can be used from both a driver and a passenger perspective. Go through it twice, once from each perspective and compare the results. How many of these items apply to you as a driver? How many have happened to you as a passenger?

1. ____ I've yelled at passengers when they complained about my driving.
2. ____ I've ignored passengers when they showed signs of discomfort or fear.
3. ____ I've enjoyed scaring passengers with my maneuvers.
4. ____ I insist on choosing the radio station or tape and controlling the volume while I'm at the wheel.
5. ____ I insist on controlling the temperature, the fan setting, and where the vents are aimed while I'm driving.
6. ____ I've denied doing something a passenger saw me do.
7. ____ I've ridiculed passengers for telling me to turn somewhere, even when they were right.
8. ____ I've refused to stop and ask for directions when my passenger tells me to, even when I'm sort of lost.
9. ____ I've insisted on choosing the route and speed when the passenger wants it another way.
10. ____ I've insisted on smoking with the windows up.
11. ____ I've deliberately refused to stop when a passenger asked to use the restroom.
12. ____ I've punished passengers for talking about my driving mistakes.

CHECKLIST: HOW PASSENGER-FRIENDLY ARE YOU?

How many of these items are true of you as a driver?

1. ____ I always consider my passenger's feelings.
2. ____ I adjust my driving to accommodate to my passengers' comfort.
3. ____ I let my passengers influence my driving for the better.
4. ____ I want my passengers to think of me as a good and safe driver.
5. ____ I try to avoid making driving mistakes even more when I have passengers.
6. ____ I think that passengers should just sit back, relax, and leave the driving to me. But if they feel more comfortable participating, I let them if it's safe.

7. ____ My passengers can control the air conditioning and windows.
8. ____ Passengers have the right to criticize the driver's behavior.
9. ____ I want my passengers to be grateful and show appreciation, but if they don't I won't resent it or hold it against them.
10. ____ My passengers can select the music.

EXERCISE: PARTNERSHIP DRIVING

It's normal and expected to experience initial resistance to changing driving philosophy and style. Most people have never even thought about their driving "philosophy." We just don't like to admit that there might be something very wrong with our driving; it's always the other drivers who need to change their attitude and behavior. For instance, 70 percent of drivers complain about the aggressiveness of others, but only 30 percent admit to their own aggressiveness. After witnessing our own road rage habit and hostile attitudes, we may want to change, but lack the will to do it. To resolve this problem, a "partnership" approach to driving self-improvement training utilizes social influence to help us change ingrained habits that are difficult to recognize on our own.[12]

The purpose of this exercise is to develop an objective view of yourself as a driver. It's as revealing as looking in a mirror to see how you appear to others. A driving partner functions as a human "mirror," reflecting what your driving looks like to others. Confronted with an objective view of themselves, many drivers get the shock of their life: "I can't believe that's me!" We recommend switching roles whenever possible, alternating between being the driver and the driving partner. By experiencing the role of driving partner, you can see what it's like to be denied or contradicted by the driver. By repeating the cycle several times or making it into a regular practice, you obtain experience that builds emotional intelligence.

Instructions for the driver:

Before you begin, the driver signs a partnership driving agreement that protects the driving partner. An example:

DESIGNATED DRIVING PARTNER AGREEMENT

1. I, _____, the driver, designate you, _____, the passenger, as my driving partner for this trip: _____
   (date, time, destination)
2. As my driving partner, I authorize you to express yourself freely about my driving, and promise not to retaliate in any way.

3. If I lose my cool and you find that I'm retaliating against you, I agree to compensate you for each incident (*Note*: negotiate and agree upon specific penalties prior to the trip. If appropriate, add it to the bottom of this agreement). You, as my designated driving partner, will make the final decision as to whether or not I retaliated. I agree to abide by your judgment even if it doesn't agree with my vision.

4. I agree that the purpose of designating you as my driving partner is to help me gain objectivity as a driver. This means letting you observe me and comment on my driving in accordance with your perceptions, feelings, and analyses of incidents. This kind of exchange will help me reach my goal of becoming an emotionally intelligent and supportive driver.

5. I thank you for helping me and am grateful to you for it. I'm willing to be your designated driving partner whenever you ask.

Signed: _____ Date: _____

Day One: Ask your driving partner to comment on your driving and give him or her the signed Designated Driving Partner Agreement. Make a commitment to allow your partner complete freedom to react to your driving style. We recommend that you tape record the trip and listen to it together later. Or ask the driving partner to take notes during the trip, and review the notes together for further discussion. We recommend that you also make notes after the trip and discuss those details with your driving partner. All discussions with the driving partner should be directed toward the main purpose of how you can improve your driving in three areas: emotions, thinking, and actions (see chapter 6).

Day Two: Select one of the partner's recommendations and work on it during the second driving session. Recording and note keeping will again facilitate discussion of your behavior during the debriefing session. Ask your driving partner to comment on how well you followed the recommendation and what you can do to improve further. Write a description of the two days and discuss the differences.

- What kinds of resistance did you experience?
- How did the driving partner help you?
- What new awareness did you gain about yourself as a partner?
- What changes will you work on next with your driving partner?

Repeat with other recommendations, one at a time. Partnership driving is an excellent approach for the three-step program described in chapter 6.

Instructions for the passenger:

On Day One, your driving partner drives as usual and you make comments as a passenger on whatever you observe and whatever you feel. Avoid criticizing the driver personally. To be objective, start with yourself in each comment, for example:

- I feel anxious about how fast we're going.
- I would feel more comfortable if you would drive in the right (slower) lane.
- I'm upset about the way you denigrated that driver with negative comments.
- I don't agree with your logic that we should still be in the middle lane now because we need to exit very soon.
- I notice you're driving over the speed limit and I wish you wouldn't.
- It bothers me that you switched lanes without signaling.
- I feel anxious when you take the turn so fast.
- I feel upset when you approach pedestrians so fast.
- I think this music is distracting.
- I'm afraid you're not fully alert right now.
- I keep thinking you're too sleepy to drive right now.

In the meantime, keep encouraging the driver to think out loud. Take notes during the trip as well as after the trip when you discuss the experience. The goal to achieve on Day One is to have you, the passenger, react freely and frequently, and for the driver to be merely exposed to your feedback without fighting back, feeling criticized, or getting into a bad mood.

On Day Two, for the duration of the trip, the driver agrees to drive according to one of your recommendations. Keep the focus on a single behavior. Later, as you gain experience and cooperation and the two of you work well together as a team, you can focus on more than one item. Keep encouraging the driver to think aloud, for example

- What are your thoughts right now?
- Are you upset at that driver?
- Do you feel very impatient right now?
- How do you explain that?
- What would you rather do?
- Do you think it's going to upset him?
- Do you care if he gets there before you do?
- On a scale of 1 to 10, how frustrated do you feel right now?
- How would you phrase this principle you believe in?
- On a scale of 1 to 10, how important is it to do that (or not to do that)? **187**

ROAD RAGE AND AGGRESSIVE DRIVING

Take notes during the trip and after, following the debriefing session. Write a description of the two days and discuss the differences. Focus on resistance to change and how it affects you, for example:

> I'm not comfortable with your driving and it often scares me. You could be more considerate to your passengers. When I complained you quickly brought to my attention the many times that I happened to lose my temper, and I admitted that I have lost control at times, and I always try to change the situation by acknowledging that I'm being inconsiderate or hostile. But when I try to bring up things about your driving, you just insist that your anger is justified.

Driving partners influence each other by giving alternative justifications or philosophies:

Driver: I don't know. Sometimes I like to be angry and mentally torture other drivers. I makes me happy.

Partner: To be happy being angry is logically impossible. The whole reason you're angry is because you're *not* happy. So it doesn't make sense for you to be happy with rage. Saying you're happy is just an excuse for not dealing with the real issue of taking a look at yourself. By saying you're happy, you're trying to justify your anger as harmless. But it still hurts your immune system.

From a debriefing session:

Driver: I tailgate because other people make me do it. I usually start out in a good mood until someone puts me in a bad mood.

Partner: I noticed you get much more aggressive when you're in a hurry, but it's a problem all the time. I think you feel a conflict about letting others just go. You don't want anyone to get the best of you. I see you weaving through traffic, changing lanes without signaling, speeding, and tailgating other cars over and over. Each time I bring it up you say it's not your fault because you have to drive that way whenever the other people are driving aggressively. While we were waiting at one red light you said, "I should've gone instead of waiting at this light." Another time you insisted on taking a detour to try to beat a light.

Several weeks later the social influence of the partnership driving team began to have an effect on this driver:

When she was stopped at a red light, she reminded herself that it wouldn't make much of a time difference by waiting. At one point when a driver cut in a bit close, she at first started cussing but then recovered herself and said, "Oh, well, he's probably afraid to miss the off-ramp exit. Bon voyage!" She still has the tendency to attack other drivers when they upset her, but she shows more awareness of the implications of her negative habit. She still had a hard time remembering to signal every time she wanted to change lanes or make a turn. I advised her to use post-it-notes on the dashboard as a reminder. Best of all, I think, is the way she felt better at the end of the trip. She's beginning to realize that it's easier and more fun to give up some of her usual driving intensity.

Partnership driving reports written by people who tried it can be found on our Web site.[13]

NOTES

1. Personal anecdotes quoted throughout this chapter were sent to us by e-mail correspondents.

2. National Motorists Association, "NMA's Seven Sensible Signals" [online], www.motorists.org/issues/safety/seven_signals.html [May 20, 2000].

3. "Drivers Supposed to Be Nice to Each Other Today," CNN.com, October 7, 1995 [online], www.cnn.com/WORLD/fringe/9510/10-07/index.html [May 20, 2000].

4. Leon James, Diane Nahl, and Richard Kirby, "Youth Against Road Rage (YARR)," DrDriving.org [online], www.aloha.net/~dyc/yarr [May 20, 2000].

5. Envoy Vehicle Courtesy System Web site, www.envoyusa.com [May 20, 2000].

6. William Beatty, "Traffic Waves: Physics for Bored Commuters" [online], www.eskimo.com/~billb/amateur/traffic/traffic1.html [May 20, 2000].

7. "Apo sa tuhod," October 9, 1997 [online], members.tripod.com/New Vizcaya/joy.htm [May 20, 2000].

8. K. T. Berger, *Zen Driving* (New York: Ballantine Books, 1998); we also recommend an audiocassette by Allen Liles, *The Peaceful Driver: Steering Clear of Road Rage* (Unity Village, Mo.: Unity House, 1999).

9. Ibid., pp. 31–73.

10. Ibid., p. 148.

11. "Random Acts of Kindness by Drivers," DrDriving.org [online], DriveAloha.com [May 20, 2000].

12. Leon James and Diane Nahl, "Partnership Driving," DrDriving.org [online], www.aloha.net/~dyc/partner.html [May 20, 2000].

13. Ibid.

9 –

LIFELONG DRIVER EDUCATION

TEENAGERS AT RISK

Teach teenagers in high school driver's education class how to be non-aggressive. Show them plenty of videos of fatal car accidents with the blood and gore that was caused by aggressiveness behind the wheel.[1]

Most adolescents look forward to getting a driver's license. But the love affair between teenagers and cars is often deadly. Car crashes kill more young people fifteen to twenty years old than any other cause. About 14 percent (8,054) of drivers involved in fatal crashes in 1996 were in that age group. Most of the fatalities of inexperienced sixteen-year-old drivers are the result of driver error (eight out of ten crashes).[2] According to the National Highway Traffic Safety Administration, a sixteen-year-old driver is 42 percent more likely to be involved in a crash than a seventeen-year-old, who has just one additional year of driving experience. In 1996, sixteen-year-old drivers were involved in 10,337 crashes, while the crash rate was two-thirds less for seventeen-year-olds (3,229). Parents are right to be concerned about these alarming statistics, since nearly half of the sixteen-year-olds in the United States are licensed drivers.

Besides inexperience in handling emergencies, young drivers often engage in more risky behaviors. Research sponsored by the International Association for Accident and Traffic Medicine (IAATM) shows that inexperience combines with immaturity and risky driving practices to increase the fatal crashes of sixteen-year-old drivers. Researchers examined the nighttime fatal crashes of sixteen-year-old drivers in California between 1989–1994 using police reports and newspaper accounts.[3] The data indicate that the crashes of sixteen-year-olds are more often single-vehicle events, more likely to result from driver error, and involve speeding and higher passenger occupancy rates (often other teenagers).

In response to the appalling statistics and the mounting concern over teen drivers, many states and some countries have instituted a graduated licensing approach that provides for several licensing phases: learner's permit, intermediate or provisional license, and then full license. A graduated licensing system supervises young, novice drivers in progressively more difficult motoring experiences at a controlled pace. Proponents believe that the more supervised practice teen drivers obtain the more experience they gain, so it is less likely they will be involved in a crash. Since young people typically have difficulty resisting peer influence to take risks and show bravado, proponents also hope more supervision will help build safer attitudes. Restrictions may include:

- Six months of crash-free, citation-free driving
- Zero tolerance for alcohol
- No driving between midnight and 6:00 A.M. without authorization
- Color-coded provisional driver's licenses
- Successful completion of a driver education course

During the permit stage, at age fifteen or sixteen, young drivers must be supervised by an adult, pass a driver education course, and remain citation free to proceed to the next level. The provisional or intermediate license includes on-road testing and a requirement to remain citation-free for the license period. Other restrictions often apply, such as more supervised driving and a curfew or prohibition against late-night driving. The third stage of full licensing occurs after successful completion of the first two stages and includes a zero-tolerance alcohol law. After New Zealand adopted a graduated licensing system, studies showed that the injury and fatality rate among young drivers decreased. By 1999, twenty states had enacted some form of graduated licensing.[4]

ROAD RAGE AND AGGRESSIVE DRIVING

Clearly, the need for driver education is high especially among teens, yet states rarely require it or fund it at insufficient levels. Driving courses are seldom available in public schools, and those that offer courses cannot meet the demand. Private driving schools often service the courts as a form of reeducation or rehabilitation for driving offenses. Officials frequently comment that the weakening of society's resolve to deliver driver education knowledge is associated with the worsening driving environment. The American Driver and Traffic Safety Association believes that the majority of drivers are rude, simply ignoring traffic rules. In the 1970s, 90 percent of people took driver education courses, in contrast with 35 percent today:

> Driving instructors say it's hard to preach proper driving when so few practice it. In a survey of more than 1,000 adults, the consumer coalition found that 64 percent believed people are driving much less courteously and safely than five years ago. The solutions they offered include more driver education, warnings or tickets from law enforcement officers and refresher driving courses for all adults similar to those required in some states for senior citizens.[5]

In addition to teaching their kids to drive skillfully and appropriately, parents can take steps to help prevent or reduce the number of crashes involving teen drivers:

> We need to target children aged 11–15 for education, and follow up with kids later—they are learning aggressive driving behavior from day one, even from parents who only get angry occasionally. Parents have to tell their kids at a young age that they are wrong when they overreact to mistakes made by other drivers. We all need to remember and recognize that everyone makes mistakes sometimes—assume that the person who angers you either didn't do it on purpose, or is a misguided soul who should be pitied, not hated.

For example, parents can:

- Supervise teens' driving time
- Give teens sufficient supervised practice during the learner's permit period and throughout the first year of licensed driving
- Put a limit on the number of passengers allowed
- Limit teens' driving during periods of increased risk such as weekends and particular holidays such as New Year's Eve
- Establish a curfew
- Insist that teens and passengers wear safety belts
- Set limits on the areas and locales where teens are permitted to drive

- Prohibit teens from driving under the influence of drugs or alcohol
- Encourage teens to use good judgment both as drivers and as passengers
- Be a good role model as a driver

The potential for a crash can heighten with aggressive driving, driver inexperience, and inappropriate interaction with passengers. Along with parent supervision, graduated licensing allows initial driving experience to accumulate under less hazardous conditions, and prohibits recreational nighttime driving that has proven to be particularly dangerous for young, beginning drivers. Driving instructors are aware that teenagers often lack the ability to exercise rational control over their behavior when driving a vehicle in a reckless manner. Today's more complex driving conditions demand that traditional driver education be redesigned to incorporate judgement and self-control in addition to the rules of the road and handling techniques.

DRIVER-ZED

The AAA Foundation for Traffic Safety created the driver-ZED program. The project was broadly supported by the American Automobile Association (AAA) and the Canadian Automobile Association (CAA) through their affiliated motor clubs, and by thousands of individual AAA members and affiliated insurance companies. The foundation developed this new program in response to "a serious need for better training of teen drivers—sixteen-year-olds have 20 times the number of crashes per mile as the average driver."[6] The interactive CD-ROM program focuses on teaching appropriate risk management. Their Web site states that "driver-ZED™ has now been evaluated under real driving conditions and has been shown to produce statistically significant improvements in the risk management skills of young teen drivers."[7]

What kind of driver training would reduce or eliminate the aggressive driving problem? In testimony before Congress in 1997, Dr. John Larson (consultant for driver-ZED) declared that "curing road rage and stopping aggressive driving practices is possible within the next five years, if a vigorous program is instituted to teaching five alternative beliefs to those currently held by aggressive drivers."[8] The beliefs that make drivers act aggressively include:

- The fastest possible traveling time is the most desirable.
- Driving competitively, and not losing in incidents, is a self-esteem issue.

- Rude drivers need to be opposed or thwarted in their forward progress.
- Drivers who don't fit the right profile are irritating and deserve to be ridiculed.
- Drivers who endanger us or insult us should be punished with some form of retaliation.

Dr. Larson believes that in order to cure aggressive driving we need to eliminate these faulty beliefs and their underlying attitudes. Since their negativity is "fostered by our culture" it is necessary to create a new set of positive driving beliefs. Dr. Larson conducted one-day seminars in 1997 in collaboration with the AAA Foundation for Traffic Safety and AAA chapters in Connecticut, and reported that some participants improved their beliefs and attitudes as a result.[9] At the same time he urged law enforcement to focus on the "more subtle" aggressive driving violations such as not signaling, not yielding, following too close, and making obscene gestures.

Throughout this century we have relied on the traditional driver education approach of teaching and testing safety knowledge, while hoping to instill responsibility. Affective driver education remained on the back burner of the driver education curriculum during the past three decades while aggressive driving and road rage were seething below the surface. Society is sensitized to the cultural inroads of general disrespect that are expressed daily in aggressive driving practices. In response to this new awareness, a new driver education paradigm has stimulated the creation of the Novice Driver Education Model Curriculum Outline sponsored by the AAA Foundation for Traffic Safety and authored by a panel of experts.[10] The intent of the project was to "reinvent driver education into a form that reduces crashes by novice drivers":

> Curriculum time and space are needed for shifting DE's focus toward motivation, and more efficient teaching of abilities could help provide this time. It will remove teachers from the more mechanical parts of the training and allow them to concentrate on facilitating development of motivation and responsibility.
>
> What drivers are able to do and what they choose to do are two different things. Knowledge of how to control a car is not as critical to safety as individual motivation: Strong motivation makes up for weak skills better than strong skills make up for weak motivation. Without strong motivation to reduce risk, advanced skills training can lead to more crashes, not fewer.[11]

Motivation and responsibility are essential components of affective education. The new paradigm in driver education shifts the focus from just safety knowledge to a more integrated driver education that imparts affective or emotional skills. There is a new recognition that training traffic emotions is both possible and necessary. This focus on the importance of values looks toward a new philosophy of driving that is community oriented rather than individual centered.

> The most critical areas of integration are personal and social values, risk-taking, self-esteem, feelings of power, sense of community, and interest in health. These feelings motivate pro-social and self-protective behaviors. Participation in peer group learning activities can help integrate safety-promoting values into all areas of students' lives.[12]

Driver education can alert people to the personality factors that tend to take over our style of operating a vehicle: our self-esteem or a sense of personal power, our prudence or riskiness, our competitiveness or sense of community support. Since these personal traits stem from the cultural norms and social values in society, it's important to employ a social style of driver instruction that enables students to influence each other through dialog and modeling. One particularly noteworthy recommendation of the new driver education approach is to "expand the integration of driver education topics into other school subjects, particularly health, community service, and other values-related activities."[13] This statement recognizes that driving is not an isolated activity done alone, and that it is part of our general values and character and our culture.

DRIVING PSYCHOLOGY CURRICULUM

When the federal government stepped up its involvement in aggressive driving initiatives, legislation, and research in 1997, we proposed a Lifelong Driver Education framework in congressional hearings.[14] There is a new readiness in the nation's judiciary system to play a more significant role in driver supervision and retraining. The stick is the presence of new aggressive driving laws that increase misdemeanors to felonies, and the carrot is supplemental driver training as an alternative to going to jail and receiving points on their licenses from citations. The *RoadRageous* self-study video course, described later in this chapter, exemplifies the new focus on social responsibility and conscience in driver education, and is used in Florida.

> In addition to assessing fines, Miami-Dade judges may now order repeat traffic offenders to attend an eight-hour class on how to curb antisocial behavior on the highways, said Chief Circuit Judge Joseph Farina. The Florida Highway Patrol wants the Legislature to define aggressive

195

driving, make it a crime and establish penalties. If that happens, courses such as *RoadRageous* could pop up statewide. The course is a turbo-charged version of defensive-driving classes offered nationally for people with reasonably clean records who get tickets. If people opt to take those four-hour classes to brush up on their driving skills, their driving records do not collect points that could raise their insurance rates.[15]

Since we acquire aggressive driving attitudes riding in our parents' cars, lifelong driver education makes sense. Lifelong driver education creates a K–12 curriculum that formalizes, augments, and transforms the current informal negative training into positive concepts and standards.

A lifelong driver education curriculum must employ findings from psychology about human development, that is, that development proceeds according to learning phases during which appropriate instruction can be effectively delivered.[16] The new driver education curriculum ought to be a *driving psychology* curriculum because the entire personality of the individual is involved in driving. According to our research, driving behavior involves the three basic aspects of personality:

- affective—the driver's feelings, emotions, attitudes, and values
- cognitive—the driver's thoughts, judgment, and knowledge
- sensorimotor—the driver's vision, motor reactions, fatigue, stress, and pain

These three aspects of our driving personality jointly determine driving behavior, so it's important to assess each of the three areas. Good driving requires that we engage in an endless task of preventing overt mistakes and suppressing irrational decisions. Since they are the source of irrational judgments and costly mistakes, we have to understand our traffic emotions.

In general, a focus on "affective instruction" is effective in the early years, introducing basic attitudes of sociality such as obedience, respect, and conscience. This is followed by a focus on "cognitive instruction" in the middle years, involving reasoning, decision making, and problem solving. There is a continued focus on emotions and attitudes on the road to reinforce the early education focus and to raise it to its appropriate cognitive level. In the midteens "sensorimotor instruction" begins. This teaches how to maneuver a vehicle on public roads. Teens are also taught cognitive knowledge of traffic laws and scenario analysis of driving incidents. The new curriculum strengthens these areas and includes a strong affective component that focuses on social responsibility, human rights, and emotional intelligence. The practical focus is teaching that the driver's prime directive is to remain in control of the vehicle as well as the situation.

Affective driving skills are taught first because they establish the attitudes behind the wheel that stem from the motivational and socioemotional system. Traffic emotions govern our competitiveness and aggressiveness, as well as our peacefulness, optimism, and compassion. Our thinking follows from our attitudes and motives. Since we think in conformity with how we feel, negative feelings promote pessimistic thoughts. Our actions are the consequences of the attitudes we maintain and the thoughts we entertain. Driving is mostly accomplished by relying on automatic habits that interact in these three areas of our driving personality. Obviously, a complete change of driving habits requires a lifetime involvement. This extended quality of continuing driver education is necessary to help people adapt to the ever-increasing complexity of congested driving and the new devices used in moving vehicles, such as cell phones, computers, entertainment systems, GPS systems, and Internet access. Each new generation needs to be taught the three aspects of a driver's personality according to the natural developmental order of human growth, at the appropriate age level. The following are model instructional objectives for driver personality development in the three domains of behavior.

Kindergarten and Elementary School: Focus on Affective Driving Skills

This early component uses age-appropriate cognitive explanations and sensorimotor demonstrations to teach these affective skills. Students will learn:

- How we create stress for drivers by our behavior in and around cars
- To observe our natural competitiveness for space and how to voluntarily reduce it
- To become aware of our anger in disputes about public spaces and right of way, how we express it, how it influences others, what its health consequences are, and how to defuse it
- To avoid learned aggression by analyzing television scenes of drivers behaving badly and getting away with it
- To practice learned optimism as pedestrians, passengers, and road users by formulating positive assumptions and outcomes
- To activate natural feelings of compassion and sympathy for the basic rights and needs of strangers in public places, and to appreciate community feelings
- To practice self-witnessing activities as passengers with parents in cars

ROAD RAGE AND AGGRESSIVE DRIVING

- To practice self-witnessing activities as pedestrians and in other road uses
- To practice group discussions on civility and human rights in road situations

Middle School: Focus on Cognitive Driving Skills

This component incorporates an age-appropriate review of the affective skills and their extension to these cognitive skills with sensorimotor demonstrations. Students will learn:

- What principles are safest for children as passengers, pedestrians, and cyclists
- To become more aware of habits of thinking while walking or riding
- To develop objective judgment about strangers' behavior
- To develop emotional intelligence as drivers, passengers, and pedestrians
- To critically analyze driving incidents (scenario analysis) by focusing on identifying choice points (how to prevent or break the chain of errors that leads to catastrophe)
- To acknowledge the human rights of all drivers
- To acknowledge passengers' rights (their convenience, comfort, and safety)
- To acknowledge pedestrian rights (why they must have the right of way)
- To acknowledge the rights of bicycle riders and how to behave near them
- To acknowledge the rights of truck drivers, the need for truck deliveries, and how to behave near them
- To practice group discussions on the importance of civility in public behavior (respecting mutual rights, inalienable rights, fairness, character, community, and so forth)
- To be able to defend the ideal of social responsibility in public places
- To recognize the benefits and rewards of being supportive and positive
- To practice self-witnessing activities as passengers
- To practice self-witnessing activities as pedestrians and other road uses

High School: Focus on Sensorimotor Driving Skills

This component uses an age-appropriate review of the affective and cognitive skills and their extension to these sensorimotor skills. Students will learn:

- To practice hands-on coordination skills with a driving simulator and supervised highway experience
- To practice self-witnessing and self-regulation techniques for acquiring automotive discipline skills (see the three-step program in chapter 6)
- To develop ability to monitor and control one's risk-taking tendency under various driving circumstances
- To stay alert by acquiring attentional checking routines
- To be prepared in handling emergencies (performing appropriate safety principles under emotionally challenging conditions)
- To be prepared in handling aggressive drivers or road users (performing emotionally intelligent strategies)
- To practice appropriate and effective driver-to-driver communication by learning to control facial rage, observing local driving norms, performing random acts of kindness, and practicing supportive rather than aggressive driving strategies
- To train for multitasking (phone, dashboard dining, children, e-mail, online communication, and so on)
- To practice basic driving exercises within a group context as preparation for QDC membership (see below)
- To act with appreciation and cooperation toward traffic law enforcement and education

There may be a concern about adding another layer to the school curriculum, but the need for driving psychology cannot be questioned. There may be an opportunity to consolidate current efforts in traffic safety, nonviolent conflict resolution, and self science programs with the new driving psychology curriculum—all under the rubric of emotional intelligence training. But it's clear that driving must be addressed explicitly at all levels of education.

POST LICENSING: THE QDC APPROACH

In addition to graduated licensing and the new K–12 driving psychology curriculum described above, adult drivers need continuing training through Quality Driving Circles (QDCs). QDCs are voluntary groups of two to ten drivers who meet regularly to help and encourage one another to follow a driving self-improvement program. Some drivers have sufficient motivation to accomplish this on their own, but in our experience the majority of drivers do not. Consider the case of dieting and losing weight. A few can do it on their own and stay trim, fit, and healthy for years afterward, but the majority of Americans are overweight and spend billions each year on methods to stay trim. Support groups increase the likelihood that change will be successful. Most drivers need a social and instructional support group to maintain a lifelong motivation for self-improvement activities, such as:

- Performing self-witnessing procedures to get to know themselves objectively as drivers (see chapter 5)
- Keeping a driving log, journal, diary, or other systematic driving record on a long-term basis
- Understanding cultural road rage and how it's transmitted to the next generation
- Counteracting learned cynicism and pessimism with learned optimism and understanding its relation to health
- Learning emotional intelligence through scenario analysis of driving incidents and identifying choice points in decision making
- Practicing a supportive driving style and experiencing its benefits
- Training themselves for safe multitasking (talking on the phone, eating, reading GPS screens, checking email, and so forth)
- Keeping up with new driving and automotive information (new gadgets, laws, surveys, safety studies, QDC databases and training techniques developed in other QDC groups)

QDCs are inexpensive instructional delivery mechanisms for all aspects of driving psychology and driver training in both private and commercial settings. Currently, QDCs exist only in experimental groups of traffic psychology students.[17] As driving density and complexity increase while injuries and fatalities remain high, we will need to develop greater skill in the driving population. We foresee a future where skill-based license renewal will be required and will include QDC participation as an inexpensive and powerful delivery mechanism for universal and lifelong driver education.

QDCs can be face-to-face or virtual. Face-to-face QDCs can be physically based in the family, neighborhood, or workplace. Virtual QDCs are asynchronous telephone, Internet, or Web-based interactive experiences.[18] Members are not physically or temporally present but communicate on the telephone or electronically through e-mail, Web forums and bulletin boards, online discussion groups, online chat rooms, and the like. There are many other natural groupings.

- Dyadic QDCs are easy to set up between a driver and regular passengers, such as car pool mates or regular driving partners (see chapter 8).
- Family QDCs promote safe and supportive driving attitudes in children, teenagers, and adults.
- Court-mandated QDCs for motivating and supervising problem drivers (see the *RoadRageous* course, below).
- School QDCs group younger and older children together, so that there is a positive generational influence and connection, and help prepare the next generation of drivers to accept and support QDC membership as a lifelong involvement.[19]
- Professional QDCs for drivers of commercial fleet vehicles, trucks, and police and emergency vehicles would reduce accident rates, citations, and costs for companies and government agencies.[20]
- Senior QDCs for older drivers would promote greater safety.[21]

It's important to meet regularly and keep attendance to motivate members not to skip. Prizes, diplomas, awards, and commendations may also help keep members involved. A rotating chair calls meetings and safeguards records for a determined period. There is no limit to how long a QDC may continue. Eventually, national and local QDC conferences, newsletters, and databases may arise. We predict that the second century of car society will not end before QDCs will be part of the normal lifelong career of every driver in industrialized countries.

We developed the following instructional tools for QDC curriculum:

- TEE-Cards for traffic emotions education[22]
- *RoadRageous* video course (see description in the next section)[23]
- Activity sheets for driving personality makeovers
- Self-assessment surveys for monitoring driving style
- Checklists of driving behaviors for easy tracking (throughout this book)
- Logs or diaries to record self-witnessing observations
- Reminder cards to guide trip-by-trip planned exercises
- Audio tapes to facilitate safe behind the wheel exercises
- Fact sheets on driving statistics, news, and alerts
- Partnership Driving Agreement forms (see chapter 8), and other help-each-other arrangements
- Scenario analysis of road rage incidents in the media to teach emotionally intelligent decision making (see chapter 5)

ROAD RAGE AND AGGRESSIVE DRIVING

- Games, skits, and musicals to teach driving psychology principles
- CARRtoons and instructional vignettes[24]
- Safe activities to do with children in the car (see chapter 7)
- Diplomas, awards, and commendations for encouragement[25]

QDCs are reeducation mechanisms that promote a value shift to enable the change from aggressive driving to supportive driving. They also promise to be the best source of continuous data for tracking the level and intensity of aggressive driving. Trained volunteers tape or video record themselves in traffic and later tabulate the data, using standard checklists to track the presence or absence and the intensity of particular emotions. These real-time data would be a measure of the level of aggressiveness or stress that drivers regularly experience on particular stretches of road.

ROADRAGEOUS VIDEO COURSE

We created a novel driver education course called *RoadRageous*, co-authored with well-known road rage therapist Dr. Arnold Nerenberg. To our knowledge, this is the first driver education course designed to teach drivers the behavioral self-modification techniques they need to implement a lifelong driver self-improvement program. Traditional driver education courses include portions explaining the importance of attitude in driving, but the difference in the new curriculum is a focus on problem solving and developing emotional self-control and a sense of community. Everyone knows that attitude is important because parents tell their teenagers, teachers tell their students, police officers tell children and motorists, government officials advise the public, and safety managers tell their fleet drivers. But research and experience show that it's not sufficient to merely tell drivers to have good attitudes. In addition to good intention, they need techniques to achieve or evolve better attitudes, especially when it's "natural" to behave badly. The course highlights and strengthens the ten basic "inner skills" drivers need in order to become "driving literate" today (see Table 9.1).

The video course teaches the three-step program (see chapter 6), a behavioral method for "learning to learn" new driving skills. Driving literacy is the ability to continuously learn new driving skills in the face of congestion and ever more demanding complexities of dashboard electronics and global telecommunications in vehicles. This prototype course involves learners in activating their "driving conscience," teaching them how to think analytically while driving, how to develop greater awareness

Table 9.1
Objectives Emphasized by the *RoadRageous* Video Course

Affective objectives	Cognitive objectives
1. To strengthen the desire for lifelong driver self-improvement.	1. To understand why it's necessary for drivers to develop inner standards of behavior.
2. To neutralize or weaken existing negative driving attitudes.	2. To understand what aggressive driving is and how to assess one's aggressiveness as a driver.
3. To strengthen and inculcate positive driving values.	3. To learn to critically analyze traffic situations and events in order to identify emotional intelligence choice points where drivers could have acted differently for a better result.
4. To learn how to transform self-centered goals into highway community goals through activities that weaken identification with aggressive models and strengthen identification with supportive driving models.	4. To practice driver self-assessment and self-improvement activities, including keeping a driving log and collecting self-observational data.
5. To prepare drivers to deal effectively with aggressiveness or provocation by other drivers with their own aggressiveness and road rage.	5. To understand the basic facts about and solutions to impaired driving (DUI, anger, advancing age, inexperience, and drugs and medication).

of thoughts and emotions behind the wheel, and how to monitor actions. Drivers utilize their data to design and create new driving personalities that are supportive instead of aggressive. The course takes a few hours to complete, but provides follow-up exercises and activities useful for an entire driving career. The course is also suitable for law enforcement and commercial drivers since they need to understand the driving psychology of motorists as well as themselves as professional drivers.[26]

Our research shows that most people behind the wheel aren't clearly aware of their own mental state, including being in a bad mood, feeling tense, overreacting emotionally, and carrying on a constant mental stream of thinking critically of other drivers: ridiculing them, cussing at them, even torturing them in fantasy. Self-witnessing yourself behind the wheel is therefore a necessary step in driver self-improvement. Most people are not used to closely observing their thinking, and it's important to stress that it takes time and effort to succeed. It is not easy to overcome resistance to making the mental effort in the middle of a busy day. Nevertheless, this is what's required for change, safety, and sanity.

One way to begin is to examine in detail the thought sequence involved in a road rage exchange, especially to identify the decision points of the protagonists—where they could still back out of the sequence of choices leading to the tragic end point. The following Traffic Emotions Education (TEE) card illustrates the critical thinking process with a real-world road rage event.[27]

ROAD RAGE AND AGGRESSIVE DRIVING

Instructions: First read the entire news story in the left hand column. Then read the comments on the right, going back to the story to examine the elements being discussed.

Road Rage Shoot Out

A hit-and-run "gone terribly wrong" was how sheriff's officials described a fender-bender between two pickup truck drivers that ended in a shootout Thursday night in northeast El Paso County. One man was killed. The other remained at Penrose Hospital on Friday with a gunshot wound to the abdomen.

The shooting stemmed from a crash that occurred about 7:30 p.m. Thursday on Powers Boulevard just south of Stetson Hills Boulevard. The man in the red Dodge Dakota was "driving erratically" when he bumped Bispo's blue Ford pickup, Hilte said.

The Dakota driver then wheeled around Bispo's Ford and sped north on Powers Boulevard, Hilte said. Bispo, a civilian employee at Fort Carson, followed as the driver turned east onto Dublin Boulevard and parked on the shoulder.

"He pulled over about a car length back, and it just went bad from there," Hilte said. Both men got out of their vehicles wielding handguns.

Words were exchanged.

Shots were fired.

Blood was spilled. Bispo's girlfriend was still on the phone with 911 dispatchers when the shooting started. On-scene investigators found about a dozen shell casings—two from the Dakota driver's revolver, the rest from Bispo's 9 mm semi-automatic pistol.

While enlisted in the Army, Bispo qualified as a sharpshooter with an M-1 rifle, according to military records. The Dakota driver died of a gunshot wound to the chest shortly after the shooting. Neither driver was licensed to carry a concealed weapon.

These two drivers got into a road dispute, the result: one is dead, the other was wounded and faces serious charges. It has happened hundreds of times this year, where one driver ends up dead, while another is facing homicide charges. The one who killed had not planned to do so. Could this happen to you? The fact is that most of the "killers" in road rage disputes were taken by surprise at the ferocity of their own over-reaction.

Notice these elements in the newspaper story on the left:

The first driver was driving in an alcohol impaired state. He chose to do so, which led to the next event.

The first driver left the scene of the crash after causing a fender bender with a second car. He chose to do so, which led to the next event.

The second driver went in pursuit to obtain the license number. Pursuing another vehicle is dangerous and illegal. But the driver had a second motive: to confront the fleeing driver. Evidence: he did not just get the license number. He chose to stop, when he could have just driven off after getting the plate number, which led to the next event.

The first driver chose to stop. This may have been an attempt to confront the second driver, or something else. We do not know. The second driver saw this, and he did not know either.

The second driver chose to stop behind the first car. This then set up the next event. If he had not stopped, or if he had stopped some distance away, the first driver may still be alive.

The second driver chose to approach the first car, or at least, chose to exit his car, which led to the next event. He could have stayed in the truck and waited for police to arrive.

The second driver also chose to exit his car with a weapon. This weapon was visible to the first driver, which led to the next event.

The first driver chose to shoot, which led to the next event. If he had not started to shoot, he might still be alive today.

The second driver chose to shoot back. The first driver was hit and died.

In these 9 steps, each driver had several opportunities to back down and to choose not to make the next move that led to disaster. Is this a road rage case? Yes, because it involves two drivers making a series of escalating moves that lead to a violent exchange, when either one of them could have broken the deadly duel by not going along with the next violent step in the series of decisions to act. Remember: it takes an unbroken series of links in a long chain of bad choices to get into a road rage shootout.

EXERCISE: SCENARIO ANALYSIS TO DEVELOP CRITICAL THINKING

Dear Dr. Driving,

I'm a 16-year-old boy and I was driving in tandem with a friend who is unfamiliar with driving in that area and on the freeway. It was almost midnight and we were driving to our homes. A friend from work invited us to a party, but we couldn't find his place so we drove back. I lost the address and all we did was drive around, then started to go home. We did not have anything to drink and nobody had taken any drugs.

We got onto the freeway and while we were driving, a black SUV pulled up really fast and close behind my friend, who was in the center lane. I was in the left lane and wanted to stay close to my friend so he would not get lost. The SUV swerved around my friend's car to the slow lane and went past really fast. He started to swerve around all the other cars ahead of us and we thought he was gone.

A little bit later he was held up in the traffic and my friend and I were both in the left lane and passed him. My friend and I had to change to another freeway that had only two lanes for a while. The SUV took the same exit and my friend and I thought it was funny that he was behind us and we slowed down in both of the lanes (stupid plan). He pulled up behind me and then behind my friend and began pointing a gun. We got really scared and did everything we could to get away. He followed us really fast but never tried to pass us. This went on for miles. We were all swerving through traffic. I think I was driving about 90 miles an hour. Sometimes we thought he was gone and then we would see that he was just kind of hiding behind other cars. We got close to our exit and I started to flash my lights and honk at my friend so that he knew to take the exit. When we took the exit we saw the SUV follow us then pull over on the off-ramp.

When we got onto the road we were met by lots of police cars. We ended up with tickets for reckless driving and we are going to plead not guilty. We think that this driver did something illegal and could have caused an accident. We know that we were stupid and added to the problem but we think that he's an adult and he was the one who was making it into a battle. What do you think? Do you have any suggestions how to handle this? Thanks.

Table 9.2 identifies the specific chain of steps that together make up this road rage incident. There are thirteen bad driving behaviors these two teenagers performed in sequence, as evidenced by their own description of the events (middle column). Your comments should answer two questions: (a) How does each step contribute to their trouble? and (b) How could they have backed out of it at each step by doing something else? Have your

Table 9.2
Scenario Analysis of a Teenager's Unrecognized Road Rage Behavior

Emotionally challenged behavior	Segment from letter	How does each step contribute to trouble?	What would be smarter behavior?
1. Playing games on the highway	"I'm a 16-year-old boy and I was **driving in tandem** with a friend."		
2. Driving after curfew	"It was **almost midnight**"		
3. Losing the address but going anyway	"I **lost the address** and all we did was drive around, then started to go home."		
4. Driving abreast occupying the center lane and the left (fast) lane	"I was in the left lane and **wanted to stay close to my friend** . . . ," who was in the center lane.		
5. Blocking the way so the SUV had to pass in the right (slow) lane	". . . SUV pulled up really fast and close behind **my friend, who was in the center lane**."		
6. Discounting the seriousness of the incident	". . . **we thought** he was gone."		
7. Not realizing they were doing something provocative	". . . my friend and I were both in the left lane and **passed him**."		
8. Not realizing that the incident has now escalated into a potential duel	"The SUV took the same exit and **my friend and I thought it was funny** that he was behind us. . . ."		
9. Finally realizing this is trouble, but still acting like they're in a duel, thus escalating the fight instead of backing down	". . . we **slowed down in both of the lanes** (stupid plan). He pulled up . . . and began pointing a gun."		
10. Engaging in reckless driving—weaving through traffic at high speeds to get away from a chase	"We got really scared and did everything we could to **get away**. He followed us really fast but never tried to pass us. This **went on for miles**. We were all **swerving** through traffic. I think I was driving about **90 miles an hour**."		
11. Engaging in further provocative behavior by ignoring its potential effect on the pursuer	". . . I started to **flash my lights and honk** at my friend so he knew to take the exit."		
12. Trying to diffuse their own responsibility in the sequence of events as a sort of denial	"We think that **this driver** did something illegal and could have caused an accident."		
13. Hiding behind inadmissible excuses, avoiding admitting what they did wrong, and refusing to think objectively about it	"We know that **we were stupid** and added to the problem **but** we think that he's an adult and **he was the one who was making it into a battle**."		

friends or family members also complete the exercise, then get together to compare and discuss everybody's solutions. This exercise will strengthen your emotional intelligence as a driver by making you more aware of how your behavior influences other people's behavior on highways.

OLDER DRIVERS AT RISK

Elderly drivers have to make adjustments that challenge personal philosophy and ideology. For instance, night vision loss for some drivers is due to glare, and does not necessarily affect their day vision. Scheduling driving times to avoid night driving, and possibly rush-hour traffic and bad weather, is a good coping strategy that preserves driving freedom and maximizes safety. Automotive sociologist J. Peter Rothe has interviewed many elderly drivers and listened to them in focus groups. These conversations reveal concerns senior motorists have about themselves and concerns others have about them:

- Insufficient self-confidence due to inexperience ("After my husband passed away, everything was pushed on me.")
- Anxiety due to decline in ability ("I'm sometimes a bit nervous on the blind side on my right when I'm in the left-hand lane. The only way I can see is to turn my head and take a look.")
- Resentment due to social ostracism ("They think older drivers are worse and should stop driving.")
- Hostile behavior addressed at older drivers that they find degrading ("One time one of the ladies yelled at me in the parking lot, 'You've got all day but I haven't.' I guess what she thinks is we're just a bunch of old fogies.")
- Lack of awareness of how family members see them as drivers, and disbelief when told of their criticisms.
- Inability to see their slowness as others experience it, equating slowness with caution and patience.
- Increased difficulty in certain vehicle maneuvers such as parallel parking ("The curb disappears from your rearview mirror before you're really close so I have to kind of guess how far I am.")
- The distressing experience of information overload on multilane superhighways ("Cars are coming and going on either side and it's taken me a long time to learn to keep in my lane, to signal, to look before I get into that other lane.")
- The experience of fatigue during extended driving hours on highways ("They just go on for miles and miles and there is no stimulation. It puts you to sleep.")

- Frustration with signs whose letters aren't big enough or are too similar to each other, and other vision problems ("Driving would be easier if there were more lines, reflectors, and larger signs placed in the center, not on the side.")
- Being very fearful of hitting a pedestrian ("Pedestrian crossings should be better marked and lit.")
- Coping with disabling diseases or injuries like arthritis, loss of vision, and other health problems. ("I just hope my health stays well enough so I can drive for a long time.")
- The dread of crashing or getting into a collision ("I worry about someone going through a stop light, especially late at night with drunks."
- Rigidifying driving style due to a preoccupation with taking great precautions ("You don't take chances you did sixty years ago. When a car comes too fast to a stop I just wait until he stops, until I'm sure.")
- Strong anxiety about being tailgated, seeing it as an infringement and an attack. ("It's a selfish invasion of my rights.")
- Refusing to concede that the left lane is not a cruising lane ("I'm already driving the speed limit so I don't need to drive faster. It's my right.")
- Experiencing greater difficulty in talking while driving ("My friend was talking but I tried not to talk because it could have distracted me.")
- Lapsing into daydreaming episodes ("Somehow I had missed the stop sign there. I didn't see it.")[28]

New drivers who are elderly and female have a double handicap to overcome in the eyes of society and the motorists on the road: They need to learn how to manage people's hostility toward both older drivers and female drivers. They especially need to learn to monitor their driving in relation to other motorists. Every stretch of road has regular users who develop "local norms" about how people should drive in that area. Anyone who drives differently violates their expectations, arouses ire, and is treated aggressively and with hostility by regulars. This hostile treatment adds to the stress and confusion of the novice elderly driver.

Many widows over the age of sixty-five never learned how to drive a car. Their husbands were the drivers, and when their husbands passed on, they had to become more independent, doing a lot of walking and learning how to take buses and subways. After speaking to many widows over sixty-five, most of them agreed that they did not learn to drive because their husbands didn't encourage them and/or they were very afraid of driving. Obviously, nowadays, women are not as afraid of driving anymore.

Since this is a cultural practice in certain layers of society, many sixty-five-year-old-plus widows whose husbands have passed on or are no longer able to drive find themselves in a predicament created by societal values. Besides understanding safety principles, these women need driver education that includes a driving psychology component to learn how to cope with the interactive nature of the highway environment, which can be aggressive, hostile, and overwhelming.

A common bitter complaint motorists voice about older drivers is that they travel at the speed limit in the passing lane and refuse to move over into the slower lane. This blocking behavior causes a flurry of dangerous activity around them as drivers angrily scramble to pass them in the right lane. New drivers who are older need training to remain alert to this problem of cruising in the passing lane, and how to monitor and facilitate the activity of vehicles around them. This is a special concern for older drivers because reaction time tends to slow with age. Older drivers typically take longer to get going at traffic lights and intersections, to make turns, or to park. What older drivers call "being patient" others around them call "obnoxiously slow." Since the number of older drivers will increase dramatically over the next two decades, there is a critical need for age groups to better understand each other, and this requires developing a greater tolerance for diversity.

The increasing age of American drivers is a serious national concern. Everyone agrees that drivers need additional skills to compensate for the decreased abilities due to aging. People sixty-five and older represent 13 percent of the population and 17 percent of all motor vehicle deaths. The aging process reduces the driver's ability to deal with traffic incidents both physically and mentally, and increases the seriousness of injuries. Elderly drivers are more likely to receive citations for failing to yield, improper turns, and running red lights and stop signs. The American Association of Retired Persons (AARP), the largest association of older Americans, opposes licensing restrictions and testing of elderly drivers, citing age discrimination. This powerful lobby group argues that restrictions should be based solely on driving ability, not age, and a program of universal testing for 177 million licensed individuals in the United States is not considered practical.

Several organizations have developed special training courses for older drivers. The American Automobile Association (AAA), AARP, and the National Safety Council offer refresher courses for seniors. Illinois requires a driver reexamination every three years for those over age seventy-five and Louisiana requires that drivers age sixty and over obtain a physical examination. Several states require reexamination if a driver is determined to be unsafe or mentally or physically unfit. However, there is no known test that reliably predicts how well a driver will operate a motor vehicle. Recent **209**

ROAD RAGE AND AGGRESSIVE DRIVING

Table 9.3
Aggressive Driving Behaviors in Young and Older Drivers

	Percent who admit to doing it regularly	
Aggressive driving behavior	Young drivers (15–24)	Older drivers (55–83)
Swearing	66	42
Breaking speed limit (over 15 MPH)	52	19
Changing lanes without signaling	36	13
Running red lights	16	2
Tailgating dangerously	19	6
Cruising in the passing lane	15	6
Making insulting gestures (men)	42	20
Making insulting gestures (women)	22	22

research with driving simulators is promising because the program varies light conditions as well as the dynamics of driving situations. We recommend that new drivers who are elderly participate in QDCs. Older female drivers can benefit from these group interactions that can provide support and motivation to continue to develop their driving skills.

Older drivers have two things going for them. First, driving experience accumulates with age, and since driving is a complex bundle of skills, experience is an advantage. For example, older drivers excel in the skill of assessing risk, while young, inexperienced drivers do not, so collision rates for youth are three times higher than rates for older, more experienced drivers. Consequently, insurance costs are higher for young drivers, and they have more traffic citations and license suspensions. Older drivers think more critically behind the wheel than younger drivers. Second, older drivers tend to manage their emotions and impulses better than younger drivers. The results from our 1999 Internet survey, illustrated in Table 9.3, show marked differences between young drivers and older drivers with regard to aggressive driving.[29]

The majority of young drivers swear and speed. Young men outdo older drivers in flipping the bird, while young women are either too scared or more compassionate. Tailgating, dangerous lane hopping, and running red lights, are far less common among older drivers. Other driving behaviors that decrease with age and experience include enjoying fantasies of violence, experiencing rage while driving, and feeling impatient and hostile. Older drivers "feel more compassion" behind the wheel. But when asked, "How do you rate your aggressiveness as a driver on a scale of 1 to 10?" young drivers chose 6 and older drivers selected 5. Not much difference! When asked how much stress they experience daily as a driver, the picture is reversed: Only 33 percent of younger drivers pick 5 or above, while 50 percent of older drivers experience higher stress. Driving stress thus increases with age, and there are both physical and psychological consequences to consider. Stress kills by weakening immune system functioning and raising the concentration of potentially harmful chemicals in the blood. If one in two older drivers experience high stress while driving, a certain percentage of them will suffer physically unless they learn to manage driving stress. Psychologically, stress is a depressant. People tend to be more pessimistic when in a depressed state, they're less happy and contribute to the unhappiness of others. It makes sense for older drivers to use their experience and maturity to practice stress management skills while driving. Here are two useful techniques.

1. Learn to be a supportive driver. Even in Hawaii, it's easy to forget about Aloha in traffic. As drivers, we all need to reaffirm the value we place on human compassion as opposed to selfishness. Supportive drivers graciously tolerate others' mistakes; they overlook, forgive, and forget. Wisdom teaches that no one can reform the driving behavior of other motorists. Next time you feel angry behind the wheel, start making funny sounds to slow down your breathing. It may also make you laugh. Then talk sense to yourself. Think of the luxury of driving without having to get mad or upset. Cultivate an attitude of latitude.

2. Come out swinging positive. Remember the driver's prime directive: retain control of the vehicle and the situation. Supportive driving behavior gives us more control over the situation than aggressive behavior. If another driver picks on you, you're faced with two choices: escalate or de-escalate. Escalating amounts to visibly expressing displeasure to the other. The moment you express it, you've relinquished control of the situation because you can't predict how the other person will respond to provocation. But ignoring the driver can also be dangerous and may result in needlessly giving up control. Instead, actively try to provide a remedy, to do a "repair job" to the other person's hurt feelings. What's appropriate depends on the norms and expectations of other drivers in that area. Sometimes smiling or waving is appropriate, but not always. When you're already in verbal communication, like in a parking lot, you have the opportunity to better control things by acting benign, nonblaming, and concerned about the other person's frustration. The point to remember is that you control the situation by taking charge with positive behavior.

ROAD RAGE AND AGGRESSIVE DRIVING

Both technology and the ever-increasing number of aging drivers are creating new demands for society to implement a lifelong driver education program. Driving psychology shows that the act of driving has deep significance for the self. The way we drive reflects the quality of our thinking and feeling and of our character. Drivers of all ages are emotionally unprepared to handle traffic congestion and multi-tasking activities in cars. There are three million two-car crashes in the United States each year, involving at least six million drivers, passengers, pedestrians, and cyclists. Over a ten-year period, sixty million people will be involved in car-related injuries, and about 400,000 lives will be lost. In terms of economic cost, the driving crash figure for the decade will cumulate to $2 trillion. Why must we endure these consequences in an educated democracy? The answer is that we'll continue to pay the awful cost unless car society shifts to the new lifelong driver education paradigm. The program we have proposed can be used as a starting point for evolving a viable universal delivery system for lifelong driver education.

CHECKLIST: POSITIVE DRIVING BEHAVIOR

Check those you would be willing to adopt.

1. ____ Putting on the turn signal in consideration of others; thinking of how to reduce stress for others
2. ____ Feeling responsible for creating stress for other road users; wanting to evolve an altruistic attitude in traffic
3. ____ Concentrating on developing better on-ramp merging skills by focusing on leaving enough space to pick up speed
4. ____ Creating positive mental scenarios and avoiding pessimism; saying, "Traffic is not too bad. I'll just relax," versus "Traffic is awful. I'll never get home."
5. ____ Driving with greater awareness; understanding the difference in people's expectations in the left and right lanes; consciously managing following distance to keep it safe, following the three-second rule
6. ____ Consciously practicing how to handle common obstacles to traffic flow; for instance, when a lane is closed and merging is required
7. ____ Compensating for the "blind spot" by always using both side- and rearview mirror and turning your head for better view
8. ____ Merging properly when a lane is closed by remaining in your lane until reaching the merge point

9. ____ Learning to avoid mental violence as retaliation; not letting frustration lead to aggressiveness and hostility

10. ____ Avoiding the symbols of competition in driving, like racing to get there first, wanting to pass all cars, feeling ridiculed when a lot of cars pass you, impulsively cutting in

11. ____ Practicing nodding instead of shaking your head at traffic

12. ____ Recognizing higher motivations in driving, like fairness, civility, morality, altruism, religion, or spirituality

13. ____ Giving up a "laissez-faire" attitude toward other drivers, such as "What's happening to that driver is not my problem."

14. ____ Being willing to figure things out ahead of time, like how late to leave, when to turn, which way to go, when to change lanes, with the goal of avoiding making unpredictable, impulsive moves that other drivers can't interpret

NOTES

1. Personal anecdotes quoted throughout this chapter were sent to us by e-mail correspondents.

2. National Highway Traffic Safety Administration (NHSTA) Web site, www.nhtsa.dot.gov [May 20, 2000].

3. A. F. Williams, D. F. Preusser, and S. A. Ferguson, "Fatal Crashes Involving 16-Year-Old Drivers: Narrative Descriptions," *Journal of Traffic Medicine* 26, no. 1–2 (1998): 11-17.

4. James B. Reed, Janet B. Goehring, and Jeanne Mejeur, "Environment, Energy and Transportation Program Reducing Crashes, Casualties and Costs—Traffic Safety Challenges for State Legislatures," National Conference of State Legislatures, Environment, Energy and Transportation Program, Transportation Series No. 5, February 1997 [online], www.ncsl.org/programs/esnr/transer5.htm [May 20, 2000].

5. American Driver and Traffic Safety Association [online], adtsea.iup. edu/adtsea [May 21, 2000]; CNN.com, August 26, 1997 [online], www.cnn.com [September 3, 1997].

6. AAA Foundation for Traffic Safety, "Driver-ZED" [online], driverzed.org [May 20, 2000].

7. Ibid.

8. John Larson, testimony before House Transportation and Infrastructure Committee, Surface Transportation Subcommittee Hearing on Road Rage: Causes and Dangers of Aggressive Driving, July 17, 1997 [online], www.house.gov/transportation/surface/sthearin/ist717/larson.htm [May 20, 2000].

9. "Driver-ZED," driverzed.org.

10. Lawrence P. Lonero, et al, "Novice Driver Education Model Curriculum Outline," AAA Foundation for Traffic Safety, March 1995 [online], www.

aaafts.org [October 20, 1997]; selections are available at www.aloha.net/~dyc/yarr/aaa97.html [May 21, 2000].

11. Ibid.

12. Ibid.

13. Ibid.

14. Leon James, "Aggressive Driving and Road Rage: Dealing with Emotionally Impaired Drivers," testimony before House Transportation and Infrastructure Committee, Surface Transportation Subcommittee Hearing on Road Rage: Causes and Dangers of Aggressive Driving, July 17, 1997 [online], www.house.gov/transportation/surface/sthearin/ist717/james.htm [May 20, 2000]; also available at www.aloha.net/~dyc/testimony.html.

15. Jack Wheat, "Program Soothes the Savage Driver," *Miami Herald*, November 18, 1999.

16. R. A. Thompson, ed., *Socioemotional Development. Nebraska Symposium on Motivation*, vol. 36 (Lincoln: University of Nebraska Press, 1990); David Hamburg, *Today's Children: Creating a Future for a Generation in Crisis* (New York: Times Books, 1992).

17. Updates on the QDC movement are posted at DrDriving.org [online], QualityDriving.com [May 20, 2000].

18. Leon James and Diane Nahl, "Quality Driving Circles—QDCs: What Are They and How Do They Work?" [online], QualityDriving.com [May 21, 2000].

19. Leon James and Diane Nahl, "CARR—Children Against Road Rage" [online], CARRworkbook.com [May 20, 2000].

20. Leon James and Diane Nahl, "Aggressive Driving Prevention Course for Law Enforcement" [online], www.aloha.net/~dyc/police/teecards.html [May 20, 2000]; *RoadRageous Aggressive Driver Course for Law Enforcement* (N. Miami: American Institute for Public Safety, 2000).

21. Leon James and Diane Nahl, DrDriving's Page for Older Drivers [online], DrivingWise.com [May 20, 2000].

22. Leon James and Diane Nahl, "DrDriving's TEE Cards—Traffic Emotions Education for All Drivers" [online], www.aloha.net/~dyc/tee.html [May 20, 2000].

23. Leon James and Diane Nahl, "*RoadRageous* Video Course Objectives and Modules" [online], www.aloha.net/~dyc/video [May 20, 2000].

24. Leon James and Diane Nahl, "Instructional CARRtoons for Aggressive Driving Prevention" [online], CARRtoons.org [May 20, 2000].

25. Leon James, "DrDriving's Vision Statement for YARR—A New Socio-Behavioral Proposal," keynote address, YARR Foundational Conference, Edmunds College, Seattle, June 19, 1998; Richard Kirby, "The Mission of YARR," YARR Foundational Conference [online], www.aloha.net/~dyc/yarr [May 20, 2000].

26. Leon James, Diane Nahl, and Arnold Nerenberg, *Road Rageous Aggressive Driver Course* (N. Miami: American Institute for Public Safety, 1999); James and Nahl, "*RoadRageous* Video Course Objectives and Modules."

27. Debra Franco, "Road Rage Not to Blame—Shootout Victim Drunk, Autopsy Finds," *Colorado Springs Gazette*, July 7, 1999.

28. J. Peter Rothe, *The Safety of Elderly Drivers* (New Brunswick, N.J.: Transaction Publishers, 1990), pp. 185–302.

29. Leon James and Diane Nahl, "Aggressiveness in Relation to Age, Gender, and Type of Car," DrDriving.org [online], www.aloha.net/~dyc/surveys/survey2/interpretations.html [May 20, 2000].

THE **FUTURE**
OF **DRIVING**

PART **3**

THE **WAR** AGAINST **AGGRESSIVE DRIVING**

10

How long can we continue as a society when people die on our highways at an annual rate five times greater than wars have killed U.S. soldiers since the beginning of the century? This year at least forty thousand people will lose their lives on highways and more than three million will go to the hospital with injuries and economic losses will reach over $200 billion. In 1999 more than a dozen states passed aggressive driving laws and law enforcement around the country has stepped up initiatives to curb aggressive drivers.

DIRECT AND INDIRECT COST

- Fatalities (425,000 per decade)
- Injuries (35 million per decade)
- Dollars (250 billion per year)
- Long-term ill health

ROAD RAGE AND AGGRESSIVE DRIVING

- Increased daily stress (hassles and concerns)
- Fear and threat on streets and highways
- Learned negativity in public places leading to automotive vigilantism and widely deployed electronic surveillance systems
- Reduced productivity when arriving at work mad and exhausted
- Learned cynicism (aggressive driving norms and disrespect for regulations) leading to alienation
- Greater air pollution due to emotional use of the gas pedal (getting fewer miles per gallon)
- Breeding the next generation of aggressive drivers

In March 1999, the *Daily News* published a list of the ten worst cities in terms of *road rage deaths*, or the number of fatalities due to aggressive driving per one hundred thousand residents.[1]

• Riverside-San Bernardino, Calif.	13.4
• Tampa-St. Petersburg-Clearwater, Fla.	9.5
• Phoenix, Ariz.	9.2
• Orlando, Fla.	8.1
• Miami-Hialeah, Fla.	8.1
• Las Vegas, Nev.	8.1
• Ft. Lauderdale-Hollywood-Pompano Beach, Fla.	7.8
• Kansas City, Mo.-Kan.	7.1
• Dallas-Ft. Worth, Texas	7.3
• San Antonio, Texas	7.0

CONGRESSIONAL HEARINGS

In 1997, Ricardo Martinez, M.D., then Administrator of the National Highway Traffic Safety Administration (NHTSA) testified in congressional hearings on aggressive driving and reported that:

(1) After years of steady decline, the total number of highway deaths increased slightly in each of the last four years.
(2) In 1996, 41,907 people died and over 3 million more were injured in police-reported crashes.
(3) These collisions due to aggressive driving cost the nation $150 billion each year.
(4) About one-third of these crashes and about two-thirds of the resulting fatalities can be attributed to behavior associated with aggressive driving.[2]

The media picked up this bombshell and started the national debate on road rage. This statistic did not sit well with the population of "tough-minded" drivers, such as the supporters of the National Motorists Association (NMA) and millions of drivers who describe their vehicle operation style as "assertive" (see chapter 12). Dr. Martinez later explained that this figure is an estimate and not a scientific finding. Nevertheless, many sources have repeated the two-thirds formula to figure out fatalities due to aggressive driving. For instance, in 1996 about forty-two thousand highway fatalities were recorded and two-thirds of that—twenty-eight thousand deaths—were attributed to aggressive driving in that year, and one-third of three million is one million injuries due to aggressive driving that year. This pattern continued throughout the late 1990s, and the nation's media declared that aggressive driving had replaced drunk driving as our worst highway problem.

The federal government's intervention through the NHTSA was influential in extending the limits of outlawed driver behavior:

> The Department defines aggressive driving as driving behavior that endangers or is likely to endanger people or property. This definition includes a broad spectrum of driving behaviors, ranging from risky driving and escalating to dueling and violence on the road. Aggressive drivers are more likely to: Speed, tailgate, fail to yield, weave in-and-out of traffic, pass on the right, make improper and unsafe lane changes, run stop signs and red lights, make hand and facial gestures, scream, honk, and flash their lights, climb into the anonymity of an automobile and take out their frustrations on others at any time, allow high frustration levels to diminish any concern for fellow motorists, be impaired by alcohol or drugs, and drive unbelted or take other unsafe actions.[3]

This new definition introduces two revolutionary ideas about driving and law enforcement. First, many common driving behaviors are now defined as crimes—misdemeanor or felony. By 1999, this idea has become a legislative reality in sixteen states, and more states were poised to enter the new age of driving behavior legislation. Years before this move by NHTSA, the U.K. and Canada developed aggressive driving laws that mandate jail time for a driver threatening another driver and large fines for motorists who endanger the lives of others. But the second revolutionary idea in the government's definition of aggressive driving—that offenses can be defined by a driver's mental state—has not yet been debated in public. We think it should be.

The two categories of behavior in the official definition cover overt and covert behavior. Overt behavior can be easily observed by camera, such as making improper lane changes, tailgating, making obscene gestures, and so on. The unobservable mental state of the driver is uncharted **221** territory: "Aggressive drivers are more likely to . . . climb into the anonymity of an automobile and take out their frustrations on others at any time, allow high frustration levels to diminish any concern for fellow motorists." The legislative implementation of these ideas will be challenging, beginning with the problem of highway troopers making stops on the basis of a driver's facial expression or perceived frustration level. These are troublesome issues we will face in the near future. We discuss these concerns below as we review the language of the new aggressive driving bills of 1999.

Our research has identified the psychological components of aggressive driving, developed an empirically based theory of the causes of aggressive driving, and specified behavioral techniques to measure and control it. It has become clear that, to some degree, nearly every driver has feelings of rage and thoughts of retaliation. We're confronted with some basic questions for which there are few scientific answers:

- Is aggressive driving increasing?
- Are there differences in aggressive driving across the cities and states—is it a universal epidemic?
- What causes the increase in aggressive driving and how can it be controlled?

New forms of record keeping are needed to track the incidence of aggressive driving in society because there are no before-and-after statistics available to answer these questions. New legislation addresses this problem by specifying offenses in terms of particular behavior. Since drivers frequently make unfortunate choices based on intense emotions, our proposal to Congress included:

- New K–12 driving psychology curriculum focusing on systematic self-assessment skills and emotional intelligence for road users
- Children Against Road Rage (CARR), a family prevention activity with children to help them avoid adopting the aggressive driving mentality
- Quality Driving Circles (QDCs), small, informal driver support groups for encouraging lifelong driver self-improvement exercises[4]

Health experts have responded to road rage by viewing it as a psychological disorder that can be treated with anger and stress management therapy. Our approach emphasizes systematic self-observation and lifelong self-improvement within a cultural context. After years of listening to hundreds of drivers speaking their minds into a tape recorder while **222** driving, it became obvious that feeling hostile and violent behind the wheel is a cultural norm rather than a psychological disorder.[5] The new federal initiatives support this orientation.

FEDERAL AGENCIES UNITE AGAINST AGGRESSIVE DRIVERS

One of the follow-up initiatives to the hearings on aggressive driving was that the Department of Transportation proposed the National Economic Crossroads Transportation Efficiency Act of 1997 (NEXTEA) that provides for the development of comprehensive state and community programs aimed at combating aggressive driving. The keystone of NHTSA's efforts in highway safety, jointly administered with the Federal Highway Administration (FHWA), is the state and community highway safety grant program, known as the "Section 402" program of the U.S. Code.[6] This act would reward states that have integrated safety plans by giving them new funds for transportation infrastructure and safety, including law enforcement initiatives, public awareness education, and the deployment of Intelligent Transportation Systems (ITS).

Also in 1997, the American Association of State Highway and Transportation Officials (AASHTO), with the assistance of the FHWA, the NHTSA, and the Transportation Research Board (TRB), assembled a group of national safety experts in driver, vehicle, and highway issues from various organizations representing the private and public sectors. The purpose was to implement a plan dealing with key areas that impact the aggressive driving problem, among them:

- Curbing aggressive driving
- Graduated licensing for young drivers
- Sustaining proficiency in older drivers
- Reducing impaired driving
- Keeping drivers alert
- Increasing driver safety awareness
- Ensuring safer bicycle travel
- Improving motorcycle safety and awareness
- Making truck travel safer

The Highway Safety Act of 1996 authorizes the U.S. Department of Transportation (DOT), through its separate agencies, the NHTSA and the FHWA, to fund traffic improvement programs implemented by state and local governments, including funding safety improvements in the areas of occupant protection, emergency medical services, police traffic services, roadway safety, impaired driving, speed control, motorcycle safety, traffic records, and pedestrian and bicycle safety.[7]

The federal government maintains a technology clearinghouse for law enforcement programs to promote the effective management of aggressive drivers.[8] One of its projects is cooperating with the International Association of Chiefs of Police (IACP) that has established a database of traffic records and enforcement technologies to share among members. Agencies are permitted to access information, submit data, and provide comments about specific technologies in the database. Other programs in the database include the speed and unsafe (aggressive) driving database of crash investigations set up by the National Automotive Sampling Sites (NASS), and the youthful impaired driver project, backed by the National Sheriffs' Association (NSA).

The NHTSA has issued an aggressive driver advisory telling motorists what to do if confronted.[9] These helpful hints have become standard on the Web, in newspaper stories, insurance company pamphlets, health organization magazines, automobile club newsletters, and public service announcements on radio and television.

(1) First and foremost, make every attempt to get out of their way.
(2) Put your pride in the back seat. Do not challenge them by speeding up or attempting to hold your own in your travel lane.
(3) Wear your seat belt. It will hold you in your seat and behind the wheel in case you need to make an abrupt driving maneuver and it will protect you in a crash.
(4) Avoid eye contact.
(5) Ignore gestures and refuse to return them.
(6) Report aggressive drivers to the appropriate authorities by providing a vehicle description, license number, location, and if possible, direction of travel.
(7) If you have a cell phone and can do it safely, call the police.
(8) If an aggressive driver is involved in a crash farther down the road, stop a safe distance from the crash scene, wait for the police to arrive, and report the driving behavior that you witnessed.

This advice is intended to help people avoid confrontations with aggressive drivers and to support law enforcement efforts to reduce road rage incidents.

AGGRESSIVE POLICE INITIATIVES

Safety legislation in vehicle and highway design has played a crucial role in reducing the number and severity of highway injuries. Legislation covering driver behavior has also had significant results in increasing seat belt usage and imposing stiffer penalties for driving under the influence of alcohol. Currently, legislators at federal, state, and city levels are enacting aggressive driving bills to assist law enforcement efforts to fight dangerous and illegal driving. Dozens of police initiatives to curb aggressive driving are described on police department Web pages.[10] Many attempt to combine enforcement with public awareness by enlisting public participation in identifying and reporting aggressive drivers, and stealth is still a common technique used by law enforcement:

> Marked patrol cars create a deterrent effect when present, but this deterrence is lost when they leave the area. When motorists see a marked patrol car, they are usually on their best behavior and stay that way until it is out of sight. Use of unmarked, nontraditional vehicles for aggressive driver enforcement in the community will contribute to public awareness by increasing motorist uncertainty about which vehicles are used for enforcement. It will also generate free publicity about the enforcement program. The use of both unmarked cars and motorcycles increase the effectiveness of any aggressive driving enforcement program.[11]

In 1999, police in Florida mounted a stealth aggressive driving initiative:

> In a region where commuting conditions are so notorious that gun-waving motorists barely rate headlines, the state highway patrol just launched one of the latest programs in the nation to define and decrease aggressive driving. Operating so-called "stealth" vehicles confiscated from criminals, undercover officers will be equipped with video cameras to record fast and furious driving from West Palm Beach to Miami. All 1,800 Florida troopers also will see training videos on bad road habits to watch for.
>
> The congested highways of south Florida provide the perfect pressure cooker for the experiment. The number of vehicles on the road in metro Miami has nearly doubled in the past decade, to 2.4 million. Driving on Interstate 95 and other major arteries is a nightmare. Among other things, impatient motorists weave from lane to lane and flash their brights inches from the bumpers of the unwary. Troopers say at least one-third of nonfatal crashes are linked to aggressive driving.
>
> State troopers hope that capturing aggressive drivers on videotape will strengthen court cases. Initially outfitted with just two undercover Jeeps, both flashy and late model, the program expands next year to

225

include a camera-carrying fleet of nontraditional vehicles—motorcycles to lumbering trucks.[12]

Communities have responded to aggressive drivers by initiating aggressive enforcement programs in an attempt to reduce illegal driving behavior and protect the community. In July 1998, the Michigan Office of Highway Safety Planning (OHSP) released a statewide survey that measured driver stress and aggression.[13] The study concluded that one million Michigan drivers, or 16 percent, are in immediate danger of committing road rage and that the associated costs will be unbearable. Clearly, reducing the incidence of aggressive driving behaviors reduces the psychological, physical, and financial burden society bears. Not only could we save money, but we could enjoy freedom from injury, peace, security, and greater community among road users. Most importantly, we could curtail the savage behavior of those who permit emotions to rule their actions, as in this 1999 story:

> Second-degree assault charges have been filed against a man accused of striking a motorist with a baseball bat in a road rage incident. The 19-year-old is currently free on $30,000 bail and will be arraigned Wednesday. Bail was set at the same amount for the 18-year-old passenger, also charged Monday with second-degree assault for allegedly joining the attack.
> The attack occurred July 13 after the driver of a black Infiniti passed a Honda at an on-ramp to Interstate 90 on Mercer Island. Words were exchanged, then both vehicles pulled over. When the driver of the Honda approached, the driver of the Infiniti punched him in the face, court papers say. He then hit the 22-year-old victim's face with a baseball bat taken from the trunk of the Infiniti, three witnesses said. Police were able to trace the Infiniti after he drove off because passengers in the victim's car noted the license plate number.[14]

The Roadwatch Program began in Caledon, Ontario, in 1993 and combines citizen observations with law enforcement.[15] Citizen Report Forms identify these aggressive driving behaviors: speeding, following too close, failure to yield, improper lane changes, improper passing, and disobeying traffic signs and signals. The forms have spaces for noting the license plate of the aggressive car and the reporter's name, address, and telephone number. The reporter's information is kept confidential and the owner of the car receives a letter from the police detailing the aggressive driving complaint. Subsequent offenses are followed by a police visit or enforcement action.

New York officials became concerned when a Department of Motor Vehicles review of police accident reports concluded that aggressive driving was a contributing factor in 70 percent of fatal accidents. In 1997 the New York State Police made aggressive driving a major target in its enforcement strategy. State Police deployed a number of minivans, called Road Rage Vans, loaded with video equipment to record aggressive driving. Thousands of drivers received citations for speeding, unsafe lane changes, and following too closely. Nineteen ninety-eight saw the introduction of the nation's first tough-minded laws to fight "drivers who exhibit dangerous 'road rage' tactics." Thousands of drivers are cited for aggressive driving in New York City each year. "Too many collisions are not accidents" according to officials. The bill creates new categories of crime called "criminal aggressive driving in the third, second and first degrees" The official definition of aggressive driving in the New York penal law is

> the unsafe operation of a motor vehicle in a hostile manner, without regard for the safety of other users of the highway. Aggressive driving includes frequent or unsafe lane changes, failing to signal, tailgating, failing to yield right of way, and disregarding traffic controls.[16]

The time has apparently come to put an end to "mayhem on wheels." For cutting someone off to "harass, annoy, or alarm a person," a motorist now risks a Class A misdemeanor with a maximum penalty of one-year in jail and license suspension. The same is true for "increasing or decreasing the speed" if there is "intent to harass, annoy or alarm another person."

A motorist is guilty of a Class E felony, which carries a maximum penalty of four years in prison and license revocation, if an object is brandished as a weapon or dangerous instrument, either to injure or to threaten to injure. A Class D felony carrying a maximum penalty of seven years in prison and license revocation is mandated for a driver who intentionally strikes a person or vehicle. In addition, penalties for repeat offenses at a less severe level are jacked up. Besides specifying penalties, the New York law also mandates aggressive driving education as a prerequisite to obtaining a driver's license, and authorizes judges to require offenders to attend driver education programs.

In 1999, at a unique symposium in Washington, D.C., called "Aggressive Driving and the Law," the secretary of transportation stated that the administration's highest priority in transportation is the aggressive driving problem. Nearly $7 billion has been allocated over the next six years to fight the epidemic on the nation's highways.[17] The government released a survey showing that aggressive driving is one of the leading safety concerns among America's drivers. Two-thirds of the drivers in the NHTSA survey admitted to unsafe driving. The most common reasons people give include: late for meetings, traffic congestion, and frustration.

ROAD RAGE AND AGGRESSIVE DRIVING

The report asserts that "we all, at one time or another, have either purposefully or unwittingly taken on the role of an aggressive driver."

> We can and must do better—which is why we are here today. We must raise the bar on safety. It requires a three-pronged approach—education, enforcement, and strong judicial efforts—to prevent this life-threatening behavior from occurring again and again. A majority of drivers from the NHTSA survey believe that the amount of law enforcement is about right. At least twenty-two states and the District of Columbia currently have active programs to reduce aggressive driving violations. The Federal government, law enforcement agencies and local communities are partnering through programs like "Smooth Operator" to combat aggressive driving and we are seeing results.[18]

A federal grant of half a million dollars was announced for an aggressive driving demonstration project for the Milwaukee Police Department. Another $600,000 went to support the national Red Light Running Campaign that so far has resulted in significant drops in the number of crashes at thirty-one sites. The federal government is interested in supporting new legislation specifically aimed at aggressive driving behaviors in order to help law enforcement and the criminal justice system deal with these crimes. According to the transportation secretary, new sentencing guidelines need to be created to provide stiffer penalties for aggressive driving offenses.

AGGRESSIVE DRIVING BILLS

The federal initiative quickly paid off. According to a 1998 report by the National Conference of State Legislatures, several aggressive driving bills have been approved and several more are being introduced.[19] Excerpts from some of these bills and new laws are presented in Table 10.1 in enough detail to illustrate the specific language used to define offenses. In many instances the law makes reference to unobservable mental states of drivers such as their intention, attitude, or intensity of emotional involvement. Such subjective assessments will present problems in future court cases. Until the issue of what is observable about drivers is resolved, new aggressive driving laws may have to alter some language in the face of legal challenges.

Law enforcement officers must be able to identify the aggressive driver's specific behavior. For instance, New Jersey police use the language of traffic violations to help officers observe specific driver behavior:

- Speeding
- Following too closely
- Unsafe lane change
- Driving while intoxicated
- Reckless, careless, or inattentive driving
- Disregard of traffic signs and signals
- Improper passing
- Driving while suspended[20]

Some tricky psychological issues may be involved in making distinctions between aggressive driving infractions and nonaggressive violations. The federal government recognizes that "just because drivers are stopped for speeding does not mean they were driving aggressively."[21] The guidelines call for citations to be marked to identify true aggressive driving violations. In our opinion, officers may have difficulty reliably profiling the aggressiveness of a driver who has committed a visible infraction. For instance, when a driver is stopped for speeding, what criteria are involved in making a decision about the driver's "intentions" that permit the officer to check off "merely speeding" versus "reckless speeding"?

To avoid potential police abuse as well as problems in the courts, various mechanical schemes will arise to define specific behaviors that are not subject to interpretation by officers. This is why traffic law enforcement between 1970 and 1990 has successfully focused on three driver behavior–detection technologies: radar detection, breath analyzers, and seat belt use (including child restraints). In each case, officers are able to provide the courts with mechanical measurements or direct observation to show whether an infraction occurred. But beginning in the late 1990s, new aggressive driving legislation has progressed faster than our ability to provide law enforcement with a behavioral technology that can objectively detect aggressive intentions in the majority of cases. As a result of the vigorous deployment of the new photo-radar technologies, speed, and blood alcohol levels are joined by "red-light running" and "improper turning" on the list of objective measurements available to police. Nevertheless, many aggressive infractions cannot be measured with these devices.

In order to identify aggressive driving through observed motor vehicle violations, the language of these offenses must always be behavioral, describing the observable behavior of drivers, not their intentions or motives. Many law enforcement units are working to resolve this ambiguity, and it may take some time to standardize language that is acceptable to courts.

The new aggressive-driving bills, introduced in many states in 1999 and being prepared in many others, share certain features. One is the def- **229** inition of offenses and the other is the cumulative severity when an offense is repeated. The bill introduced in Washington State specifies that drivers must commit "two or more of the offenses within five consecutive miles."[22] The state's comprehensive list of aggressive driving offenses includes:

- Breaking the speed limit
- Cutting drivers off when passing, not allowing someone to pass safely
- Driving across highway dividers
- Driving through a crosswalk occupied by a pedestrian
- Driving too slowly when unwarranted
- Driving with one or more wheels off the road
- Exceeding 20 MPH speed limits in school zones when kids are present
- Incorrectly yielding when entering traffic
- Knocking over traffic signs
- Making unsafe U-turns
- Not signaling before slowing for a turn
- Not stopping at railroad tracks when directed to do so
- Not stopping or yielding according to signs
- Not taking care to avoid hitting pedestrians
- Not yielding at intersections to the driver on the right when arriving simultaneously
- Not yielding when making left turns
- Opening vehicle doors unsafely and leaving them open too long
- Passing in no-passing zones
- Passing stopped school buses when warning lights are flashing
- Running traffic lights or signs
- Speeding in marked construction areas
- Tailgating
- Throwing bottles, nails, wire and other dangerous items from moving vehicles
- Turning incorrectly at intersections

This list is an indication of the many weaknesses of licensed drivers, but the language used in aggressive driving legislation across the nation varies considerably. Table 10.1 gives some examples of current or proposed legislation in several states, identifying the features that determine vague or specific enforcement language.

Table 10.1
State-to-State Comparison of Aggressive Driving Law Language

State	Language of Aggressive Driving Laws	Rating	Analysis
Washington	committing any two or more acts of aggressive driving within five consecutive miles	specific	Assumes that "acts" is also defined. The expression "two or more" is measurable.
Washington	passing improperly	vague	What is "improperly"? Needs specific behavioral description.
Virginia	operating a vehicle in a threatening or intimidating manner with the intent to cause others to lose control or be forced off the highway	vague	"Threatening manner" is unclear. "Intent" of driver is unknown to officer and calls for judgment that can be questioned in court. Forcing off the road is observable.
Virginia	operating a vehicle with a reckless disregard for the rights of others or in a manner that endangers any property or person	vague	"Reckless disregard" is a judgment call. Better to describe the observable behavior.
New York	driving with intent to harass, annoy, or alarm another person in a manner contrary to law	vague	"Intent" is difficult to prove and calls for judgment. Better to describe the driver's behavior, e.g., "honked repeatedly while tailgating."
New York	changing lanes or speed in a manner that serves no legitimate purpose and creates a substantial risk of injury or death to another	vague	Difficult to prove "no legitimate purpose." Better to describe the driver's behavior, e.g., "switched lanes ten times in one mile while speeding."
Nebraska	repeatedly honking horn	specific	Observable behavior.
Connecticut	failure to stop when directed by a police officer	specific	Observable behavior.
Arizona	Drivers could be charged with aggressive behavior if they are cited for a combination of any three of the following charges, committing two or more listed offenses that include • failing to obey a traffic control device • passing on the right or on the shoulder • tailgating or following too closely • failing to signal lane changes • failing to yield the right of way • running a red light or a stop sign • passing a vehicle on the right by traveling off the pavement	specific	Good examples of behavioral language; all are observable by an officer.

ROAD RAGE AND AGGRESSIVE DRIVING

TRAFFIC ENFORCEMENT EDUCATION

The concept of educating motorists while enforcing the law is taking hold in police departments everywhere. According to Ontario Provincial Police Superintendent Bill Currie, who is concerned by the five hundred calls per week received from drivers complaining about road rage, the provincial Highway Rangers in the Greater Toronto Area deliver "roadside interventions." Stopped drivers fill out "a questionnaire designed to help motorists see whether their anger is under control or if they're headed for a road rage situation."[23] The California Highway Patrol has mounted a campaign using billboards and public service announcements to remind motorists of the importance of following the rules of the road. The traffic division of the San Antonio police force is using our TEE Cards to train officers as well as handing them out to motorists. TEE Cards represent the essential partnership that must exist between law enforcement and traffic education in a new dual role for officers on the road.[24]

Government officials recognize that aggressive driver programs should try to increase voluntary compliance with traffic laws and not merely focus on catching and punishing offenders. Public awareness of a program is essential for two reasons: first, to send a message that aggressive drivers will not be tolerated and, second, to promote community support. The current model favors a multiagency approach to pool resources and expertise. Some highway law enforcement practices rely on stealth to surprise and catch offenders, but the new approach promoted by the government switches from stealth to awareness and readiness to comply. "Publicize to maximize!" could be the motto that describes the new law enforcement philosophy. The intensifying involvement of government in the driving arena has produced a novel mixture of enforcement and education that introduces new roles for the police and citizens alike. The motive to gain public acceptance of these special enforcement efforts reflects the desire to teach drivers about highway responsibility and intelligence. Now patrol officers are expected to deliver a driver education mini-lesson along with a warning or citation.

A new, paternalistic approach to drivers is evolving in government. At first, aggressive driving initiatives used dedicated personnel and targeted specific areas on streets and highways. The government's new attitude is that aggressive driving enforcement must be a priority to everyone on patrol, not just traffic units, regardless of their assignments. Along with this broader motivation comes a new focus on data collection on aggressive driving violations and the creation of shared databases that keep track of trends over time in particular areas. Legislative bills in many states mandate collecting data to track driver behavior changes objectively using baseline-intervention methods.

The War against Aggressive Driving

The new standard for an integrated approach to fight traffic violators involves several agencies to achieve adequate ground-air coordination. The government recommends the deployment of

> fixed-wing aircraft or helicopter to work aggressive driving details. The aircraft is used as an observation platform, while marked law enforcement vehicles on the ground stop the identified violators and take the necessary enforcement action. Ground units represent state, municipal and county law enforcement agencies from the area. One ground law enforcement vehicle has a television reporter and camera crew riding along to report on the enforcement activity.[25]

Following a trend that has been successful with C-SPAN and Court TV, government agencies involved in traffic enforcement encourage the deliberate use of media coverage, through ride-alongs and live-remote broadcasts. More states are equipping highway patrol cars with video-recording equipment that provides a legal record of what happens during traffic stops.

The war against aggressive driving is intensifying, but it can hardly succeed by relying exclusively on the deterrence effects of surveillance and punishment. We believe that a full answer to the aggressive driving problem requires that we rethink driver education and training by including traffic emotions education and making it a lifelong process. Traffic emotions literacy is as important as safety literacy in today's high-density, high-performance commuting. In the meantime, citizen activism against government paternalism is also stiffening and expanding, and our nation suddenly finds itself polarized between sentiments of fighting for highway independence and those who agitate for getting tough with more legislation and enforcement.

NOTES

1. Don Russell and Bob Warner, "City's Roads Have No Rules, and It Seems Even the Cops Don't Care," Philadelphia Online [online], www.philly.com/packages/hellonwheels/hell10.asp [May 20, 2000].

2. Ricardo Martinez, "Statement of the Honorable Ricardo Martinez, M.D., Administrator, National Highway Traffic Safety Administration, before the Subcommittee on Surface Transportation, Committee on Transportation and Infrastructure, U.S. House of Representatives," July 17, 1997 [online], www.house.gov/transportation/surface.sthearin/ist717/martinez.htm [May 20, 2000].

3. National Highway Traffic Safety Administration (NHTSA), "Strategies for Aggressive Driver Enforcement" [online], www.nhtsa.dot.gov/people/injury/enforce/aggressdrivers/intro.html [May 20, 2000].

ROAD RAGE AND AGGRESSIVE DRIVING

4. Leon James, "Aggressive Driving and Road Rage: Dealing with Emotionally Impaired Drivers," testimony before House Transportation and Infrastructure Committee, Surface Transportation Subcommittee Hearing on Road Rage: Causes and Dangers of Aggressive Driving, July 17, 1997 [online], www.house.gov/transportation/surface/sthearin/ist717/james.htm [May 20, 2000]; also available at www.aloha.net/~dyc/testimony.html.

5. Leon James, "Traffic Violence: A Crisis in Community Mental Health," *Innercom—Newsletter of the Mental Health Association in Hawaii*, June 1987. Available online at www.aloha.net/~dyc/violence.html.

6. Martinez, "Statement," www.house.gov/transportation/surface.sthearin/ist717/martinez.htm.

7. James B. Reed, Janet B. Goehring, and Jeanne Mejeur, "Environment, Energy and Transportation Program Reducing Crashes, Casualties and Costs—Traffic Safety Challenges for State Legislatures," National Conference of State Legislatures, Environment, Energy and Transportation Program, Transportation Series No. 5, February 1997 [online], www.ncsl.org/programs/esnr/transer5.htm [May 20, 2000].

8. National Highway Traffic Safety Administration (NHTSA), "Traffic Law Enforcement" [online], www.nhtsa.dot.gov/people/injury/enforce/tleFeb99.htm [May 20, 2000].

9. Ibid.

10. Leon James and Diane Nahl, "Police and Legislative Initiatives" [online], www.aloha.net/~dyc/police.html [May 20, 2000].

11. NHTSA, "Traffic Law Enforcement," www.nhtsa.dot.gov/people/injury/enforce/tleFeb99.htm.

12. Deborah Sharp, "South Florida Tries 'Stealth' Campaign," *USA Today* [online], www.usatoday.com/news/special/agdrive/drive004.htm [May 20, 2000].

13. Michigan Office of Highway Safety Planning (OSHP) Web site, www.ohsp.state.mi.us/pages/default.htm [May 20, 2000].

14. MariLynn Terrill, "AP Wire News Briefs," *Western Front*, July 21, 199 [online], westernfront.wwu.edu/1999/July/news1854.html [May 21, 2000].

15. Community Roadwatch Report [online], www.polcomms.org.nz/Forms/Roadwatch%20Report.htm [May 21, 2000].

16. "Governor Pataki Announces Legislation to Fight Road Rage," New York State Government Press Release [online], www.state.ny.us/governor/press/feb9_98.html [July 23, 1999].

17. U.S. Department of Transportation, "Remarks Prepared for Delivery, Secretary of Transportation Rodney E Slater, Aggressive Driving and the Law: A Symposium," January 22, 1999 [online], www.dot.gov/affairs/12299sp.htm [May 21, 2000].

18. NHTSA, "Traffic Law Enforcement," www.nhtsa.dot.gov/people/injury/enforce/tleFeb99.htm.

19. Jan Goehring, "Aggressive Driving, Background and Overview Report," *NCSL Transportation News*, November 1998 [online], www.ncsl.org/programs/esnr/498rage.htm [March 3, 1999].

20. New Jersey Aggressive Driving Program, "Aggressive Driver/Aggressive Enforcement Report Issued for 1997" [online], www.state.nj.us/lps/p80418a.htm [May 21, 2000].

21. NHTSA, "Strategies for Aggressive Driver Enforcement," www.nhtsa.dot.gov/people/injury/enforce/aggressdrivers/intro.html.

22. Goehring, "Aggressive Driving," www.ncsl.org/programs/esnr/498rage.htm.

23. Bob Mitchell, "Aggressive Drivers Face Road Rage 'Test'—Education Needed on Stress, Experts Say," *Toronto Star*, March 25, 1998.

24. Leon James and Diane Nahl, "Aggressive Driving Prevention Course for Law Enforcement" [online], www.aloha.net/~dyc/police/teecards.html [May 20, 2000]; *RoadRageous Aggressive Driver Course for Law Enforcement* (N. Miami: American Institute for Public Safety, 2000).

25. NHTSA, "Strategies for Aggressive Driver Enforcement," www.nhtsa.dot.gov/people/injury/enforce/aggressdrivers/intro.html.

SPEED LIMITS
THE GREAT
MOTORIST REBELLION

AGGRESSIVE VERSUS ASSERTIVE DRIVING

I break the law every time I drive on the highway. There's nothing unusual about that: The vast majority of American drivers are law-breakers, too. We American drivers have always decided for ourselves how fast to drive. Whenever arbitrarily low speed limits have been imposed, we've just disregarded them—or fought back with radar detectors and CB radios.[1]

What is speeding? Most drivers admit to going over the posted speed limits at times, but they vary in how much over and how regularly. This is what's called the "speed limit + x" rule. For example, for drivers who consider the "start of speeding" to be $x=15$ miles per hour above speed limit, in a 35 MPH zone, speeding begins at 50 MPH! The size of the x varies according to neighborhood norms, and it tends to remain constant. Police say they consider speeds measurable above the posted limit to be speeding. Clearly there is a 15 MPH divide between the law and the cultural norm. This is the source of the great American speed limit rebellion that is fomenting in activist groups around the nation and on the Web.

The topic of speed limits arouses vehement reactions from drivers who meet in online discussion groups. First, they believe that fixing speed limits is a government ploy for levying additional unauthorized taxes, which arouses resentment against police who enforce the limits. Second, they feel that good drivers who can handle higher speeds are being made to suffer for bad drivers whose "stupid" and "mindless" errors cause most accidents, forcing lower limits on everyone:

> Almost all speeding tickets are bad. It's not because the officers don't follow procedures, it's the speed limits themselves that are too low. Instead of attempting to make our roads safer by aiming laws at those in society who don't know how to properly drive, why don't we just remove these idiots from the road?

• "Slow drivers" arouse fury:

> Every night this week I've seen some corny story on the news about "road rage," wherein a supposedly maniacal individual kills innocent soccer moms by way of aggressive driving on the highway. If "road rage" is real, isn't it actually due to the frightening number of moronic wood-paneled-minivan-driving soccer moms going 47 MPH in the left lane on America's highways?

This attitude is summed up in another driver's conclusion: "No caskets needed for fast drivers who are attentive," reciting this common line of reasoning:

> Federal studies show that drivers at 10–15 above the average actual speed have the lowest accident rate, and even those 20–25 over have no more than the average driver. The real killers are at 10 or more under, and 30 or more over.

There is a widespread belief that speed is relative and that "speed in itself" isn't an important contributing factor in highway collisions. As one driver argues:

> There are times when doing 80 MPH is unsafe and there are times when it's perfectly safe. Unsafe would be going 80 MPH in heavy rain when traffic is flowing at 55–60 MPH. Safe would be passing someone at 80 on a clear day when traffic is flowing at 70–75 MPH. Note that the posted speed limit has nothing to do with either case. My point: The posted speed limit doesn't determine the danger factor in either of those two

ROAD RAGE AND AGGRESSIVE DRIVING

cases and it doesn't for many other real-world situations either. I witnessed a terrible accident caused by some moron who was going about 90 when everyone else was going around 65. I also saw an accident caused by some idiot trying to merge at 50-ish when traffic was flowing at 65–70 (rear-ended).

This was a response to a driver who pleaded "I'm just saying that driving the speed limit should not be considered a safety hazard." A typical point of view states that speed limits are only intended for poor and inexperienced drivers:

Where does it say that the lawmakers are good judges of what is proper speed limit? Why are speed limits in the United States so low, when Europeans can drive legally at higher speeds without having their highways drenched in blood? I think I can decide for myself what is a reasonable speed, given road, weather, traffic conditions. I think you'd have to be pretty naive not to work out that the speed limits are set for drivers that are either poor or not confident on the road, as well as those driving older vehicles. Applying a 55 limit regardless of where the road is, what kind of road it is, how wide it is, how much traffic it carries, and how twisty it is, is plain brainless. On main highways I stay under the limit because I don't want to answer to a cop. But on deserted, unpatrolled back roads, I drive like a bat out of hell. Damn anybody who doesn't like it.

There is, for some, a certain pride in rage and retaliation:

I believe that just because someone has road rage does not constitute them as being a bad driver, in fact makes them more aware of other vehicles around them that are driving in a hazardous fashion. Any fellow road ragers out there? I want to hear a similar point of view.

A 1999 Central Michigan University study of both victims and perpetrators of road rage found chilling results that provide further evidence of the cultural roots of aggression on the road and its relationship to social identity. The majority of convicted road ragers in this study remained self-righteous:

Most drivers who engage in "road rage"—from tailgating and honking to sideswiping and drawing weapons—believe their aggressive behavior is inherited from a parent and their victims deserve what they get. The exploratory study also found that while some victims of road rage are so shaken by the experience they no longer drive, others transform themselves into the offensive, aggressive drivers they once condemned—they will no longer let others get the upper hand.

More than 70 percent of the perpetrators felt that justice was served for having engaged in road rage behavior. In addition, the majority of the perpetrators in the study felt that their road rage activities elevated their self-identities and self-esteems because they were "correcting a wrong" or "standing up for oneself."[2]

CITIZEN ACTIVISM AGAINST GOVERNMENT PATERNALISM

In the 1990s, as government stepped up its fight against aggressive driving, two ideological groups of drivers emerged, taking opposing sides on government intervention in controlling motorists. The ideological "right" consists of "assertive" drivers who take driving seriously, consider themselves skilled, complain bitterly about law enforcement practices, and uphold an aggressive attitude toward many drivers whom they consider incompetent, inconsiderate, and responsible for most accidents. The ideological "left" promote more government intervention and legislation restricting the behavior of motorists, such as aggressive driving initiatives by police, electronic traffic control devices, neighborhood traffic calming strategies, total speed enforcement, maintenance of a national database of aggressive drivers, and a national hotline for reporting license numbers of cars observed driving aggressively. Interestingly, both sides support better driver training, but neither side sees training as the central issue.

An increasing polarization is taking place between those who pressure government officials to initiate more aggressive approaches against aggressive drivers, and those who oppose further government intervention as intrusive and unnecessary. Each side is well prepared with its own ideology, logic, and statistics to back up its arguments. A variety of individual and collective efforts are active across the country, such as the group Citizens For Roadside Safety:

> The goal of this organization is to save lives and force the Federal Highway Administration (FHWA) and the states to dedicate more time and money to highway safety. In the past there has been an attitude that if a driver runs off the road they deserve to die. Due to pressure from many people and organizations like ours, this attitude is gradually changing.[3]

However, the problem isn't that simple, according to groups on the other side who believe that inviting more regulation incurs hidden costs and unacceptable disadvantages, particularly when it comes to speed limits. The National Motorists Association (NMA) was established in 1982

ROAD RAGE AND AGGRESSIVE DRIVING

"to represent the interests and rights of North American motorists."[4] Both at the national level and through a system of state chapters, it has organized a widespread movement of resistance to speed enforcement on highways. Members share the philosophy that highway authorities wrongly attribute the cause of accidents to going faster than the posted speed limit. They question the scientific validity of studies cited by authorities to justify setting the same policy toward speed limits on all types of roadways. They charge that governments at the county and state level set speed limits below the rate most drivers actually travel, in violation of federal regulations, and they believe that this is done to increase revenue through ticketing. From this ideological perspective, anything that leads to more government regulation of driving is viewed with suspicion, for example, recent legislative activity on aggressive driving:

> Road rage and aggressive driving has been a hot topic with the Michigan media. This is not a coincidence. The battle against road rage and aggressive driving was thought up in Washington, D.C. The insurance industry and the safety lobby thought up the campaign. The government is providing grants to the states to combat road rage. . . . Michigan is using funds to purchase laser speed detection devices to write more speeding tickets. This is not getting unsafe drivers off the road. The unsafe drivers are tailgating, hogging the left lane, weaving through traffic, or driving too slow. If we want to combat road rage we should use the publicity and funding to target the problem—not collect more revenue from those driving a reasonable speed.[5]

The Association of British Drivers (ABD) like the NMA, opposes current speed limit policies in the U.K. and questions the veracity of official reports attempting to prove that "speed kills." According to the ABD, there is no justification for the oft-quoted government assertion that "one-third of accidents are caused by excessive speed."[6] When ABD researchers analyzed a 1999 report by the British Transport Research Laboratory (Report 323), they concluded excessive speed was a relatively minor causal factor in accidents (4 to 5 percent) in comparison to inattentiveness or "careless or incompetent inability to judge a situation involving another road user." Still, the battle to slow cars is intensifying in many communities with intrusive tactics.

To buttress its position, in 1999 the National Motorists Association Foundation (NMAF) released a study on speed limits and highway safety. It reviewed data since 1995, when the national maximum speed limit was repealed, allowing each state to establish its own speed limits. Thirty-three states raised freeway speed limits in 1996, while seventeen did not. What happened when the study compared the accident rate for the two groups of states?

Speed Limits—The Great Motorist Rebellion

Comparing the group of limit-raising states and the group of unchanged states, the study demonstrated that fatality rates dropped in both groups, essentially equally. Raising speed limits did not affect overall safety. The study examined fatality rates on all roads in each state, so that the expected usage shifts from less-safe undivided highways to safer and faster freeways were accounted for, helping to explain the favorable safety results associated with higher freeway limits.[7]

According to the report, these findings are similar to other studies that have reported a 5 percent reduction in traffic accidents for all states, regardless of their policy toward highway speed limits. While the National Highway Traffic Safety Administration (NHTSA) and others warned in 1995 that raising limits would kill sixty-four hundred more people each year, the national fatality rate actually dropped to record lows in each subsequent year.[8]

Many drivers refuse to acknowledge that speed is a contributing factor to crashes because it reduces the time available to react in an environment where mistakes are common.

> Speed does not kill; it takes an idiot behind the wheel to kill. Don't be an idiot. The whole idea of driving is that you're not supposed to hit things. That's why every car on the road has a steering wheel. If a driver doesn't hit a barricade, the driver won't be killed, irrespective of the speed at which the driver is traveling.

Still, some drivers seem to prevail with a cool logic that's closer to the truth:

> Speed increases the likelihood of impact and since most recreational drivers are indeed "lousy, lazy, or stupid" at times, there's a pretty good chance that someone will do something stupid while somebody else is going too fast to react to it. That's a fairly common theme in most straight-road highway accidents I've been to.
>
> In spite of the propaganda that you've swallowed . . . speed limits do involve safety issues. The idea, broken down into it's most simple elements, is to keep traffic moving at a safe and predictable speed, so that traffic crossing (at intersections) or merging (at on ramps) or simply changing lanes (anywhere) can correctly estimate closing speeds.

In other words, predictable speeds are critical for drivers to gauge their decisions and the anticipated responses. Without predictable speeds, the element of risk increases sharply, which in turn sets up a classic recipe for road rage. This sounds reasonable, because we need predictability to reduce errors, yet it's not acceptable to emotional logic:

ROAD RAGE AND AGGRESSIVE DRIVING

Please present some proof that going faster will increase the likelihood of hitting something. You can't, because there isn't any! Some very basic driving habits that apply to lower speeds also apply as the speeds go up. If you follow them then you can safely travel at higher speeds. If you maintain a safe following distance, keep right and pass left, and pay attention to the road then you can safely drive much faster than most highways are posted. Not all drivers are as stupid as you think they are. They drive around obstacles at speeds above 55 MPH. An extra 20 MPH does not cloud their brain and force them to aim for the concrete barriers.

Many traffic engineers agree with the theory that driving is safest when speed limits reflect actual driving rates on that road rather than being set lower as an attempt to slow down the traffic. Drivers will drive at their confidence level for conditions, and that is always higher than the legal limit when it is set too low. It creates hazardous conditions because it breaks up the homogeneity of drivers flowing at a similar speed. It promotes a diversity of speeds, and this, the engineers say, is more dangerous than setting the flow at a higher legal rate. In addition to being more dangerous, citizens get slapped with a scary traffic stop, an expensive traffic citation, and a higher insurance rate. Finally, they believe that it's unjust and unconstitutional. Clearly, citizens are passionate about speed, speed limits, and speed enforcement. To many, it is obvious that speed kills, while others deny it and remain unconvinced that speed enforcement is justified. Nevertheless, government is extending its efforts to regulate speed and some citizen groups are taking charge in their own way.

POLICE PRESENCE

Police patrols put a damper on aggressive driving and encourage quick reductions in speed:

What bothers me most about Texas drivers is when they see a cop on the road. They usually hit their brakes and everyone behind them freaks out and has to hit their brakes too. Then, most of the people just congest the road because they are too afraid to go around the cop. Stupid Drivers.

An officer confirms it:

When I drive below the posted speed limit on the freeway I create traffic jams because everyone seems to be afraid to pass me.

One driver complains that police officers often drive over the speed limit even when they don't have to:

The Virginia state police came up behind me doing 85-plus, I moved over, and then they stop dead and pull into one of those emergency vehicle only lanes to set up a speed trap. Admit it, you never drive the speed limit, and you probably don't even have to when not on duty, since the cop who pulled you over would recognize you and let you go. As a police officer you should not only be enforcing the laws but also setting an example for others to follow.

But when the police car goes over the speed limit, it's not smart to pass:

I was driving on M14 in Michigan, west of Detroit heading toward Ann Arbor. I merged onto the expressway with a Michigan state police car about three vehicles in front of me. He was traveling at about 62 MPH (the speed limit at the time was 55), so I set my cruise at 62 and followed him. I gradually crept up on him and finally passed. It took seven miles, so we were going at virtually identical speeds. As soon as I went by he put his flashers on and pulled me over. As he walked up to the car he said, "Passing a police car; that's not too smart." Apparently not. Even dumber was when I replied, "A police car speeding, then pulling me over for the same thing; that's not too smart either." Surprise. I got the ticket.

A commonly expressed attitude among drivers is that police should spend their time fighting crime in the city, not patrolling roads to check on drivers:

My eyes are not on the road for a significant chunk of time while I'm driving—not because I'm spacing out, but because I'm looking for cops. If I didn't have to watch for cops, I'd be a much safer driver. I'd think that cops would want to eliminate traffic violations, because then they'd only be going after murderers, robbers, and other nastiness that the vast majority of people think should be punished. Imagine the community support they'd have! Right now I can't stand the police in my home town, because I picture them as dweebs who lie in wait trying to ambush people like me going over the limit.

TRAFFIC CALMING

According to the Institute of Transportation Engineers (ITE), "Traffic calming is the combination of mainly physical measures that reduce the negative effects of motor vehicle use, alter driver behavior and improve conditions for non-motorized street users."[9] Years before the phrase "traffic calming" became widely known, we learned to accept traffic lights, stop signs, yield signs, speed bumps, and rumble strips to manage and control traffic flow for safety and efficiency. According to ITE, traffic calming goals aim to develop indirect methods of influencing the behavior of drivers to:

- Increase the quality of life
- Incorporate the preferences and requirements of the people using the area (e.g., working, playing, residing) along the streets, or at intersections
- Create safe and attractive streets
- Help to reduce the negative effects of motor vehicles on the environment (e.g., pollution, sprawl)
- Promote pedestrian, cycle, and transit use

Since traffic-calming objectives focus on increasing safety and the perception of safety for nonmotorized users of streets, physical barriers and designs are used to force motor vehicles to slow down, including speed humps or bumps, chokers, traffic circles, closures, diverters, median barriers, raised crosswalks, raised intersections, roundabouts, rumble strips, and chicanes. Many drivers lack the skills and persistence to train themselves to cooperate with the spirit of traffic-calming programs in the neighborhoods they travel through. It helps to think of the positive aspects of traffic calming as we drive through and slow down despite our impatience to move on. Consider the benefits of traffic calming cited by ITE:

- Allows your own neighborhood to protect the young and old
- Reduces the need for police enforcement
- Enhances the street environment (e.g., street scaping)
- Encourages water infiltration into the ground
- Increases access for all modes of transportation
- Reduces cut-through motor vehicle traffic

Traffic control is an issue that pits various constituencies against each other. Public pressure sometimes determines a traffic policy that is suitable for cyclists but not for drivers, and vice versa. People who live where rush hour traffic zips by every day want traffic-calming devices to slow things down on their block. Bicycle advocacy groups want more restrictions on the movement of cars, which drivers oppose. Controversy surrounding the issue is inevitable since the parties involved protect contrary interests, and because it amounts to speed control, traffic calming tends to set opposing lines between neighborhood constituencies, including:

- Motorists in transit versus local residents
- Drivers versus bicyclists
- Drivers versus pedestrians

Speed Limits—The Great Motorist Rebellion

- Bicyclists versus pedestrians
- Private versus commercial drivers
- Four-wheel drivers versus truckers

Authorities set speed limits according to traffic engineering studies. They find that the best way to ascertain the appropriate speed limit for a stretch of road is to survey the speed of free flowing traffic and to set the speed limit at the eighty-fifth percentile, the speed exceeded by 15 percent of the vehicles.[10] This practice minimizes accident risk and maximizes motorist compliance. The NMA argues that instead of following this approach, current speed limits are based on political considerations, such as making it easier to gain court approval for convictions or relying on fines as revenue.

Many concerned motorists believe that exceeding speed limits can be safe under favorable conditions, so citations could be dismissed when the court ascertains that there was probably no safety hazard involved. They support allowing traffic engineers to set or change statutory limits only if the observed and measured eighty-fifth-percentile speed differs from the statutory speed limit for that classification of road. They want speed zoning to be tied to speed measurement data, obtained unobtrusively under favorable weather conditions, in the absence of construction work or visible police presence. The NMA does not object to separate speed limits for other vehicle classifications, such as big trucks, nor does it object to law enforcement charging a driver with excessive speed regardless of the posted limit, as long as the officer can prove in court that the speed was unsafe for prevailing conditions. In short, citations should be withdrawn if motorists can prove they were not exceeding the eighty-fifth-percentile of the actual traveling speed on that road, regardless of the posted or statutory limit. Obviously, their intent is to return some judicial control to motorists.

The NMA cites a number of traffic-engineering studies showing that "arbitrarily interrupting traffic with 'nuisance' or 'speed-breaker' stop signs increase intentional violation and can actually increase the overall speed on the road where they are used." The Manual on Uniform Traffic Control Devices (MUTCD) forbids the use of stop signs for speed control because unnecessary stop signs encourage aggressive driving and make it less safe for pedestrians. Studies have shown that using speed bumps for speed control only works for traffic adjacent to the bump, and does not reduce the average speed on a street. While humps and bumps can be dangerous to cyclists and a nuisance to pedestrians, each bump slows down emergency vehicles by fifteen seconds. All vehicles are forced to decelerate and accelerate, using more fuel and creating more pollution than traffic passing through. As a result, Michigan has outlawed bumps as a traffic control device.

ROAD RAGE AND AGGRESSIVE DRIVING

ELECTRONIC TRAFFIC SURVEILLANCE

Red-light running is the leading cause of urban crashes and annually kills eight thousand people and injures one million more. A study by the Insurance Institute for Highway Safety looked at seventy-eight cities in the United States with populations of over two hundred thousand and found an average of 2.5 fatal red light running crashes per one hundred thousand people per year.[11] The range was substantial with top-ranking areas like Fresno, Los Angeles, and Sacramento experiencing nearly twice the national average. In 1998 U.S. Secretary of Transportation Rodney Slater announced a nationwide campaign against red-light running, calling the practice one of the most dangerous aspects of aggressive driving. The new campaign provides federal and private funding for additional red-light cameras to augment local law enforcement. Photo radar consists of a camera, computer and radar. The radar detects the speeding car, the camera takes a picture of the driver and the license plate, and the computer records the time and place, storing the information in an accessible database. The registered owner of the vehicle receives a citation by mail and drivers can make an appointment to view their pictures.

A 1995 federally funded pilot program in thirty-one U.S. cities cut red-light collisions by as much as 43 percent in some communities. In 1997, the governor of California signed a bill that increased fines for running red lights to $271. Half of the money collected from the tickets goes toward enforcement and creates a self-funded program for the cameras. The use of cameras to enforce traffic regulations has been authorized by legislation in several states, including Delaware, District of Columbia, Illinois, and Maryland. North Carolina and Oregon have limited authorizations for particular cities. Illinois, California, and Texas authorize the use of rail-crossing cameras. Colorado requires warning tickets for first-time offenders if the violation is less than 10 MPH over the limit, and caps fines at $40, denying license renewal requests from drivers with unpaid fines. On the other hand, New Jersey and Wisconsin prohibit the use of camera radar for traffic enforcement. New York and Virginia set a maximum limit of twenty-five photo monitoring devices for specified localities; Utah limits camera radar to school zones; and Hawaii has placed cameras at key intersections and plans to implement photo radar ticketing in 2000.

Supporters of the new traffic technology believe that photo radar cuts accident rates at intersections where they are installed. This is significant because more than one million collisions occur at intersections with traffic signals each year in the United States.[12] But opponents disagree with the interpretation of the evidence. They object to a system of electronic surveillance on highways, and enforcement that is triggered by a "ticket machine." They don't believe that slowing traffic leads to greater safety, and want speed limits to be "realistic," to reflect what most drivers are doing on a stretch of road. So opponents push for techniques that are known to reduce accident rates without slowing traffic, such as improvements in light synchronization and road design. Others who see traffic cameras as an invasion of privacy that ushers in the era of big brother nevertheless accept camera enforcement as the lesser of two evils, the other being their terror of aggressive drivers.

The benefits of the greater use of electronic traffic surveillance are said to result in fewer police officers needed on traffic duty, more pressure on drivers to comply with regulations, reducing the number and severity of collisions, penalizing violators with fines to pay for a control system that protects everyone, and avoiding discriminatory treatment of drivers.[13] These benefits ensure that traffic control technologies will continue to be deployed for some time. It is reported that by 1998, traffic cameras to control speed were in use in over seventy countries. Despite legitimate fears of invasion of privacy and fraudulent misuse, traffic surveillance technologies will be integrated with intelligent transportation systems (ITS). A vehicle's location may be tracked or monitored continuously throughout a trip, by road and satellite remote control devices, creating a permanent digital record of a trip with associated details about location and places visited, speed, length of stops, and any other detail obtainable from the car's computer. Precursors to integrated systems are seen in 1999 auto models equipped with GPS services such as OnStar and Visteon. If legislation permits, integrated traffic management systems could be used as a system of taxation based on the number and kind of violations found in the database at the end of each year.

As expected, the National Motorists Association opposes photo radar on principle:

> NMA opposes the use of photographic devices (video, motion picture, or still), including the citing of vehicle owners with moving violations that may or may not have been committed by the vehicle's owner. With properly posted speed limits and properly installed traffic-control devices, there is no need for camera-based traffic law enforcement devices. Taking a reckless driver's picture does not stop that incident of reckless driving.[14]

Many objections have been raised by the NMA to all aspects of photo-enforcement approaches, from inadequate notification of defendants (by mail) to failure to positively identify the driver of the vehicle and promptly notify the defendant. Photo radar evidence leaves out the context of the incident, and no witnesses are present to explain the situation. Since photo-enforcement devices have not been proven by independent researchers to reduce violation rates, some question the claims of manufacturers that their devices improve safety. The NMA points out that the United States has a lower fatality rate than most of the countries that regularly employ photo enforcement devices.

Another serious concern is that photo radar can generate faulty speed readings, raising the specter of thousands of tickets being issued between routine maintenance and calibration inspections. Tests done by the University of Virginia on high-speed, multilane highways found that fewer than 3 percent of the photos taken of vehicles on interstate-type roads provided a clear image of a single vehicle, the license plate number, and the driver. The NMA also objects to cameras because they are intrusive and unnecessary. They argue that most red-light runners are inattentive and would not be influenced by the presence of a camera, but no evidence is presented for this theory. Instead they believe that red-light cameras might be an easy way for authorities to postpone needed improvements such as traffic light synchronization, elimination of unneeded controls, and partial deactivation of traffic lights during periods of low traffic volume. The NMA takes the position that government officials have abandoned their traffic-engineering responsibilities, relying instead on electronic surveillance systems to generate new income.

Citizen opposition to electronic enforcement is widespread, for example:

> This petition of British Columbia Voters and other concerned citizens is to request the cancellation of the use of photo radar cameras on British Columbia Roadways. We request that speed limits be adjusted to reflect the speeds that the majority of drivers want to travel, thereby reducing speed variation and the necessity for unreasonable speeding fines. Your petitioners respectfully request that you immediately take such action as deemed appropriate.
>
> It is imperative that the provincial government be made aware of the level of opposition to their policies on photo radar speed enforcement and the setting of speed limits. Our goal is to collect 250,000 signatures (10 percent of the motoring population in B.C.) on the petitions and will officially present them to the Minister of Transportation and Highways.[15]

Nevertheless, public-opinion surveys by the Insurance Institute for Highway Safety and Behavior Research Center of Arizona show general support for photo-enforcement systems. In 1998, Advocates for Highway and Auto Safety, an alliance of consumer safety, law enforcement, public health, and insurance organizations, released the results of a Harris Poll showing that two out of three Americans (65 percent) "want their state legislatures to authorize the use of cameras at intersections to take a picture of the license plate of every car that runs a red light."

Red-light running is one of the most frequent traffic offenses occurring as often as once every five minutes. Red-light-running camera enforcement is a proven countermeasure to help reduce violations and intersection crashes. Preliminary crash data from localities employing red light running cameras already indicates their effectiveness. Victoria, Australia experienced a 32 percent reduction in intersection crashes in just the first six months after camera installation, and Los Angeles, CA, found that red-light-running camera use at railroad grade crossings reduced crashes by 42 percent in the first six months.[16]

In general, American drivers support installing cameras at intersections to reduce violations, collisions, and injuries. But many do not, and some have made it a political issue.

SPEED TRAP REGISTRIES AROUND THE WORLD

Citizen activism against speed enforcement has taken a new twist on the World Wide Web. The idea for a directory of speed traps to alert travelers began in the United States.[17] Thousands of entries organized by state can be accessed; for example, this one from Texas:

290 northwest freeway road
Mile Marker: between Fairbanks N Houston and Pinemont
Date Added: Sat Jul 5 02:59:12 CDT 1997
Speed Measuring Technology Used: radar
Average Ticket Cost: unknown
Group Running Trap: Local PD
Type of car used: marked
Used: weekly
Scanner Frequency:
Latitude: 29.879613
Longitude: -95.529969

Additional Info: There are several traps here: Southbound (toward downtown Houston):

1. At top the hill approaching the Fairbanks N Houston exit, a Houston Police Dept (HPD) Camaro sits on the downslope just out of detector range.

2. On the service road after exiting @ Fairbanks N Houston, two HPD Camaros sit on a side road. One tags the other tickets.

3. Just past the Pinemont exit, sitting under the Pinemont overpass, same HPD Camaro. Northbound (toward Austin): 1. Same as Southbound 3.[18]

ROAD RAGE AND AGGRESSIVE DRIVING

According to the Speedtrap Registry, law enforcement agencies are not against these information-sharing activities, viewing them as just another method of exerting pressure on drivers to manage their speed. The worldwide reach of this movement, extraordinary in its dedication to fighting vehicular speed control by government, reveals the depth of the issue in many people's minds. Excessive restrictions on rate of travel are seen as illegitimate encroachment on constitutional freedom. With this conviction comes an interpretation of scientific findings that disagrees with that of the government and antispeed citizen groups.

ACTIVISM AGAINST AGGRESSIVE DRIVERS

Citizens Against Speeding and Aggressive Driving is a nonprofit grass-roots organization that sponsors an annual National Road Victims Remembrance Day:

> CASAD is dedicated to making the roads safe for drivers, pedestrians, and bicyclists alike. Our mission is to reduce auto-related deaths and injuries by eliminating speeding and aggressive driving, and to offer assistance to victims of car crashes and their families.[19]

The organization encourages communities to introduce traffic-calming methods, lobbies for more legislation and law enforcement against aggressive drivers, and pressures car manufacturers to change their focus in commercials:

> It is a familiar scene during prime-time television: A young woman is shown driving a red Mitsubishi Eclipse down a country road at very high speed. The woman is on her way to her grandparents' home, and the car is going so fast that it makes the house rumble when she arrives. Meanwhile, the announcer declares: "It's uncommonly fast, and fun to drive, and it makes quite an entrance."
>
> The steady stream of advertisements like these, which continue to promote dangerous driving behavior despite enormous publicity about the epidemic of aggressive driving, has shocked many CASAD members. In March, CASAD's public policy committee sent letters to the CEOs of 14 major automakers in the United States, urging them to stop promoting speeding and reckless driving in their television commercials. The committee expressed particular concern about the potential of these ads to influence the behavior of young drivers.[20]

Ontario's Oro-Medonte County launched a road safety program involving King Township called Road Watch:

Speed Limits—The Great Motorist Rebellion

Our mandate is to reduce fatalities and collisions through awareness, education, and enforcement. Our roads have Road Watch signage and all citizens receive a packet of Citizen Report Forms. When they observe dangerous aggressive driving they can fill in the form and describe the behavior, action, location, etc., and the information can be faxed to the Ontario Provincial Police or placed in a drop-off box made by our high school students. Funds were raised for this project and this September [1999] we have Education Resource Kits for primary, junior and intermediate students (K to grade 8). We have the permission of both school boards to do this and the Road Safety Program has been tied in with the school's curriculum.[21]

The Knoxville Road Rage Action Page urges motorists to go on the offensive against aggressive drivers:

Now, something can be done!! With a short form, you can keep a record of the objectionable driver for other Knoxvillians to view. Data on these pages will also be submitted to insurance companies on a regular basis. Now we'll know to keep away from that idiot with that certain license plate number. If nothing else, filling out this form and seeing the offending party on the Internet will make us feel better, no?[22]

Some typical examples of these emotionally charged reports:

Make/Model/Description: Dark Green Chrysler New Yorker
License: (KY) DXL568
Date Observed: 10/28/97

Driver's Actions: Old fart tailgates, even though there is plenty of room in the passing lane!

===

Make/Model/Description: Black Ford Econoline Van
License: 373 DLG
Date Observed: 10/30/97

Driver's Actions: This thing burns a few quarts of oil every hundred feet, putting out more smoke than a California wildfire. An environmental disaster on wheels. Can't drive behind it without supplemental oxygen.

A related organization calls itself DUD, and its theme is "Don't Get Mad—Get EVEN!"

You are cruising down the freeway, windows open, and the woofers are cranking the tunes. You don't have a care in the world. Suddenly the idiot in the car next to you does something real stupid, and unlawful.

ROAD RAGE AND AGGRESSIVE DRIVING

> The cops are never around when you need them. You give the jerk a blast on the horn. Your indignation is met with an upraised finger. Your blood pressure skyrockets, and your blood boils. Wait a minute—don't get mad—get even. Let the world know what a jerk he or she is. Put the license number up for the world to see. Register the dangerous driver as a DUD—the Database of Unsafe Driving.[23]

There are two emotional dynamics in the activism directed against bad drivers: (1) undergoing an agonizing or scary experience while driving, and (2) the compulsion to vent and retaliate. We think about frightening events over and over again and vent by retelling the story on many occasions. During each of these mental "rehearsals," the emotions of fear and vengeance are ignited. The terrifying part is often dramatized, and the retaliation part is often expressed in derogatory remarks about other drivers. Continuing to obsess about the incident rather than limiting our thoughts and feelings to the incident itself, we kick it up a notch by attaching it to ideology and the politics of emotions.

The road rage culture promotes cynicism toward agencies and officials who make road regulations, from police who enforce, to politicians who legislate, judges and county officials who administer, and engineers who advise and design. The logic is that "these people should stop telling us how to drive." And it deepens with the resentment felt against the rule makers of the road, "especially since they don't know what we know, so they end up causing more accidents instead of less." Nowhere is this attitude more visible than the issue of speed limits and their enforcement. Electronic and physical traffic control systems continue to be deployed even as citizen activism against speed control and government paternalism is increasing. Two motorists' ideologies are clashing in our neighborhoods.

NOTES

1. Personal anecdotes quoted throughout this chapter were sent to us by e-mail correspondents.

2. "Road Rage Drivers Show No Remorse" [online], www.newswise.com/articles/1999/4/ROADRAGE.CMU.html [May 21, 2000].

3. Citizens for Roadside Safety Web site, www.98.net/road-safety [May 21, 2000].

4. National Motorists Association (NMA) Web site, www.motorists.org [May 21, 2000].

5. "Road Rage," *Michigan Motorist News* [online], www.motorists.org/MI/roadrage.html [May 21, 2000].

6. Association of British Drivers, "U.S. Evidence Refutes Banal 'Speed Kills' Message," September 1997 [online], www.abd.org.uk [May 21, 2000].

7. National Motorists Association, "Foundation Study Shows: Safe to Raise Freeway Speed Limits" [online], www.motorists.org/pressreleases/safetoincreasespeedlimits.html [May 21, 2000].

8. National Highway Traffic Safety Adminsitration (NHTSA), "Strategies for Aggressive Driver Enforcement" [online], www.nhtsa.dot.gov/people/injury/enforce/aggressdrivers/intro.html [May 20, 2000].

9. Institute of Transportation Engineers (ITE), "Traffic Calming for Communitites" [online], www.ite.org/traffic/index.htm [May 21, 2000].

10. Insurance Institute for Highway Safety, "Speed and Speed Limits" [online], www.hwysafety.org/safety_facts/qanda/speed_limits.htm [May 21, 2000].

11. Ibid.

12. "Shelley Fights to Keep Red Light Cameras in California" [online], democrats.assembly.ca.gov/members/a12/press/p1298003.htm [May 21, 2000].

13. Ibid.

14. NMA Web site, www.motorists.org.

15. Alex Campbell, "Photo Radar as Deployed in British Columbia" [online], www.islandnet.com/ITE_BC/Jan97_Photo.html [May 21, 2000].

16. Ibid.

17. Speedtrap Registry Web site, www.speedtrap.com [May 21, 2000].

18. Speedtrap Registry, www.speedtrap.com/ShowTrapList.asp?country=38 [May 21, 2000].

19. Citizens Against Speeding and Aggressive Driving (CASAD), "Partnership for Safe Driving" [online], aggressivedriving.org/index.html [May 21, 2000].

20. Ibid.

21. County Web site, www.township.king.on.ca/rwgen.htm [April 4, 1999].

22. Knoxville Road Rage Action Page, www.geocities.com/TimesSquare/Castle/3130/complain.html [May 21, 2000].

23. Database of Unsafe Driving, "Don't Get Mad, Get Even" [online], www.comnet.ca/~chezken/duds.html [May 21, 2000].

DREAM CARS AND DRIVING REALITIES

IN THE DRIVER'S IMAGE

What do we look for in a car? One 1986 report describes an experiment to discover hidden or unconscious motives for buying certain kinds of cars.[1] The researchers compared responses to what people liked about cars, first in a normal state and then in a hypnotized state. Their answers were revealingly different. In the normal state people mentioned pragmatic things that are ordinarily important to car owners—price, reliability, comfort, and appearance. In the hypnotized state they spoke of the liberating sense of freedom that motoring brings and the sense of exhilaration that comes from driving fast. Precautions like wearing seat belts were dismissed as timid and unnecessary. They imagined that driving in busy traffic is a pleasant and interesting experience. All drivers were perceived as friendly "beings of power" controlling wonderful machines in beautiful highway settings. The cars they were driving in their imagination were dream cars—ultrafast, amphibious, and powerful, with luxury features. Of course, none of these people actually drove cars like this and they didn't see many drivers that behaved like those in their idealized imagination. Could it be that people drive in their imagination more than on the real road? Some psychiatrists believe that our fantasies are driven by unfulfilled desires. According to Freud, every fantasy contains the fulfillment of a wish. An idealized image of ourselves in cars "improves" the unsatisfactory reality.

Car commercials appeal to unfulfilled fantasies of distinction, uniqueness, independence, and superiority. The implied message is, "Own this particular car and you'll have these desired qualities." Buyers are influenced by such commercials because cars confer a special social identity on their owners. Self-witnessing reports of drivers frequently reveal that they correlate the car's appearance with its driver. When they see a luxurious or unusual car, in their mind its owner also takes on these characteristics—rich, educated, competent, good-looking, and well dressed. Old and unattractive cars had unkempt, lazy, unreliable owners who made driving blunders. Though their expectations were not necessarily met, drivers continued to perceive car and owner in this way.

A cover story in *Psychology Today* recognizes that people have revered cars for a century, and there's no "slowing down our ongoing love affair with the car."[2] The automobile has radically altered the way we live and build our homes, and is certainly one of the most significant objects of our age. Ego and self-image are intertwined with a sense of control and power expressed in the names manufacturers give to their models: Jaguar, Cougar, Eagle, Mustang, Blazer, Wrangler, Taurus, Viper, Cobra, Range Rover, Explorer. Car ads use words that describe cars in terms that evoke human drama and emotion: impulse, wild, spirit, dream, passion. Marketing appeals to our sense of ultimate attainment when the car in the ad is described as "beyond unique" or "supra distinctive" or "ultra-knockout." This is not simply a male preoccupation with power and dominance. Kate Culkin writes in *Ladies, Start Your Engines: Women Writers on Cars and the Road*:

> Speeding down I-80 in my El Camino, I am the most powerful woman in the world. Look out plastic import, I think, take that, puny sports car; if push comes to shove, I'll crush you without a second thought. Eating with one hand, steering with the other, I realize women with big American cars don't need self-assertiveness training—a V-8 engine would empower anyone, male or female.[3]

Back in the 1930s there was a popular stage song that went,

ROAD RAGE AND AGGRESSIVE DRIVING

I'm wild about horns on automobiles that go "Ta ta ta ta" "Ta ta ta ta"
Thirty-five bucks I'm glad I saved my dough to buy one
To be in style you ought to try one
For Sirens or Klaxons, the girls never fall
But I get attention when they hear that call
I'm wild about horns on automobiles that go "Ta ta ta ta ta ta ta."[4]

Many songs featuring the romance of cars and driving have made it to the top of the music charts. Songs like "Hey Little Cobra," "Hitchin' a Ride," "Car Wash," "Mercedes Boy," and "Pink Cadillac" celebrate taking pride in your vehicle, feelings of superiority in speed and horsepower, independence, partying, and a freewheeling lifestyle.

Automobile poetry and nicknames for cars reflect the enthusiasm people feel for their cars, but there may be a downside when these mental images are internalized and used as symbols of how we should be driving and how we should perceive other cars and their drivers in relation to ourselves. According to the world portrayed by automobile ads the car we drive must be super-charged with power and a competitive spirit. Commercials portray the new car that's "just for you" zipping around corners, climbing rugged country hills, flying through water, and zooming up palace staircases. A new car is sold as a status symbol, an extension of the self, competitive, exclusive. The car is portrayed as a home, fort, or castle; tank or missile; dream machine; great for getaway and escape.

The exaggerated way we normally talk and think about cars, fueled by super-charged automobile ads, could contribute to the current negative culture on highways by encouraging and romanticizing status competition, aggressiveness, hostility, envy, intolerance and disrespect for other drivers. A heightened sense of emotional territoriality promoted by some ads draws drivers into a me-against-them attitude that could lower the threshold for aggressive driving. While helping drivers with road rage containment and recovery, we have noticed a strong resistance to adopting a more supportive or prosocial driving style. Many of us who have grown up in the car culture have developed a subconscious fear of looking like wimps on the road. We are supposed to think and feel in superlative terms. The extreme has become the norm. This has become a deep-seated cultural value. This dramatic inner outlook unknowingly influences how people feel behind the wheel, what thoughts they have when driving, and how they treat each other on the road.

In and of itself, the passion for beautiful, high-performance cars doesn't require a high-handed attitude of disrespect toward other drivers. A love of cars can be compatible with supportive driving. Motorists who take car ownership and driving seriously stay knowledgeable about technical details, performance, and safety. They feel deeply about the importance of doing the right thing, whether it's buying, maintenance, or handling on the road. If they see a dirty, shabby looking car, they feel the owner is neglecting or mistreating the vehicle. In an important sense they're on the right side because many accidents are caused by drivers who are insufficiently caring or alert to problems with their cars. The problem starts when "being right" turns into "being righteous." The self-image game has then gone too far. We predict that as more people become involved in lifelong driver self-improvement, the symbols of excellence in the marketing world will turn to supportive driving portrayals.

DRIVING MUSIC

Music has become an integral part of the driving experience. Sound systems are the most popular accessory, and drivers often spend hundreds of dollars on good ones. Drivers are affected by music, carefully selecting types that have the desired effect for them, and avoiding others. For some, music is used to create a loud interior environment

> Personally I like Fear Factory. Gets you in a wickedly hyped up mood (not road rage) and lets you concentrate on driving like never before, also keeps you awake on those long drives.
>
> I don't know about going on a drive and listening to *Dark Side of the Moon*, too many quiet bits.
>
> For me it's the *Delicate Sound of Thunder* (Comfortably Numb version) turned up to about 20 going through a good ten-speaker system. Of course it sucks when you've only got a six-minute drive to get somewhere, and are forced to sit outside your mates' house for the last minute with the stereo that loud because it's sacrilege to turn it down or off before it finishes.
>
> You can't go past a bit of ZZ Top to get you in the driving mood.[5]

However, not everyone wants music to influence them while driving:

> For a few months I didn't have the money to replace my broken car radio. I was saving for a Blaupunkt. So for awhile, I drove a cappella, so to speak. Strangely, I grew to like not having a car radio. When I finally saved enough money to buy a radio, I didn't. I enjoyed the sounds of silence. My daily commute became intellectually interesting. I started thinking about all sorts of things about my personal philosophy. I realized that the lack of a car radio had liberated me. All along I believed the

music coming from the little speakers in the door set me free. Now I realize that it was limiting me.

I got caught speeding twice in my life and both of the times it was because I was listening to the music in my car and did not realize how fast I was going. When my favorite music comes out, I just lose myself! On a different day, I was driving and realized that the music was off. It was a bit of surprise because I was so calm and relaxed that it was almost like I was meditating. So I recommend that you sometimes stop listening to the music in your car. It's really different!

One of our correspondents sent us a school report in which she showed that her teenaged friends took longer to apply the brake when a sign came up while driving to loud music. They responded to signs faster when there was no loud music playing.[6]

Contrary to common belief, music may not immunize drivers from feeling enraged during routine traffic events:

There was no traffic. Everyone was signaling. I was happy. On the way, I even noticed that I was singing. It was weird because I came to a realization that when I drove, I usually only sing during slow songs and not the fast songs. There happened to be a stalled car on the far right shoulder lane. When the cars began to brake to "rubberneck," I became enraged, and I started swearing and cussing to the cars in front of me for slowing down. I even remember pretending that my hand brake was a machine gun and I "shot" all the cars in front of me.

Music has the power to calm or excite, to sooth or to inflame. If listening to music works to ease aggressive thoughts and feelings while driving, it can be an effective preventive agent. If drivers choose provocative music that encourages aggressive thinking, it may exaggerate emotional reactions in routine incidents.

DASHBOARD DINING

Besides mutating into moving communication platforms, twenty-first-century cars are being equipped for safer and more comfortable eating experiences. The latest in-car appliances include:

- mini-microwaves
- refrigerated glove boxes
- coolers designed for autos, trucks, and utility vehicles
- trays that fold down, as in passenger aircraft

- warming cup holders
- trash compactors

Dashboard dining is fast becoming part of the daily life of Americans, who have long been perfecting the practice of eating on the run. Fast-food chains are responding by designing specialties that are easier to eat behind the wheel.

- Taco Bell folds tortillas a particular way to hold food and juices inside; the tortillas are made more durable and taco shells less crumbly.
- Kentucky Fried Chicken offers a pita sandwich, with a pocket on the bottom to catch chicken, dressing, cheese, or anything else that might fall into a lap.
- IncrEdibles offers push n' eat scrambled eggs with cheese and bacon.
- Others make breakfast sandwiches more moist and crumble-proof.
- Some are designing omelets and hamburgers in the shape of a hot dog, making them easier to hold and eat with one hand. For instance, 7-Eleven convenience stores had an ad campaign depicting the stores as "Dashboard Diners," and introduced a hot dog-shaped quarter-pound hamburger.
- McDonald's has the McSalad Shaker. Salad comes in a plastic container that fits in a cup holder. Add the dressing, fasten the top, shake it up, and eat with a long fork.
- In-N-Out Burger in San Francisco supplies a "lapmat" with its juicy burgers, to help keep clothes and vehicle spotless.
- More car-friendly foods resemble egg rolls and burritos, with slender shapes or ingredients stuffed into wrappers.
- One-handed salad wraps and other easy-to-eat finger foods are replacing dipping sauces and shredded lettuce.
- Jack-in-the-Box offers an array of "finger foods," including French toast sticks.[7]

Eating while driving is common, but risky. A business executive, hurrying between meetings, took her eyes off the road to take a bite of a hamburger and went right through a red light. "It was really an eye-opener on how dangerous it is," she said, and since then she rarely eats and drives. Others believe they can steer, eat, and shift gears at the same time. One driver admitted, "Safety might sometimes be compromised, but yeah, I can do it." Still, the automobile is one of the favorite places to eat. It has been estimated that Americans eat about 18 percent of their meals in cars (that's nearly one meal in five!).[8] Car salesmen report that a car is **259** scarcely considered worth buying without multiple cup holders in the front and back with slide-out racks. Fast food restaurants report that 50 percent of their sales occur at the drive-through window.

According to the *San Francisco Chronicle*, the California Highway Patrol frequently fields calls about drunken drivers weaving on Bay Area freeways. But whiskey bottles and beer cans aren't always to blame. One officer complained about having to wait while a stopped motorist finished the last few bites of her burrito before she would sign a ticket for a lapsed registration, not to mention a driver with French fries between the legs and ketchup on the fingers who received a ticket for weaving and drifting across lanes while focusing too much on munching.

The point is not that people should stop eating in their cars but that, like other forms of multitasking while driving, one needs to train oneself to do it safely, to dashboard dine with emotional intelligence!

CAR PHONES

The National Highway Traffic Safety Administration estimates that there will be eighty million cell phone users by the end of 2000. Experts have calculated that in that year, 1 percent of traffic accidents will be due to car phone use, at a national cost of $3 billion. Several countries already have laws restricting drivers from using cellular phones, including Australia, Brazil, England, Israel, and Switzerland. Whether handheld, with headset, or built-in, car phone use is on the rise. More drivers use them and more people complain about drivers who do. It seems obvious to any observer that without training, talking on the phone while driving is risky because it can be distracting and will lead to near-misses or crashes. Research supported by the AAA Foundation for Traffic Safety in 1991 concluded that "use of cellular phones does not interfere significantly with the ability to control an automobile except among the elderly, where potentially dangerous lane excursions can occur."[9] The finding was based on the reactions of drivers in a traffic simulation task on a computer. Despite the optimistic conclusion, the data they report show that motorists who get involved in "complex conversations" have slower reactions to routine events, such as a stop sign, traffic light, or oncoming car, and fail to react altogether to some events to which they normally react when not on the phone. The study found that older drivers (fifty-five-plus) are twice as likely to be distracted by phone use as younger drivers. We emphasize that these results are based on drivers who did not put themselves through a training procedure. We believe that future research will show that multitasking while driving can be safely carried out if the drivers train themselves with appropriate exercises. Some drivers may require more training than others.

In an effort to reduce the number of motor vehicle accidents in New York, a state senator introduced legislation in 1999 to prohibit drivers from talking on cellular phones while traveling on roadways throughout New York State. The senator cited a 1999 study published in the *New England Journal of Medicine* showing that "dialing and driving can be just as dangerous as drinking and driving." The study indicates that the risk of having an automobile crash increases fourfold when the driver is talking on the telephone:

> Under the Queens lawmaker's legislation, people who talk on hand-held cellular phones or cellular car telephones while driving would be charged with a traffic infraction and pay a fine. A first offense could cost a driver up to $50, second offenses $100 or more, and third offenses $200 or more. Drivers would have a 60-second grace period to make and receive calls before pulling their vehicles off the road and parking in a safe location. The legislation also addresses circumstances in which drivers are alone and can demonstrate that they either needed to use the phone to protect their life or safety, or believed they were at risk of becoming a victim of a crime.[10]

Clearly, driving and talking on the phone can be dangerous if you don't train yourself. This is the critical issue in a world where this technology, along with Internet access or telecommuting in the car, probably will not be banned or restricted. Industry officials suggest that drivers pull off the road when they want to use the car phone. Is this realistic? We think it's more pragmatic to become competent and safe car phone users with a self-training program that includes these steps:

- Training yourself before using it in the car: how to hold the phone, how to answer it, how to dial it, how to give other commands (listening to voice mail and so on)
- Training yourself as you sit in the car before driving
- Training yourself gradually, while driving:
  * First, pretend you're calling and go through the steps.
  * Second, make training calls to a cooperating friend. Have a passenger present who can assist you.
  * Third, make and receive brief calls. Have a passenger present who can assist you.

Once you've learned the mechanics of calling, you need to train yourself for driving and talking on the phone:

ROAD RAGE AND AGGRESSIVE DRIVING

- How to stay alert
- How to give the appearance of being alert

Both aspects are important. When motorists see you talk on the phone many will be scared or annoyed at you, possibly even be hostile. The best way to demonstrate alertness is to respond clearly and predictably to changes in traffic situations. This is an important clue that other motorists use to gauge your alertness while on the phone. Keep up with the flow of traffic and practice executing lane changes and turns at the same rate as everyone else. The phone cannot be used as an excuse for slowing down or interfering with the expectations of other drivers. Unless we train ourselves in how to multitask efficiently while driving, we will disrupt the orderly flow of traffic and evoke hostility.

MOBILE COMPUTING

We are beginning to see sophisticated onboard, online personal computers that enable drivers to retrieve e-mail and pager messages and check for stock quotes, sport scores, lottery numbers, or horoscopes, as well as back-seat games and movies. One in-dash device fits in a single-bin compartment and provides a combination of information, entertainment, telephone communication, traffic alerts, voice e-mail, global positioning system (GPS) navigation including NavTech Map Data featuring moving maps and voice-announced next-turn directions, and security features. This is the beginning of a new phase for automobiles which manufacturers have come to see as the final frontier of unstructured time left in America—the commuting hours, or about 12 percent of waking time.

Auto suppliers estimate that the new market for in-car computers, called "automotive telematics," will quickly reach $10 billion in the United States alone. Visteon's system for the 2000 models is designed to be compatible with more than sixty-six foreign and domestic models. And General Motors has deployed its OnStar system in many of its 2000 models. Automotive computers work with flashing lights and icons on small vivid screens mounted on a center console. Drivers can use voice commands or switches for scrolling and changing functions. The computer robot reads your e-mail aloud, and eventually will be able to take dictation. The Delphi system will integrate steering-wheel controls with heads-up windshield displays to allow drivers to read e-mail without taking their eyes off the road or their hands off the wheel.

The politically correct way to refer to a car now is to call it your "mobile environment." Marketers predict that vehicles will become communication platforms. IBM is the latest in a string of technology heavyweights to move into the automobile space, working with some U.S. automakers on projects combining computing and automobile technology. "It's very much an extension of our strategy," said Ed Holden, director of IBM's global automotive marketing. "There are a lot of people on the road, and they'd like to be able to keep working while they're in their vehicle."[11] Microsoft introduced a Windows CE-based car computer that comes installed in the radio slot. It offers basic features such as voice-activated messaging and GPS navigation, and is designed to synchronize with handheld devices. Others, such as General Motors' OnStar system, have portable devices with mapping and navigation features that can be moved from car to car. IBM has teamed with DaimlerChrysler to create a mobile office that will include a desk, an IBM ThinkPad with ViaVoice speech recognition software, and a mobile Internet link.[12] The console sits in the back seat of the car so that people can't drive and surf simultaneously. The business console can also track the condition of the vehicle, navigate, and entertain passengers with Internet-based games.

Computer makers are expecting that the demand for car PCs will rise. Intel is reported to lead the list of mobile-electronics companies targeting the family car, and developers are looking closely at the Java programming language for development of key interfaces as the number of Windows CE-based auto-PC systems grows. Even dashboard displays are contemplated by some developers, despite the problem of driver distraction with graphic systems. Currently, GPS satellite receivers and digital video disk (DVD) navigation systems are the leading PC applications used in car navigation systems. Backseat video entertainment systems for passengers based on DVD technology are available; for instance, Ford Motor's Visteon Automotive Systems unit is a rear-seat entertainment system for minivans with plug-and-play capability for video games, and at the 2000 North American International Auto Show in Detroit, Ford announced its alliance with Yahoo! that will connect its customers to the Web.[13] Ford also offers rear-seat cameras to enable parents to watch their children.

eGo, a portable digital audio device launched late in 1999, gives commuters and mobile workers a way to conduct business from their cars. The "Audio PDA" includes a text-to-speech engine that converts e-mail messages into synthesized speech. Audio responses to e-mail are recorded and sent as e-mail attachments. Motorists can use speech prompts to navigate through their folders on the device. This device can be plugged into an A/C adapter and into a car's cigarette lighter, is equipped with two AA batteries for portable use, or may be hard-wired to a car stereo.

The General Motors e-GM unit is in full swing with the first GM "Web car" offered on a 2000 Cadillac, and featuring in-car services such as:

- Access to the Internet and World Wide Web
- Route support (communication with a service center for asking directions)
- Theft protection (tracking a stolen car)
- Air bag deployment notification
- Summoning an ambulance after a crash
- OnStar MED-NET (stores your personal medical history and allows emergency personnel access to this information)
- Concierge services, including remote door unlock, road side and accident assistance[14]

Up to one million GM owners are expected to subscribe to the OnStar service in 2000. These dramatic new technological services for motorists are exciting, but we must ask what are we doing to equip motorists to drive these dream cars? What new skills do drivers need to handle these "mobile environments" safely? Using these electronic devices while driving adds to the risk of driving. The official advice is that drivers should pull off the road into a parking lot before using them. We doubt that this is practical, since most drivers won't choose to stop. Again, we need to help drivers train themselves to use the increasing numbers of new gadgets safely. The training can be connected to the purchase, and manufacturers could play a significant role in facilitating this. We believe that QDCs are well suited to help millions of drivers train themselves in the intelligent use of the computing car. If, during the first century of car society, the automobile was your castle, in the next century the car will be your planet.

INTELLIGENT TRANSPORTATION SYSTEMS

The 1990s marked the first decade of the second century of car society, as well as the beginning of the deployment in the United States of a national architecture of intelligent transportation systems (ITS) that integrate vehicle and traffic control. By July 1996, the U.S. Department of Transportation had completed its ITS plans. In 1998, Congress authorized an additional $1.2 billion to the year 2003. By 1999, a number of statewide systems were already in place. According to some estimates, the global market for ITS products will exceed $200 billion by the year 2015. States use electronic transportation technology to integrate traffic control and traffic management at all levels of public and commercial transportation. The main functions are used to:

- Manage traffic electronically
- Make the roads safer
- Provide travel information
- Control environmental pollution
- Route commercial carriers
- Manage parking
- Quicken toll operations

Minnesota has a statewide system called Guidestar that integrates city and rural infrastructures, providing road and weather information statewide as well as information delivery systems for commercial vehicles. The TranStar system in Houston, Texas, is reported to reduce delays caused by traffic incidents, saving the city about $8 million annually. Electronic toll lanes on the Tappan Zee Bridge in New York have doubled traffic capacity from five hundred to one thousand vehicles per hour. The automated incident response system in Atlanta, Georgia, helped cut response times to emergencies in half, gaining precious minutes that save lives. Crash rates dropped by 38 percent in the six years after ramp meters were installed along Interstate 5 in Seattle, Washington, to control the flow of traffic entering the freeway.[15]

Legislation in Colorado has authorized the deployment of ITS-based services for traveler and road information, emergency medical response, traffic management and operation, safety monitoring systems, and commercial fleet management. Tennessee legislation focusing on traffic congestion and relief is officially committed to considering ITS as a potential solution. In 1997, the Pennsylvania legislature appropriated funds to deploy IT systems. Separate urban and commercial traffic management systems are also being created. It is reported that the Commercial Vehicle Information System Network (CVISN) will connect states through online technology for automated inspections and vehicle registration. Ten states have been selected by the Federal Highway Administration in a national pilot program for the deployment of CVISN.[16]

A list of ITS services currently offered or contemplated in diverse agency reports, demonstrates how rapidly the world of driving has been transported to the online world:

- En-route driver information
- Route guidance
- Traveler services information
- Online concierge service
- Traffic control incident management
- Travel demand management
- Pretrip travel information

- Ride matching and reservation
- In-car videoconferencing
- Electronic payment services
- Emergency notification and personal security
- Advanced vehicle control and safety systems
- Collision avoidance sonar
- Sleep monitors to wake the driver
- Vision enhancement with night vision technology
- Safety readiness
- Precrash restraint deployment[17]

The equipment involved in ITS management integrates highway electronics with in-car computer controlled sensors:

- Automated incident response systems
- Collision avoidance systems
- Dynamic traffic signs
- Electronic toll plazas
- Electronically encoded fare cards
- Global positioning system (GPS) and onboard navigation systems
- Intelligent cruise control and proximity warnings
- Panic buttons and "mayday" systems
- Radio updates on traffic conditions
- Ramp meters that measure and regulate traffic
- Roadside sensors that can detect tailpipe emissions
- Smart cards
- Tollbooth scanners
- Traffic flow detectors embedded in roads
- Travel kiosks

Intelligent transportation systems are designed to reduce the driver's involvement with certain details by automatically taking care of routine requirements such as electronic fare cards, toll-booth scanners, roadside sensors, intelligent cruise controls, and proximity warnings. The ultimate effect of ITS on aggressive driving has not been investigated, but while electronic assistance for motorists may compensate for driver error and improve both monitoring and communication functions that drivers depend on, drivers must wait many years before these enhancements are affordable. Currently, radar collision avoidance systems used in commercial trucking adds 3 percent to the cost of the vehicle.

The National Motorists Association stated in 1994 that

Dream Cars and Driving Realities

Intelligent Transportation System technology offers many opportunities to serve and benefit motorists. It also has the potential for great abuse on the part of government and industry. To the extent that ITS technology can expedite traffic, reduce delays, forewarn motorists of delays and/or dangerous conditions and improve the capacity of the highway system it should be supported and encouraged. Conversely, the NMA will oppose efforts to use ITS technology to ration highway capacity, dictate travel routes, enforce traffic laws or expand tolling.[18]

The NMA acknowledges the benefits of ITS, but it worries about potential uses of ITS to slap on new surveillance, regulations, and taxes:

Imagine driving down the highway, a sound alerts you and a message is displayed on an in-car screen, "You are speeding." This information is transmitted to the local authorities. The next day you receive a traffic citation in the mail. Or, you are on a rural highway with a speed limit of 45, and your vehicle's speed is automatically limited to 50 mph. If this sounds like something out of Star Wars, believe me, it is feasible.[19]

Car manufacturers have installed black boxes, similar to those in aircraft, that record data about trips such as speed. If there's a crash, it records the speed on impact along with other data that can be used in court cases. The NMA also opposes this unobtrusive observation technology though it has been deployed in many models in the 1990s.

MANAGING IN THE NEW WORLD OF DRIVING

We haven't achieved the jet cars portrayed in science fiction movies and television, but there are experimental flying car models available today. Robert Fulton designed a flying car in 1946, but Moulton "Molt" Taylor is known in the United States as the father of the flying automobile. He developed the modern Aerocar in the 1950s, and since then other inventors have developed the Cafly, the Jetcar, and the Air Car, among others. Enthusiasts predict that flying automobiles will enter the market by the year 2005. Driving has taken on new meaning as an interactive, multitasking operation that involves piloting a heavy, moving communication platform or mobile office, complete with dashboard dining and backseat multimedia. The new technologies in cars may contribute to motorists' bubble-environment mentality. Inevitably, cars will continue to evolve technologically, integrating functions that permit drivers to communicate and work on the road at a distance. The wise course is to acknowledge that drivers require training in these new technologies, in fact, each gadget requires a training process.

267

ROAD RAGE AND AGGRESSIVE DRIVING

It has not yet entered the consciousness of the automotive world that specific training is needed for using devices, such as cell phones, e-mail, GPS communications, and map reading, while driving and dashboard dining. But because people need to learn the new and ever more complex skills of "driving informatics," in the near future training will take a prominent role because of its impact on safety.[20] This new driving information literacy encompasses the ever-widening definition of what we do in and have to understand about cars: transportation, automotive repair, insurance, travel, communication, eating, grooming, reading, entertainment, work, education, and social relations among motorists and with police, truckers, passengers, pedestrians, and cyclists. Driving informatics represents the integration of the complexity of our intellectual, financial, and civic investments in the grand driving enterprise.

In this new world of driving, motorists face increasing "commuting stress." The stressful consequences of daily commutes include:

- Increased production of gastric acid
- Increased risk for gastrointestinal disorders
- Increased production of "fight or flight" hormones
- Reduced blood supply to the brain
- Lowered immune response for several hours
- Increased blood pressure
- Higher heart rate[21]

A recent poll reports that 49 percent feel some or a lot of anxiety sitting in traffic, 35 percent somewhat or very overwhelmed, and 51 percent feel some or a lot of stress in traffic.[22] People think it's just the congestion and delays, but most stress is due to aggressive and incompetent driving, exacerbated by the increasing pressure to multitask in vehicles. Since our driving environment will continue to increase in complexity, the real solution to combating commuting stress lies chiefly with the individual. Aggressive driving is a cultural habit learned from parents and reinforced by TV. It is ingrained in our personality and character through the culture of disrespect, the argument culture, and the culture of entitlement. It is exposed in traffic congestion, which presents plenty of opportunities for expressing displeasure. Congestion and construction would not lead to driver stress in a supportive and community-oriented highway atmosphere. The cultural inheritance of aggressive driving and road rage is spreading with each new generation. This inheritance can be checked if an entire generation of drivers declares itself against highway cynicism, and collectively adopts and supports new norms of civility and skill on roads.

NOTES

1. Peter Marsh and Peter Collett, *Driving Passion: The Psychology of the Car* (London: Jolmathan Cape, 1986).

2. Peter Marsh and Peter Collett, "Driving Passion: There Seems to Be No Slowing Down Our Ongoing Love Affair with the Car," *Psychology Today* 21, no. 7 (June 1987): 16–24.

3. Elinor Nauen, ed., *Ladies, Start Your Engines: Women Writers on Cars and the Road* (Boston: Faber and Faber, 1996).

4. Clarence Gaskill, "I'm Wild about Horns on Automobiles" [online], www.lib.duke.edu/cgi-bin/texis/searchdb/asl/search/+kx6ZePVpw/more.htm?id=3797441a137 [May 21, 2000].

5. Personal anecdotes quoted throughout this chapter were sent to us by e-mail correspondents.

6. Susan Strick, "Music Effects on Drivers' Reaction Times" [online], www.aloha.net/~dyc/misc/music_strick_report.html [May 21, 2000].

7. Bob Muessig, "Dashboard Dining" [online], www.rvsafety.com/dash-boar.htm [May 21, 2000]; "Breakfast Break," *Honolulu Star-Bulletin*, November 18, 1999, p. A7.

8. Ibid.

9. James McKnight and A. Scott McKnight, "The Effect of Cellular Phone Use upon Driver Attention" [online], www.aafts.org/Text/research/cell/cell0toc.htm [May 21, 2000].

10. "Senator Stavisky Introduces Legislation to Prohibit Drivers from Using Cellular Phones: Cites Study Finding that Cellular Phone Use by Motorists Can Be As Dangerous As Drunk Driving," New York State Senate News Brief [online], www.sendem.com/carphone.html [May 21, 2000].

11. "IBM's Auto Computer Takes a Back Seat," Zdnet.com [online], www.zdnet.com/zdnn/stories/news/0,4586,2226314,00.html [May 21, 2000].

12. Ibid.

13. George Leopold and Terry Costlow, "Car PCs Move into the Fast Lane," CMP's TechWeb [online], www.techweb.com/wire/story/TWB19990115S0003 [May 21, 2000].

14. Brian S. Akre, "GM Launches Web Plan," *Washington Post*, August 1999 [online], www.washingtonpost.com/wp-srv/business/daily/aug99/gm10.htm [May 21, 2000].

15. Matt Sundeen, "Intelligent Transportation Systems (ITS)," NCSL Environment, Energy and Transportation Program, November 1998 [online], www.ncsl.org/programs/ESNR/ITS.htm [May 21, 2000].

16. "CVISN," Intelligent Transportation Systems for Commercial Vehicle Operations [online], www.Avalon-ais.com/itscvo/cvisn.htm [May 21, 2000].

17. Texas Transportation Institute (TTI), "Urban Mobility Study," 1998 [online], mobility.tamu.edu [May 21, 2000]; "On the Road Ahead: Smart Automobiles," *Honolulu Advertiser*, December 17, 1999, pp. C1, C3.

18. National Motorists Association (NMA), "NMA's Position on ITS" [online], www.motorists.org/issues/its/NMA_position_on_its.html [May 21, 2000].

19. Ibid.

20. Diane Nahl and Leon James, "What Is Driving Informatics?" DrDriving. org [online], www.aloha.net/~dyc/informatics.html [May 21, 2000].

21. Frank J. McGuigan, "Aggressive Driving," in *Encyclopedia of Stress* (Needham Heights, Mass.: Allyn & Bacon, 1999).

22. "Kensington Stress and Technology in the Workplace," *PC Computing*, December 1999, p. 38.

INDEX